Living in Language

Living in Language

The Literary Word at Work in the World

DAVID BOSWORTH

Front Porch Republic *Books*

LIVING IN LANGUAGE
The Literary Word at Work in the World

Copyright © 2024 David Bosworth. All rights reserved. Except for brief quotations in critical publications or reviews, no part of this book may be reproduced in any manner without prior written permission from the publisher. Write: Permissions, Wipf and Stock Publishers, 199 W. 8th Ave., Suite 3, Eugene, OR 97401.

Front Porch Republic Books
An Imprint of Wipf and Stock Publishers
199 W. 8th Ave., Suite 3
Eugene, OR 97401

www.wipfandstock.com

PAPERBACK ISBN: 978-1-6667-7449-8
HARDCOVER ISBN: 978-1-6667-7450-4
EBOOK ISBN: 978-1-6667-7451-1

05/13/24

To all my teachers—in person or in print, living now or dead—whose mood-soaked words still haunt my head, with gratitude: reheard, revoiced, your tales live yet, your songs play on . . .

*But in the mud and scum of things,
There something alway(s), alway(s) sings.*

"Music," Ralph Waldo Emerson

Contents

Acknowledgments		ix
Living in Language		1
1	Mythos-Minded Thinking	5
2	The Most Precious Square of Sense	19
3	Saving the Appearances	40
4	Two Sides of a Tortoise	67
5	In the Beginning	96
6	A Prescription for Contemporary Fiction	116
7	Real and Fake Accounts	123
8	Toward a Literature of Awe	135
9	Phoenix?	153

Acknowledgments

Portions of this book first appeared, in altered forms, in the following publications: *The Georgia Review, Raritan Quarterly Review, Michigan Quarterly Review,* and *The Hedgehog Review.* My thanks to the editors for providing an early public forum for the reflections that follow. The Hasidic oral tale "Hovering above the Pit," excerpted from *Hasidic Tales of the Holocaust,* is reprinted here with the permission of the estate of Yaffa Eliach, who was that anthology's editor.

Living in Language
(a Reply)

"THIS DAY IN HISTORY"

October 14, 1066: King Harold II of England [was] defeated by the Norman forces of William the Conqueror at the Battle of Hastings fought on Senlac Hill . . . At the end of the bloody, all-day battle, Harold was killed—shot in the eye with an arrow, according to legend—and his forces were destroyed. He was the last Anglo-Saxon king of England.

—@History.com

Near the start of his fifty-minute talk on postmodern fiction, the lecturer paused, and supplying perhaps some prefatory context for his thoughts to come, he said to us then with a knowing smile: "If I had a half-hour, I could prove to you that language only refers to itself." That assertion made, our learned guest, a professor of French at a prestigious private school, pivoted back to the topic at hand by parsing a novel whose many words, in a notable feat of monastic restraint, never included the letter *e*.

The audience was small: to leave would seem rude. And so it appeared, from my conspicuous seat in the second row, that *I* would have the time, a half-hour at least—while our speaker lightly glazed with ironic praise more self-referential works of prose—to weigh the claim he hadn't proved.

Unschooled by theory, so many, it seemed, had been so wrong. The list was long and would have to include every oral tribe who strove so hard to marry each word in its native tongue to the feature it best fit—whether rock or river, otter or ox—in the natural world. I thought of all their prayers and pleas, their carefully composed poems of praise or woe, and of those dire distinctions that each group made between the sounds of the sacred and those of the profane, with punishments in place for speaking out of bounds. I remembered, too, how Inuit midwives would call out names, seeking that one-and-only word, which, they knew—or *thought* they knew—would beckon each baby out of its womb. What a waste, all that ardor spent on superstitiously matching our verbal abstractions to the tangible assets of what proves to be instead an unnameable world—what a squandering of wit and will. A sad assessment, but apparently true now that we knew that language only refers to itself.

In the beginning was the Word? . . . not really, it seemed. And thinking then in biblical terms as I shifted in my seat, I recalled those scriptural accounts of a Middle East little changed in three thousand years—then as now a land that seethed with fratricidal rage. Even "the seed of Abraham," who shared a tongue and a jealous God, had too many separate, feuding tribes. I recalled in particular how the soldiers of Ephraim were said to be slain by their close Hebraic cousins from the land of Gilead. And how, while trying to sneak away from their battlefield defeat, the survivors were challenged by enemy guards at every ford in the River Jordan. I recalled how they were made to speak then a single Hebrew word, and how that was a test that these desperate imposters, otherwise indiscernible in speech or cast from those who quizzed them, couldn't quite pass. And when I recalled that *shibboleth* meant "a stalk of grain," I was appalled at how the verbal sign for what was, after all, the very source of civilized life ironically became the final word that each would speak.

Ignoring the lecture, picturing instead that long-ago scene, I shivered in my seat at its implications. To think that it only took this much, a demiquaver of difference in pronunciation, *hissing* where their tribal enemies *hushed*, to unleash the swords that cut their throats, each and every one . . . the blood of Ephraim, 42,000 husbands and sons, staining that holy river red. Clearly they didn't know, those feuding "people of the Lord"—those farmers turned to soldiers, those password police guarding each ford—that language only refers to itself.

But as I glanced around the hall at the gathered few, it occurred to me that our postmodern group was not so different, after all. I thought of a young couple I knew and the wedding vows they had so earnestly composed. I thought of all the many promises that each of us makes—to call, to care, to arrive on time; and of the formal contracts we're given to sign, for loans, for jobs, and of the subsequent sorties of legal indignation when one of the parties has "failed to comply." I thought of judges and juries carefully assessing what each witness says, and of the intimate whispers of weary fathers reassuring their daughters as they tucked them into bed.

Graver still, I thought of the slang of corner gangs and the threat to passersby who couldn't comprehend their cryptic codes of disrespect—recalling then, too, those comic nicknames, inside jokes, that bound as one the members of other, less menacing cliques and clubs. I thought of the women I knew who, rereading Jane Austen, still hoped to be wooed by the old formulaic professions of love, and how they weren't alone. For even as we sat there, millions elsewhere were turning pages, scrolling down screens, sifting through poems and other novelists' scenes for nuggets of meaning, models of feeling—worlds made of words to inspire or console. All leading me to ask if anyone I knew actually behaved as if they believed the lecturer's claim.

Certainly not that boy I had recently seen jump from his car and onto a curb; how he stood there exposed, in t-shirt and jeans, equally unaware of the evening's freezing rain and the unmanly shame of his needy pleas, while shouting at a house: *Mandy, come out, come out! Mandy, come out!* If only he had known that Mandy's words of rejection, whether mocking or meek, had been referring to *themselves* and not to his hopes of being held close on a wet winter evening.

And then I was struck by an odd association, the abstract claim of the lecturing theorist resurrecting in my mind a singsong rhyme from grammar school days: all those times we were told *sticks and stones may break my bones, but words will never hurt me.* Now I have to ask, though, what I never did back then: which belittled kid, weeping in the dirt by a jungle gym, ever believed that peacekeeper's lie? Who hasn't learned by the age of five that, just as we crave to be touched and are sometimes punched, we live to be told that we're liked or loved only to risk being cursed or mocked.

And staring at our guest, I was tempted then to test him. Just how would *he* respond if, interrupting his talk, I hurled some verbal sticks and stones at him, yelling at him then: *You're full of shit, you pretentious dick! You derivative, status-grubbing, Frog-loving twit!* Reminding him then if he bristled or flinched: *Hey, dude, no offense meant; no harm, no foul to one-and-all when language only refers to itself.*

Ten minutes to go, and as I shifted in my seat, the air seemed to roil in sonic revolt. The words themselves rebelled against the man who spoke them, reasserting then, if only to those ready to discern it, the story of their origins in other times and places—in Danish marshes, Spanish mansions, in slave-tilled fields and oppressive factories. In my archeologist's ear, it seemed that I could hear the hybrid evolution of the language that we shared, all its fusions and fractures—some words expunged, others torn from foreign shores and rudely worn like looted rings on Vikings' thumbs. I recognized then all the booty of battle and of exploration, the pidgin of trade and of illicit love, strangers then exchanging not just goods and genes but alien words, which mated then with other words, so many mongrel terms quickly put to use to sieve and hold, like nuggets veined with gold, the metamorphic features of our otherwise inconceivable world.

Our speaker didn't seem to know that, beneath the precious mask his theory wove, the very sounds he spoke were pulsing with the passions of past events. He couldn't sense, as I could then, all the *living* that infused the language that he used: the rage for order, the hunger for more, the all-enduring grief that revived the dead on the ghostly breath of holy verses. Deaf to our dependence on the sins and suffering of those who came before us, our lecturer couldn't catch, as I did then, the subliminal sounds of long-ago incursions, each Anglo-Saxon word he said a fricative sledge crushing the skull of a Celtic farmer.

And yet, I'm sorry to confess, I said none of this then. Instead, a choice I've long regretted, I fled as soon as the lecture ended. And so to make amends, here it is now, the climax to my belated reply—what I should have but didn't say during the Q & A that followed your talk, sir. Although I don't "do theory" or earn my living declining French verbs for the well-endowed, I *have* acquired an ear, equally armed with gratitude and fear, for the presence of the past in the English that we do share.

Which is why I don't intend to end by mustering a set of abstract proofs. Instead of arguing with you, I'll only testify now to what I heard resounding in your words on that autumn afternoon. First, the drumming of hooves on a field near Hastings. Then the clangor of axes battering shields. Then the terrible plucked chord of a thousand Norman bowstrings set loose at once. And then, moments later, the eerie whistle of their missiles as they bolted down, followed by the sound of a single final jolt.

Almost a thousand years old, this is the news that, staying news, reemerged that day from your lecturing mouth. I heard it *then*, followed by a man's agonizing cry. I hear it *now* in every Franco-Norman word we unknowingly pronounce: that arrow piercing King Harold's eye.

1

Mythos-Minded Thinking

*If you can write a nation's stories,
you needn't worry about who makes its laws.*[1]
—George Gerbner

In an age that officially endorses science and whose formal validation of truthful doctrine is usually swaddled in the scriptural reassurance that "studies have been done," we also commonly hear the dismissive phrase, "it's just a myth." But that is the prejudice of the rational materialist mind speaking, a mind whose formal means for knowing the world, however acute and useful, cannot fully measure or appreciate, much less produce mythological truths. We remain a storytelling species. And because the stories we habitually tell ourselves about ourselves become crucial mental tools in the maintenance of both stable communities and coherent personalities, the supposedly trivial pursuits of our entertainment industry are not trivial in effect when taken as a whole. What I'm going to call "mythos-minded thinking" (reasoning by metaphor, music, and narrative) not only precedes "logos-minded thinking" (reasoning by formal systems of abstract logic and math) in the evolution of human

1. George Gerbner, "TV or Not TV?," *Bill Moyer's Journal*, April 29, 1979. Gerbner was paraphrasing a comment by Scottish patriot and poet Andrew Fletcher from 1704— "If I were permitted to write all the ballads I need not care who makes the laws of the nation"—whom he cited in an online article, "Private Thoughts to Free Expression": https://www.religion-online.org/article/private-threats-to-free-expression/.

consciousness and culture; such thinking remains *the* most powerful means for expressing and transmitting our cherished beliefs, and so is a key field to turn to when studying the crux of any culture's understanding of the good and the true, as well as the beautiful.

The image I hold in mind that compresses and contains this larger claim I'm making is borrowed from an anecdote I was once told: that of a toddler who so loved his favorite storybook that he opened its cover and tried, physically, to step inside. In ways less literal but, in fact and over time, more consequential, we have all entered an anthology of stories (literary and cinematic, anecdotal and formal, personal and local and sometimes even national). We inhabit those narratives, and they in-habit us in the literal sense: that is, they *in*-form and construct, usually subliminally, those *habits* of mind that drive and shape our everyday decision-making. They calibrate our private expectations and are instrumental in formulating our collective common sense.

Friends, families, lovers co-create a store of anecdotal stories; they mythologize their shared past as a means of binding themselves to each other. So, too, on a grander scale and with a deeper time frame, do tribes and nations: their members co-create and then ritually retell stories of origin and of crisis. Although these shared stories often begin in what we now like to call "the facts," they are never strictly factual in the historical sense, for which, in a scientific age, they are sometimes called to task. Their primary if unspoken intention, however, is not the exact preservation of a factual past but the protection and perpetuation of crucial social relationships—of romantic love, friendship, familial and tribal belonging—and to dismiss these stories as "just myths" is to misunderstand in fundamental ways what being a friend, lover, family, or nation both means and requires.

In 2008 we suffered a catastrophic collapse in our economic system—in the bleakly funny words of our president then "this sucker could go down"[2]—and in the immediate aftermath of the initial downturn we began to hear about the disastrous laws and policies that caused this crisis. But in the spirit of the quotation that opened this chapter, I'm going to insist that long before those laws were written and adopted, the stories Americans were telling themselves began to go wrong in specific ways that set the mental stage for that collapse. For although our collective

---

2. President George W. Bush, after negotiations about a massive federal bailout for the country's imploding financial system initially failed, September 26, 2008. See: https://www.politico.com/tipsheets/huddle/2008/09/this-sucker-could-go-down-003768.

myths do not have to be historically factual, they need to remain relatively truthful to the human circumstance; they have to gauge both our limits and our gifts. If they don't, and we still allow them to "inhabit" us, then we *are* more likely take the whole ship down.

Later I will examine some specific historical instances of storytelling going wrong. But first let's consider why it is—in an age of impressive scientific achievement, and in the nation that more than any other has sought to define itself by strictly rational principles—that stories have remained so influential. Why it is still true today that if you tell a nation's stories, you don't have to worry about who makes its laws.

GENESIS: THE ORIGINS OF MYTHOS-MINDED THINKING

Human beings are different from other earthly creatures in that we possess a native intelligence that allows us to extensively manipulate the material world to our own preferred ends. This capacity is itself radically empowered by our gift for language, which allows us both to convey to others the discoveries we have made (whether new tools, hunting techniques, or herbal medicines) and then to accumulate those improvements over time. This repository of communal knowledge that protects and enhances us, that has provided us with an enormous evolutionary advantage, we can loosely call *culture*. Our ability to create and then pass on cultural knowledge via language not only enhanced our so-called animal instincts; it in some ways replaced them, so that the loss of that ability, the demise of culture, can become an actual threat to the physical survival of the group.

Prior to the invention of writing and the subsequent technological refinements required to make literacy widespread, memorization of spoken language was the *only* means that could guarantee a relatively accurate conservation of vital cultural knowledge. That is to say, the capacity to memorize large stores of verbal information was not the mere parlor trick that it seems to be today, when we have the luxury of books, photos, videos, digital files, and websites to do our remembering for us, but was instead the very key to cultural (and so, too, often physical) survival. Some numbers, then, to help calibrate the likely impact of this situation on the direction of the evolution of human consciousness and culture.

The best current guess is that our species has existed for some 300,000 years. The fully phonetic alphabet—which made it possible for a large percentage of any tribal population, and not just a special expert few, to become literate—emerged in Greece, circa 800 BC, some 2800 years ago. The first printing press in the West, which was necessary for the widespread democratization of literacy there, was built less than six hundred years ago. Whichever date we choose as the better boundary, however, the overall conclusion remains the same: the vast majority of human beings who ever lived (117 billion is an estimate I once read)[3] were unlettered, were "illiterate."

The latter word is so imbued now with derogatory connotations that we are inclined to associate illiteracy with stupidity or at least ignorance, but ancient peoples—more properly call *pre*literate rather than illiterate—weren't natively stupid, nor were they necessarily ignorant. They *were* cultured, to varying degrees of sophistication, but because that culture was orally based, they produced no written record, often leaving *us* ignorant as to their most intimate beliefs.

I could enumerate here the heroic efforts of archeologists and anthropologists in slowly recovering some of those beliefs, but I don't want to drift too far from the central points of my argument, which are as follows: because the successful transmission of cultural knowledge was a significant advantage for survival, and because for most of our existence we were not a literate species, human beings were under extreme evolutionary pressure to become adept at recalling and sharing oral knowledge. Some of those adaptations must have been physiological, a transformation of our brains' hardwired ability to perceive and retain verbal cues. Others, the ones of interest to us here, were cultural and involved increasingly sophisticated developments in the use of language itself—the discovery of new ways to structure our spoken words and the experiences they conveyed that made them more impressive, that aimed to make them "unforgettable."

On the small-grained level this led to the evolution of what we now call poetic technique: the manipulation of rhythm, rhyme, and refrain, the musical patterning of words. An appreciation of patterned sound appears to be a near universal feature of our species; most people seem to find musical expression highly pleasurable. And because the other dimensions of ordinary experience that we find highly pleasurable (for

---

3. https://www.prb.org/articles/how-many-people-have-ever-lived-on-earth/.

example, food and sex) prove to be instrumental to our physical survival, it is not outlandish to assume that our native appreciation of the musical must also supply us with *some* sort of evolutionary advantage, nor to speculate that such an advantage may be rooted in our species' early use of the musical qualities of language to render its cultural content, its life-sustaining knowledge, more memorable. In any case, it is not at all speculative to say that poetic devices are also mnemonic devices, that on the small-grained level of phrase and sentence, rhythm and rhyme are powerful aids for memorization. They were some of the means that helped us remember before writing could do our remembering for us.

Here's an example of those means in ancient action, as cited in a review of a biography of Genghis Khan, the great 12th century Mongol conqueror. *We watch Genghis's Golden Horde on the march, an army organized in the tens of thousands. Because all of them, including officers, are illiterate, orders move by word of mouth, composed in rhyme for easy memorizing and set to a fixed melody known to every warrior—like learning a new verse to a song that he already knew.*[4] Once upon a time in the human story, rhyme and song were not just expressions of personal heartbreak or joy but also instrumental in the conduct of war.

If the *medium* of verbal expression was patterned in ways to empower memory, and thus assure the accurate conservation and transmission of vital cultural knowledge, then it seems reasonable to expect the same practical intention would prevail with the *content*. The patterning of the message that proved (and still proves) to be most memorable on that larger scale was, of course, the subject of this chapter. It was a narrative, a story: recognizable people, usually from one's tribal past, represented in words and set in motion, characters acting and reacting, facing travails and traced through time.

Why should stories prove so memorable? Again, we can turn to our fundamental nature as a species for clues. Human beings are intensely social creatures—that too is part of our evolutionary makeup. Because our survival depends on group cooperation, we are attracted to and provoked by other people, and have evolved a complex and powerful set of emotions linked to our sociability. By representing people in dramatic situations, stories naturally evoke those powerful feelings, and it is simply a fact, not a speculation, that experiences that are conveyed by cues that

---

4. John Leonard, reviewing *Genghis Khan and the Making of the Modern World* by Jack Weatherford, in *Harper's Magazine,* March 2004, 85.

provoke strong emotional responses prove more memorable than those that do not.

There's another reason that stories became the primary means for conveying life-sustaining knowledge, one much harder for us to imagine but nevertheless true: preliterate peoples had no real alternatives. At that point in the human story, there was no philosophy, no scientific method or theory as we now know them, very little in the way of abstract knowledge at all—that is to say, there were very few words in the vocabulary of any oral tribe that represented *kinds* of things, rather than actual specific things. Most knowledge was embodied knowledge, all learning a form of apprenticeship (that is, modeling yourself after another person who was weaving, plowing, making a fire), and the oral stories that evolved to convey vital skills and knowledge mimicked that process of apprenticeship. The standard advice in creative writing workshops has been "show don't tell," but it is important to realize that prior to a few thousand years ago, the possibility for analytical telling at all was extremely limited. At any given university today, most of the thinking we are asked to do, except in the arts, is rooted in abstract reasoning—a species of thought that didn't exist, except in a more primitive sense, for most of human existence. Which is to say, mythos-minded thinking was the only game in town.

To sum up, due to our unique nature as the thinking species, human survival and progress depended on evolving means for accurately preserving each social group's life-sustaining knowledge. The verbal form best suited to this crucial mission was a human story conveyed through poetic devices, ritually and repetitively recited. This is exactly what anthropologists found in the still existing oral tribes they studied. In some places, in a very early example of the specialization of the intellect, one or two people, sometimes called bards, would be held most responsible for performing these poetically empowered oral tales. They were, in effect, the tribe's designated memory, and therefore essential to its survival. To quote fiction writer William Gass:

> *At one time the bard's recital was the main conduit of authority, making sense of the past, fostering acceptance, and focusing pride—whether true or false or fabled mattered only to outsiders. Old anecdotes gave present circumstances heft, scope, interest, and instruction. In so many ways you were your forbearers, and the storyteller taught you whom to hate or emulate, what to aspire to, and, like the Bible, what to believe, how to behave.*[5]

5. William H. Gass, "Go Forth and Falsify: Katherine Anne Porter and the Lies of

Gass's description captures the comprehensive nature of the authority that storytelling attained in a preliterate age. "Old anecdotes," however, doesn't do justice to the astonishing complexity and sophistication some of these oral narratives attained. It has now been established pretty conclusively, for example, that the *Iliad* and the *Odyssey* were originally oral compositions, ones collectively co-created over many years, and only eventually written down and refined by someone called Homer. Hundreds of thousands of words, musically and narratively shaped, memorized and recited without the aid of the written page: imagine the mind capable of such a Herculean task, and imagine the circumstances that drove them to undertake it.

After a point, the Greek people, organized into separate small city-states, had spread beyond their initial homeland to various colonies on islands off Asia Minor and in the Mediterranean. Today, with all our forms of near-instant communication, the distances that marked the Greek diaspora would seem insignificant, but because they lacked any sophisticated system of communication except for speech, the challenge of sustaining a set of common beliefs, a shared cultural identity over time, was great. How did they do it? According to classicist Eric Havelock: through reciting together the shared lore of their tribe, the mythic history of the Hellenic people that was encoded in the various episodes of the *Iliad* and the *Odyssey*. Periodic public performances occurred, with musical instruments and with dancing, both the body and the mind engaged, the gathered community a kind of collective tuning fork receiving and transmitting the oral traditions and wisdom of the tribe, a wisdom that was almost exclusively "mythos-minded." For once upon a time, "once upon a time" was the only rigorous way to memorialize knowledge and so gain the advantages it supplied.

At this point in our story about the evolution of stories, the potential for an alternative to mythos-minded thinking finally arrives in Greece, fueled by the discovery of literacy. And not just any form of literacy. Enter, stage left, the first fully phonetic alphabet, whose exceptional efficiency meant that not only the specially trained few—the so-called scribes—could learn to read and write, but also the average tribal member, and, just as importantly, at an early age. I have to fast-forward through this part of the plot because it takes hundreds of years for the impact of phonetic literacy to reshape the underlying premises—the common

---

Art," *Harper's Magazine,* January 2009, 71.

sense—of Greek thought. But as it does, logos-minded thinking—disembodied and therefore abstract; objective, analytical, "philosophical," proto-scientific—begins to emerge as a rival way of comprehending the world and storing cultural knowledge.

I'm not melodramatizing the situation by using the word rival; that is precisely how it was perceived by some of the key thinkers of the time, especially Plato, early philosophy's greatest author and fiercest advocate. In the *Republic*, where he is trying to define the ideal society, Plato decides that he will banish Homer's epics from his Republic's schools. They are, for him, too spellbinding, too emotional, their characters too imperfect, making them "bad role models" for the youth he wishes to educate in a philosophical way. He acknowledges these epics' psychological power but also recognizes the threat that power poses to his new project. Plato is one of the first to argue that the mythic is inherently deficient, that the fabled is, in some fundamental way, not truthful.

Plato's assertion brings us back full circle to where we began. For this early philosopher intuitively grasped that those who write or tell a people's foundational stories are also inevitably shaping the nature of those people's customs or laws. Plato was correct then in evaluating the educational power of the Homeric myths, but he was wrong in presuming he could legislate that power out of existence by simply banishing them from his schools, just as he was wrong in assuming that humans either could or should be ruled primarily by abstract laws. Authoritarian leaders might succeed in excluding a particular set of stories from the classroom or the civic square, but they could never banish either the immediate allure or the ultimate influence of storytelling itself. For even though the invention of writing removed many of the evolutionary pressures that helped establish narrative thinking as a key constituent of the human mind, we have only been fully literate (if we count the Greeks as the starting point) for less than 1% of our existence as a species, not even 3,000 years out of 300,000.

The logos-minded thinking that Plato helped to advance has added greatly to our knowledge and control of the material world. But it has not and cannot replace the essential operations of mythos-minded thinking, which are far more deeply engrained in our nature, and through which we still co-create and sustain our most intimate and important social relationships as friends, lovers, neighbors, and citizens. It is still the case that we step inside the stories we share, that they *inhabit* our minds, establishing a pattern of preferences and a climate of expectation, teaching us, to quote Gass again: "whom to hate or emulate, what to aspire to, what to believe, how to behave." They still predate and powerfully influence the laws that we make, formal or otherwise.

EXODUS: THE USES AND ABUSES OF MYTHOS-MINDED THINKING

To be fair, though, I have to take pains not to overly idealize the impact of the mythic imagination. Any human trait that is powerful and primal can also be potentially dangerous. The stories we tell ourselves about ourselves not only can console and redress; they can teach us "whom to hate," can organize and animate collective rage, scapegoating the innocent and scripting disaster on a massive scale. There is, alas, no shortage of historical examples to demonstrate that danger.

For decades now white supremacists in America have been enamored of *The Turner Diaries*, a 1978 novel by the racist William Luther Pierce that dramatizes the violent overthrow of the U.S federal government and a subsequent race war that ends with the extermination of the nation's non-white population. And those fictional words, as it turns out sadly, have indeed been "fighting words": the plot has become a map multiple times for violent behavior. In 1983 in Washington state, Robert Jay Mathews organized The Order, a white supremacist cell named after the revolutionary group in the novel. Their ultimate mission was to spur just the sort of race war that Pierce depicted, and to do so, in just two years' time they robbed a number of banks and armored cars, bombed a theater and a synagogue, and murdered a Jewish radio talk show host before going up in smoke in a shootout with officials on Whidbey Island.

Nor was Mathews alone in using Pierce's plot as a personal model. When he was captured, Timothy McVeigh—who was responsible for the Oklahoma City Bombing, blowing up a federal building and killing 168 people in 1995—was carrying in his car photocopied pages from, yes, *The Turner Diaries*: a scene that depicted a mortar attack on the U.S. Capitol.

But we haven't gauged yet the full potential for harm. Take the case of Adolf Hitler, the arch exemplar of the sociopathic leader. The provocative documentary *Architecture of Doom* makes the case that Nazism was, at its core, an expression of Hitler's *aesthetic* sensibility. The would-be artist (playwright, architect, stage designer), having acquired the authority of an absolute dictator, was empowered to enact his aesthetic vision on the grandest of scales and to the detriment of millions. Hitler was a great admirer of Imperial Rome, which he took to be the historical model for his Third Reich, and given his obsession with race, he promoted a spurious racial ancestry, a mythic history, that linked the Germans to the ancient Greeks and so to the glories of the classical era. Modeling his aesthetic after the remains of that era, Hitler instructed his minion-architect Albert Speer to design buildings that would make "beautiful ruins."[6] (The stated aim was to have his Third Reich's buildings last a thousand years, but you have to wonder about the psychology of a leader who was already imagining his cities in ruins—a goal he achieved, all across Europe, in just five years.)

More relevant to the analysis here, Hitler was a passionate admirer of Richard Wagner's operas. The form itself bears notice. Operas, after all, are choreographed narratives set to music and performed in public, and as such they bear some resemblance to those public recitations of the Homeric epics in preliterate Greece—for they too were accompanied by music and sometimes even enacted through dance. In a memoir, one of Hitler's early friends claimed that the shape of his political ambitions was powerfully influenced by one particular Wagnerian opera, *Rienzi*, which they saw together in 1906, and that later, after he assumed power, Hitler told Wagner's widow that "it all began" then, when he first attended a performance of *Rienzi*: the germ of Nazism, the nightmare that would plague the mid-twentieth century, was spawned on its operatic stage. Scholars now doubt the anecdote concerning Wagner's widow, but there's no denying Hitler's infatuation with the opera. For his fiftieth birthday in 1939, the year he invaded Poland and World War II commenced, he requested and received as a gift Wagner's original manuscript.

More tellingly, this opera's plot eerily anticipates the rhythm and ruin of the Führer's political life. *Rienzi* is set in Rome, and you will recall Hitler's obsession with Imperial Rome as an inspirational model for his Third Reich. The plot is based on the career of an actual revolutionary leader, Cola di Rienzi, who, in the 1300s drew on populist support to defeat the nobles and assume power, just as Hitler did in the early 1930s. In the opera, Rienzi's ambitious plans to unify Rome and restore its grandeur are then beset by factional plots against him, as were Hitler's, including a number of failed coups and assassination attempts. Eventually, heeding the condemnation of the Church, even the people turn against

---

6. See the 1991 documentary by director Peter Cohen, *Architecture of Doom*.

Rienzi. In their counter revolt they burn the capitol, killing him and his lover, and the opera ends with the building collapsing: images of climactic destruction that recall Hitler's final days, hiding with *his* girlfriend in the bunker of a besieged Berlin in flames. In its overall narrative shape, if not every point, *Rienzi* eerily anticipates the "architecture of doom" that defined Hitler's rule. And if we ask why he would identify with a storyline that ends so disastrously for its protagonist, we might recall that he was the same leader who was instructing Albert Speer to design buildings that would make "beautiful ruins."

In turning to examples of criminal and genocidal behavior that were influenced by the mythic mindset, my intention has been to recall that any mental or material tool that is powerful can also be powerfully abused. But perhaps I have gone too far now, and some countermoves are called for. First, let's do away with the illusion that *if only* the world had followed Plato's advice, and banned the products of the mythic imagination from its schools and civic squares, humanity would have been spared such self-imposed catastrophes. Even as Hitler, the political artist, was murdering millions, Stalin, the political scientist, was doing the same in the Soviet Union, followed by Mao in China and Pol Pot in Cambodia. Which approach killed more is a statistician's game I won't pursue. I doubt it mattered much to the survivors whether the extermination of their loved ones was following a mythic-minded plot or an abstract theory of utopian governance.

It was said, in the immediate aftermath of 9/11, that irony was now dead, that we as Americans would never laugh in the same way again. The decorum of the moment did demand the gravity of grief, but the claim that such humor had become socially extinct was implausible even then. Laughter of all sorts, including the irreverent, is too essential to our makeup as human beings. Likewise, it was said in the aftermath of World War II that art and literature couldn't possibly address its dehumanizing devastation—that, to quote Theodore Adorno, "to write poetry after Auschwitz [was] barbaric."[7] But poetry and fiction are not simply the provinces of elites, meant to exemplify the refinements of the superior mind; they are, as I've been arguing, expressions of our deepest nature as human beings. They are integral features of our native intelligence, supplying our most fundamental ways of making sense of our experience—of linking the present to the past, and of motivating and organizing our future

---

7. Theodore Adorno, "Cultural Criticism and Society," Prisms (M.I.T. Press, 1982), 34.

actions. The same mythic imagination that empowers the architects and authors of infamy also empowers its victims to address and, sometimes, *redress* the suffering they experience, even suffering as intense and grotesque as occurred at Auschwitz.

To validate that claim, I'll now turn to an artifact of the mythic imagination that directly engages the horrors of the concentration camps. This brief tale is taken from an anthology, *Hasidic Tales of the Holocaust*, and a little historical background is advisable to frame its narrative. Hasidic Jews were a revivalist movement first established in Europe in the early eighteenth century. Its members turned away from what they considered to be an over-emphasis on scholarship in traditional Judaism and stressed instead prayer, ecstatic devotion to a charismatic leader, and (most relevant here) storytelling. In such a turn, we can see a revival of the tension or rivalry between logos- and mythos-minded ways of reasoning first articulated by Plato.

The form preferred by this group, though, was the parable-like tale, the traditional teaching tool of preliterate cultures, not a full-length epic like the *Odyssey*. Insomuch as they lived in central Europe, many Hasidic Jews were exterminated in the Nazi genocide, but a small group did survive, and came to America, where their oral stories and remembrances were recorded by the scholar Yaffa Eliach. This particular tale is set in Janowska, a slave labor and concentration camp set up by the Nazis in what is now Ukraine, and this originally oral story is based on a conversation with Holocaust survivor Rabbi Israel Spira, who, you will note, is also one of its two main characters.

"Hovering above the Pit"[8]

It was a dark, cold night in the Janowska Road Camp. Suddenly, a stentorian shout pierced the air: "You are all to evacuate the barracks immediately and report to the vacant lot. Anyone remaining inside will be shot on the spot!"

Pandemonium broke out in the barracks. People pushed their way to the doors while screaming the names of friends and relatives. In a panic-stricken stampede, the prisoners ran in the direction of the big open field.

Exhausted, trying to catch their breath, they reached the vacant lot. In the middle were two huge pits.

---

8. "Hovering above the Pit" is based on a conversation between the Grand Rabbi of Bluzhov, Rabbi Israel Spira, and Baruch Singer on January 3 1975, and collected in *Hasidic Tales of the Holocaust,* ed. Yaffa Eliach (Oxford University Press, 1982), 3–4.

MYTHOS-MINDED THINKING

Suddenly, with their last drop of energy, the inmates realized where they were rushing, on that cursed dark night in Janowska.

Once more, the cold, healthy voice roared in the night: "Each of you dogs who values his miserable life and wants to cling to it must jump over one of the pits and land on the other side. Those who miss will get what they rightfully deserve—ra-tat-tat-tat-tat."

Imitating the sound of a machine gun, the voice trailed off into the night followed by a wild, coarse laughter. It was clear to the inmates that they would all end up in the pits. Even at the best of times it would have been impossible to jump over them, all the more so on that cold dark night in Janowska. The prisoners standing at the edge of the pits were skeletons, feverish from disease and starvation, exhausted from slave labor and sleepless nights. Though the challenge that had been given them was a matter of life and death, they knew that for the S.S. and the Ukrainian guards it was merely another devilish game.

Among the thousands of Jews on that field in Janowska was the Rabbi of Bluzhov, Rabbi Israel Spira. He was standing with a friend, a freethinker from a large Polish town whom the rabbi had met in the camp. A deep friendship had developed between the two.

"Spira, all of our efforts to jump over the pits are vain. We only entertain the Germans and their collaborators, the Askaris. Let's sit down in the pits and wait for the bullets to end our wretched existence," said the friend to the rabbi.

"My friend," said the rabbi, as they were walking in the direction of the pits, "man must obey the will of God. If it was decreed from heaven that pits be dug and we be commanded to jump, pits will be dug and jump we must. And if, God forbid, we fail and fall into the pits, we will reach the World of Truth a second later, after our attempt. So, my friend, we must jump."

The rabbi and his friend were nearing the edge of the pits; the pits were rapidly filling up with bodies.

The rabbi glanced down at his feet, the swollen feet of a fifty-three-year-old Jew ridden with starvation and disease. He looked at his young friend, a skeleton with burning eyes.

As they reached the pit, the rabbi closed his eyes and commanded in a powerful whisper, "We are jumping!" When they opened their eyes, they found themselves standing on the other side of the pit.

"Spira, we are here, we are here, we are alive!" the friend repeated over and over again, while warm tears streamed from his eyes. "Spira, for your *sake, I am alive; indeed, there must be a God in heaven. Tell me, Rebbe, how did you do it?"*

"I was holding on to my ancestral merit. I was holding onto the coattails of my father, and my grandfather and my great-grandfather, of blessed memory," said the rabbi and his eyes searched the black skies above. "Tell me, my friend, how did you reach the other side of the pit?"

"I was holding on to you," replied the rabbi's friend.

I'm loath to add much here, letting this powerful tale speak for itself. I'll conclude instead by simply noting this. Rather than responding with silence, as some suggested, this Rabbi and others in his group remained true to their original vision, weaving a tale of ecstatic devotion, generating hope even while bearing witness to what might have seemed the most despairing and demeaning of circumstances. The mythic imagination may have helped to design and dig the murderous pit that was the Holocaust, but it also supplied to some of its survivors the seemingly superhuman capacity to hover above it.

2

The Most Precious Square of Sense[1]
(In Praise of Shakespeare's 'Politics')

Judas Kiss

In one phase of our seemingly endless culture wars, the works of Shakespeare took center stage. As his plays, long under assault for their supposedly reactionary politics, were rapidly disappearing from university reading lists, some critics responded by angrily demanding that boards of regents intervene. Although the issue of how to expand the curricular canon without diluting excellence or dissolving coherence was a serious one, and although the prospect of ex-pols and retired corporate leaders (the usual revolving-door cast of reigning regents) designing freshman syllabi by executive fiat should have sent shivers down the spines of academic radicals and conservatives alike, some amusing ironies attended the conflict. As has so often been the case in our culture wars, the most vociferous opponents shared more than they dared admit. Neither the appalled defenders of the Bard nor the "transgressive" academics who attacked him seem to note how much that faculty's career-rewarding habit of trashing old texts to boost the new resembled the marketing model of our consumer economy. Then as now, peek beneath the surface of curricular revolt and you could find, among nobler aims, the same formula

---

[1]. Most of Harold Bloom's words cited in this chapter come from two of his books: *The Western Canon: The Books and School of the Ages* (New York: Harcourt Brace & Company, 1994), henceforth referred to as *WC*; and *Shakespeare: The Invention of the Human* (New York: Riverhead Books, 1998), henceforth referred to as *Shakespeare*.

that has so enriched the very millionaires whose think-tanks were funding the reactionary attack on the academic left.

That the programmatic scorning of Shakespeare (and Emerson and Melville) might be as much commercially correct as politically correct; that politically correct (now "woke") behavior might often be a secular reflection, a kind of unintended parody, of the broader culture's habit of using Judeo-Christian rectitude to mask an unchecked pursuit of material self-interest—these were realizations unspeakable on both sides of the debate. For to admit them was to commit a genuinely transgressive act by acknowledging the one taboo truth still left in our otherwise totally unzippered public sphere: namely, that consumer capitalism is the most radically anti-conservative political economy in the history of the species, as corrosive to the continuity of art, ethics, and religion as it is to the ecology of field, forest, and stream. If, in William Irwin Thompson's words, postindustrial America is a "catalytic enzyme that breaks down all the traditional cultures of the world,"[2] that dissolution includes its own, and no literary author has more shaped our Anglo-American culture than Shakespeare himself.

But I come to praise Shakespeare, not to bury him, and what concerned me most about that debate was not his debunkers but those defenders who instead betrayed him with their kiss. In an age of salesmanship, it is the co-opting of the meaningful rather than its dismissal that tends to pose the greater threat. So it was that against the shrill accusations of misogyny, antisemitism, and royalist oppression, we began to hear the indignant counterclaim that the playwright, in his greatness, was beyond politics, that he abided in the ethereal realm of the purely aesthetic, quasi-divinely above the fray. We were told that his works were indisputably if paradoxically "good for us" without having anything practical to say about the good or the just.

Oddly, Harold Bloom became the principal public proponent of this purely aesthetic reading of Shakespeare. In a prolific burst of books, Internet postings, prefaces to anthologies, and mainstream interviews, the Yale professor rode the popular backlash against political correctness to become the most audible defender of all high art and, especially, a vociferous opponent of judging older literary works according to their compliance to contemporary political values.

---

2. William Irwin Thompson, *The American Replacement of Nature* (New York: Doubleday, 1991), 78.

The oddity of this event didn't reside in Bloom's interpretive slant, which had remained essentially unchanged throughout the years, but in the style of their delivery and the audience he targeted. Once himself a high priest of academic criticism who, from an endowed pulpit in New Haven, made his own transgressive tweakings of traditional literary readings, and whose mandarin books rarely graced the coffee tables of middle America, Bloom lost his following within the profession to the postmodern acolytes of Derrida and Foucault and their sometimes allies, the sans-culotte rebels of feminist theory and cultural studies. As the great defender of elitist status in literature ("the Muse, whether tragic or comic, favors the elite"),[3] Bloom couldn't have been happy with this fall from grace within his chosen field, and with no hope of an imminent restoration in sight, he began entrepreneurially reinventing himself in the mid-nineties by gravitating toward that oxymoronic role so favored by late consumer culture: the mass marketer of elitist taste. Disdainful of both politics and populism, he nevertheless began the essentially polemical task of pitching his case to the broader audience of the uninitiated.

To catch a flavor of the self-dramatizing gusto with which this once apolitical critic joined the fray, we can turn to the opening lines of Bloom's essay, "They Have the Numbers; We, the Heights,"[4] where he explicitly associates himself and his like-minded readers with the great Spartan army whose self-sacrificial courage in delaying the Persian invasion of 480 B.C. helped saved Greek culture for posterity:

> *My title is from Thucydides and is spoken by the Spartan commander at Thermopylae. Culturally, we are at Thermopylae: the multiculturalists, the hordes of camp-followers afflicted by the French diseases, the mock-feminists, the commissars, the gender-and-power freaks, the hosts of new historicists and old materialists—all stand below us. They will surge up and we may be overcome; our universities are already travesties, and our journalists parody our professors of 'cultural studies.' For just a little while we longer, we hold the heights, the realm of the aesthetic . . .*

"Holding the heights" had always been Bloom's preoccupation, but in books such as *The Western Canon* and *Shakespeare: The Invention of the Human*, with their more accessible prose and overtly pedagogical approach, the identity of those who shared that honor with him began to

---

3. WC, 34.
4. "They Have the Numbers; We, the Heights," *Boston Review*, April/May 1998: https://www.bostonreview.net/forum/harold-bloom-they-have-numbers-we-heights/.

shift. Rather than address the small fraternity of critics with whom he once held sway, Bloom started pitching his arguments to a much larger and potentially more profitable audience.

By doing so, he was joining that virtual horde of NEA-CONs—Nattering Exegetes of Astute Consumption—who, through their multiple columns, newsletters, documentary specials, tasting tours, and DVD lecture series, were pitching then their expert taste to the undiscriminating. In the mall of the mandarin, even the literature professor might generate a revenue stream. I never would have predicted it back in the day, but Harold Bloom, too, started writing for the People, or rather for the People as defined by PBS. The man who began as the would-be kabbalist of esoteric criticism was becoming instead a latter-day literary Julia Child.

Such a stance was not without its charms. Bloom's willingness to raise a glass not only on behalf of aesthetic pleasure but in sheer gratitude to its agents and authors—that generous *joie de vivre* of Child's signatory "*Bon appetit!*"—was especially winning when compared to the pinched, inquisitorial temper of too many of his academic opponents, whom he aptly dubbed the School of Resentment. There may be much to lament in millennial America's popular culture but, as Ken Starr belatedly discovered, the moral common sense of democracy still detests a show of sheer mean-spiritedness, and few activities seem meaner than bullying the busts of the defenseless dead. While Derrida famously aimed to "decapitate" the corpse of the canonical author and others chose to "interrogate" him in a manner shared by the East German *Stasi* or America's own Joe McCarthy, Bloom's counter mission of praise, however small the cast it admitted, seemed a relatively more decent task.

That rarity of greatness, as spied by Bloom, was more than offset by the hyperbole of his appreciation. In *Shakespeare: The Invention of the Human*, for example, this self-confessed "bardolater" pays lavish tribute the playwright's stature, assigning him a one-and-only patent for the invention of modern consciousness, and so elevating him to a divine-like status. ("Bardolatry, the worship of Shakespeare, ought to be even more of a secular religion than it already is.")[5] And in *The Western Canon* he further insists that "we owe to Shakespeare not only our representation of cognition but much of our capacity for cognition."[6] Admission to the heights of *this* heavenly sphere is limited to one, but other semi-divinities

---

5. *Shakespeare*, xvii.
6. *WC*, 40.

of creativity receive their due. Throughout these works, Bloom assumes the Thermopylaean mission of rushing to the defense of that whole long but thin line of literary DWEMs ("Dead White European Males") who have constituted the critically approved Western tradition.

The argument is consistent. In a clearly articulated, mostly jargon-free prose, these books and their shorter spin-offs both mock and lament the School of Resentment's abandonment of "all aesthetic and most intellectual standards . . . in the name of social harmony and the remedying of historical injustice."[7] Restoring those standards, Bloom's literary polemics relentlessly reassert the rights of genius, insist that great works of art are freely created by unique individuals and not by the ineluctable "social energies" of their era, and contend that a very limited number of such literary artists have had inordinate influence not only on other artists but on the very shape of contemporary consciousness. Bloom further insists that this inequality of influence is not only historically real but the justifiable result of extraordinary accomplishment, and so he roundly rejects the relativism that would render all artistic achievement—from the bedspread of an anonymous quilt-maker to the epic of a Milton—as equally noteworthy.

Bloom's defense of superiority in art might seem a tonic resistance to the wash of pseudo-idealistic egalitarian sentiment that disarms discernment, rewards mediocrity, and all too often merely masks the crassest graspings of careerism. Yet though he justifiably complains in these books about the extreme reductionism of the School of Resentment, his own views prove no less reductionist and so, too, no less a danger to artistic value in the richest sense. Against the rigid moralistic readings of both the left and the right, for example, Bloom asserts with an equivalent rigidity that the "moral values" of the canon are "nonexistent"[8] and that such literature can "not make one a better or a worse person"[9] in any discernible way. And against the materialist determinism of neo-Marxist readings and the psychological determinism of Freudian interpretations, he asserts, against all common sense, that artistic works are influenced almost solely by other works of art. The canonical novel, play, or poem owes little to the social "place" of its creation; nor is such a work dependent on the biography of the literary artist separate from his reading habits. Literature alone breeds new literature through a narrowly conceived

7. *WC*, 7.
8. *WC*, 4.
9. *WC*, 30.

struggle between the creative will of the single artist and the influence of a few earlier canonical works.

This theory of the "anxiety of influence"—through which each work of literary art struggles to remain, in Bloom's curious phrase, "uncontaminated" by the great works preceding it—was his primary claim to originality as a critic. In essence, however, this theory is merely a version of Satan's self-deceiving boast in *Paradise Lost* (Book I, 230–34) projected into the field of literary study. Flipping Milton's cautionary example into an ideal, Bloom wants to believe, like the fallen angel, that certain special authors can come close to possessing "a mind not to be chang'd by Place or Time"; that the great work of art can somehow be "its own place," divinely autonomous and immune to influence.

Here, too, Bloom retains a jeweler's eye for a similar folly in his activist opponents, mocking the "declarations of literary critics" who believe that they have freed themselves from the "anguish of contamination"—that is, from the influence of the DWEMs who dominate the canon. Each of these critics, he notes sarcastically, believes that he or she "is Adam early in the morning. They know no time when they were not as they are now; self-created, self-begot, their puissance is their own."[10] Yet this fantasy of self-genesis is precisely the one that Bloom enshrines for the canon itself by insisting that its works are largely immune to social circumstance. It is also the very drive that he elevates into the primary motive for the creation of lasting literature: "the desire to write greatly is the desire to be elsewhere, in a time and place of one's own, in an originality that must compound with inheritance, with the anxiety of influence."[11]

So it is that Bloom, no less than his activist adversaries, idealizes the mind's "own place." And his disdain for these critics emerges not from his appreciation of the folly of that aim but from their failure to recognize the cruel Darwinian reality that attends it: namely, that only a special canonical few can approach its attainment.

But if the "desire to write greatly" is simply the "desire to be elsewhere, in a time and a place of one's own," then even the very best literature is reduced to a quest for self-centered escapism, an idealized alienation from both the physical and the social worlds. By insisting "all that the Western Canon can bring one is the proper use of one's own solitude,"[12] Bloom's thinking becomes emblematic of the dangers that

10. *WC*, 7.
11. *WC*, 12.
12. *WC*, 30.

attend a decadent individualism, its tendencies toward solipsism, narcissism, and megalomania. As such, his ultra-refined boosting of "bardolatry" proves less an original project than a predictable product of the crudest "social energies" of our own time and place.

The romantic egotism of Bloom's theory is deeply akin to the false autonomy relentlessly pitched in every niche of our consumer economy, high or low. Even before he joined the NEA-CON crew, Bloom's thinking tacitly resembled their point of view, which is why his eventual conversion was not so shocking after all. In its attempt to segregate beauty from meaning, aesthetic sensibility from moral coherence, Bloom's defense of Shakespeare reduces some of the canon's greatest poetry into but one more line of gourmet delicacies, exotically spiced and elegantly arrayed, to be avidly consumed for consumption's own sake.

Morbid Magnitude vs. Moral Consequence

> ... Love cools, friendship falls off, brothers divide; in cities mutiny; in countries discord; in palaces, treason; and the bond cracked 'twixt son and father.
>
> —King Lear

In his preface to *The Western Canon*, Bloom complains that he feels "quite alone these days in defending the autonomy of the aesthetic, but its best defense is the experience of reading *King Lear*." This seems a curious statement, shadowed as it is by two extreme ironies. First, Bloom's own ideology—which asserts "the sovereignty of the solitary soul, the reader not as a person in society but as the deep self"[13]—idealizes the notion of being "quite alone"; and second, of all Shakespeare's plays, not only is *Lear* one of the most overtly political, it also supplies a comprehensive critique of the same solitary individualism that the "anxiety of influence" would celebrate. To grasp this, though, we need to recover a commonsense reading of the play that, by avoiding the rigid either/or biases of radical "interrogation" and Romantic "bardolatry," can recognize both the moral rigor of Shakespeare's lyricism and the psychological subtlety of his political compass.

---

13. *WC*, 10–11.

To grasp that compass, we need to recall the temper of the moment when the play was composed—*its* time and place and prevailing "social energies," as they were urgently expressed in John Donne's 1611 poem, "An Anatomy of the World":

> *'Tis all in pieces, all coherence gone;*
> *All just supply, and all Relation:*
> *Prince, Subject, Father, Son, are things forgot,*
> *For every man alone thinks he hath got*
> *To be a Phoenix, and that there can be*
> *None of that kind, of which he is, but he.*

By the turn of the seventeenth century, the initial joy of Renaissance creativity was curdling into dread as the inherent contradictions between medieval feudalism and modern individualism became all too apparent. As a religious conservative, Donne was deeply dismayed by the threat of disorder he found in every field from religion to politics to philosophy. He feared, correctly as it turned out, that the new "atomism"—which was redefining both material and social reality by emphasizing the uniqueness of "pieces" over the necessity of "Relation"—would result in political and moral anarchy. In *King Lear*, staged just five years before the publication of Donne's poem, Shakespeare supplies us with the most comprehensive study of this threat. He dramatizes in devastating detail the psychological sources of political anarchy, showing how, through the rise of the Phoenix in its various forms, "all" might indeed dissolve to pieces.

Bloom contends that this story of family betrayal and civil war is the "most sublime" of Shakespeare's four great tragedies, certainly a defensible position, and he makes many astute, small-grained observations concerning the inventiveness of the characterizations. But the grander reason behind Bloom's endorsement of *Lear* as the "strongest literary work" he has ever encountered clearly emerges from the utter bleakness he claims to find in its conclusion. By the end, he insists, "everything seems against itself" so that we are "thrown outward and downward until we are left beyond values, altogether bereft." We are condemned, like Lear before his death, to inhabit "a terrible and deliberate gap." We are cast into a desolate "space between meaning and truth" that, Bloom insists, is one of the supreme achievements of imaginative literature: the devastating evocation of a kind of "cosmological emptiness in which we wander and weep."[14]

Bloom's Romantic biases are revealed most clearly here with his desire to associate aesthetic sublimity with cosmological emptiness, imaginative achievement with wandering and weeping. And as *Lear* the tragedy is adjudged to be the most sublime *because* it brings us "beyond values, altogether bereft," Lear the character is said to be "the greatest of all representations of a king" not due to any real nobility of action but because he is "much the most passionate,"[15] because his raging is the fiercest, his suffering the most unbearably intense. Although these aesthetic judgments succeed in stripping moral stature from their compass, they are not themselves, of course, "beyond values" but are the expression of a Romantic calculus which projects the reductionist formula of modern quantiphilia into the arena of morbid emotions. Just as the rationalist technocrat believes that *more* (data, money, efficiency) *must equal better* (a truer, happier, safer society), the Romantic aesthete insists that the greater the intensity of the emotion evoked (especially misery), the greater the authenticity—the more terrible conclusion, the more sublime the experience.

Elsewhere Bloom asserts more specifically that "the greatness of the play has everything to do with Lear's patriarchal greatness,"[16] thus inverting into praise the School of Resentment's reductive complaint about patriarchal oppression. But look wherever we wish inside the play's five acts, we can find little sign of the old man's individual achievement in the patriarchal sense—that is, as an effectual leader or father. Though much can be deduced from his behavior throughout the play, we only have the opening scene as direct evidence of Lear's performance as king, for it is in that scene that he relinquishes his authority to the husbands of his older daughters, Regan and Goneril.

To those accustomed to democracy and the egalitarian values associated with it, Lear's desire to go into a semi-retirement and divide his kingdom among his heirs might in itself seem a sign of political greatness. The voluntary surrendering of authority and its division among equals through delegation are, after all, two of the essential characteristics of democratic governance, ones that we associate with its political and moral superiority. But in Shakespeare's time such a decision was radical and potentially destabilizing. Lacking the institutional checks and

---

14. *WC*, 67–69.
15. *WC*, 66–67.
16. *WC*, 68.

balances of modern democracy and charged with a surging individualism as yet untutored in the duties as well as the rights of freedom, the early 1600s were trapped in a dynamic of stressful contradictions, their medieval institutions unable to contain modern ambitions.

To translate Donne's version of that crisis back into Bloom's own critical terms: the new "deep self" of the "mind's own place" (with its emphasis on individual ambition) was colliding with the old expectations of "the person in society" (those feudal traditions of "just supply" and right Relation that still favored loyalty over ambition, stability over innovation, and absolute authority over delegation). Despite Bloom's wish to keep art "uncontaminated" by social influence, *King Lear* was clearly written in response to that crisis, and both the shape of the plot and the array of characters clearly favor the old order. All the heroes—Cordelia, Kent, and Edgar—are heroic through their adherence to feudal conceptions of loyalty as daughter, liege, and son; all the villains—Goneril, Regan, and Edmund—are upwardly mobile individualists who crack the bonds of domestic relations in a ruthless pursuit of private ambition, whether political, economic, or sexual in nature.

In this case, then, the School of Resentment's complaint about Shakespeare's politics might seem to have some basis in fact, but we can only make such a judgment after considering the actual alternatives available at the time. An author can't be against a political movement that doesn't yet exist, and to fault Shakespeare for being anti-democratic is akin to accusing Newton of being against relativity, or to blaming Bach's predecessors for refusing to compose in counterpoint. In any case, Lear's decision has little to do with thoughtful political reform, democratic or otherwise. Although he hints that he is retiring, in part, to prevent future strife after his death, his division of the kingdom is exercised in a fashion that emphasizes the willfulness of his authority even in the process of abdicating it. By continuing to endorse autocratic behavior while breaking up the very polity (a unified kingdom) that sustains its form of social order, Lear initiates a devolution into anarchy. Rather than reforming the monarchy according to democratic principles, his division of it atomizes autocracy, provoking a *political* version of "the anxiety of influence" and a subsequent agonistic struggle of wills, as each fractured piece fights to reassume an absolute authority over the whole.

The recklessness of Lear's decision, which engenders strife under the very guise of preventing it, is exposed in the first scene by the king's chosen means of enacting the division. Here the medium becomes the real message as he rashly invites a softer version of the divisive competition that will soon send the country into civil war.

> *Which of you shall we say doth love us most,*
> *That we our largest bounty may extend...*[17]

This is the new calculus of value, the model of merit for the governing heart now being endorsed: the right to rule has been explicitly equated not with intelligence or nobility of character or even raw military force, but with the magnitude of one's love for Lear. *More* love for me, says this supposedly greatest of patriarchs, *must equal better*. Quick to follow their father's calculus of sheer self-interest, the older daughters shamelessly accept this invitation to a flatter-fest, buying the boroughs of his Manhattan with the beaded ornaments of their sham affection. Goneril proclaims her father "dearer than eye-sight, space, and liberty."[18] Not to be outdone, Regan then insists that even that fulsome praise "comes too short," professing herself instead "an enemy to all other joys, / Which the most precious square of sense possesses."[19]

I'm citing this well-known opening scene, in part, to emphasize the importance of Regan's exact words, for they hint at the catastrophic significance of this collaborative exercise in emotional dissembling and supply the ethical hinge that links Lear's self-love to the civil war to come. If the "square of sense" is indeed *most* precious, then to proclaim herself its enemy, to favor one joy to the exclusion of all the others—in Donne's terms, to accentuate the "piece" at the expense of "Relation"—is to reject the harmonies of community for the harms of isolation, the magnanimity of love for the morbidity of obsession. (As is so often the case with Shakespeare, "square" in Elizabethan English bears a fruitful double meaning here, suggesting both the equitable balancing of all varieties of human joy, the theme I am stressing, and "the front part of a woman's dress," which implies a balance that is particular to a feminine sensibility.) Aware that the human heart not only must but should have multiple allegiances, Cordelia refuses to say that she loves her father "most" and is then banished by her furious father with the final curse: "Better thou / Hadst not been born than not to have pleased me better."[20]

---

17. *King Lear*: I, i, 51–52.
18. *King Lear*: I, i, 56.
19. *King Lear*: I, i, 72–74.
20. *King Lear*: I, i, 233–34.

In an attempt to moderate our view of Lear's offense here—which is not simply the banishment of Cordelia (and her defender Kent) from his kingdom but a radical exclusion of honesty itself—Bloom claims that the king's "principal fault in regard to Cordelia is an excessive love that demands excess in return."[21] But this is a disingenuous reading, one that discounts the danger of such love by flattering its intensity. Here as throughout, Bloom seems to blur the inherent stature of the role of the patriarch (whether as father or king) with the stature of Lear's performance in those roles, just as he confuses the cautionary quality of Lear's behavior within the play with the exemplary quality of Shakespeare's representation of it. Because the "moral values" of this or any tragedy have been explicitly proclaimed as "non-existent," because those values have been replaced by a Romantic bias for "the solitary self" over "the person in society," and (more importantly here) for sheer emotionality over nobility of character, the magnitude of Lear's patriarchal passion automatically eclipses the consequences of his patriarchal actions; the intensity of the piece obscures its disastrous effects on the coherence of relations, and Lear is praised as "great."

(It is impossible to exaggerate Bloom's sentimental inflation of Lear's status. In *Shakespeare*, he insists that the old king is "a kind of mortal god" and that within his characterization Shakespeare was seeking to portray "a paradigm for greatness." In a book that alternates deft observations with near delusional misreadings born of the author's Romantic biases, perhaps the most delusional is this: Bloom actually argues that Lear was modeled on, and the equal to, the aging King Solomon, that sage and psalmist who was thought to be not only the wisest of ancient Israel's leaders but also the most politically adept.[22])

Bloom himself has championed the inevitability and desirability of "creatively" misreading literary texts, but it would be difficult to exceed the perverse irony of this reversal of Shakespeare's intent. Bloom's confusion between the stature of a social role and the stature of the personality occupying that role, along with his critical forsaking of "the most precious square of sense" for the crude calculus that *more* (passion) *must equal better*, violate two of the play's central themes. They are the very flaws in Lear's character that drive the plot toward its catastrophic conclusion. And they are the ones that, five hundred years later, spur an

---

21. *WC*, 66.
22. *Shakespeare*, 477–79.

economy whose own excessive pursuit of *more* is fueled by the same delusory dream (and marketing scheme) of narcissistic autonomy.

All this brings us back at last to Bloom's morbid celebration of *Lear*'s bloody finale: the reading that would link the sublimity of the play as a whole to the "cosmological emptiness" its final act evokes. This interpretation might be plausible if, as in *Waiting for Godot*, we *were* cast "beyond values, altogether bereft" by the end. We're not, and Bloom's insistence that we are constitutes a misreading that violates the spirit of the play no less egregiously than the very worst supplied by the School of Resentment.

True, through most of the play's five acts, all does seem, as Kent reports to Lear, "cheerless, dark, and deadly."[23] Gloucester's astrological prediction, cited at the start of this section, has been enacted throughout: love *has* cooled, there has been discord in the country and treason in the palace, and the tender bond—not only 'twixt son and father, but 'twixt daughters and father, 'twixt lord and liege, 'twixt sisters, 'twixt brothers—has been dangerously "cracked." After Lear relinquishes his authority to his two flattering daughters, they turn on him and then on each other in an ever more bloody acceleration of betrayal in pursuit of raw power.

Yet at the play's end the anarchy has ceased, its agents completely defeated, order restored by a noble leader, Albany. The cost has been horrific—Gloucester, Regan, Goneril, Cornwall, Oswald, Edmund, the Fool, Cordelia, and Lear have all died—yet the ultimate result is not a banishment into utter emptiness but a restoration of civil order and public justice. Not only does the play end with a political redress and with a moral reckoning for all its villains; two of the three most admirable characters, Kent and Edgar, survive the carnage. And to seal and perpetuate our faith that justice will now prevail, we are left with Albany's unambiguous pledge that

> *All friends shall taste*
> *The wages of their virtue, and all foes*
> *The cup of their deserving...*[24]

Yet Cordelia does die, and most undeservedly. *Her* reckoning remains the burr in the heart that demands explaining, for she and the Fool alone, among that long list of the dead and the maimed, are wholly blameless. This princess who forfeited a kingdom rather than falsify the true nature of love, this daughter who sustained a constant yet undeluded emotional bond to

---

23. *King Lear*: V, iii, 291.
24. *King Lear*: V, iii, 303-4.

the father who cruelly cast her out, has been murdered on her own sister's orders—sororicide the ultimate "crack" in the nest of tender bonds that holds society together. And when that very father, now repentant, bears her lifeless body onto the stage as if to beg it back to life—surely one of the most crushing entrances in all of English drama—when he howls and hammers the irreversible fact of her death into his own (and our) minds, those moments mark the closest the play comes to justifying Bloom's sense of an unredeemable emptiness. "No, no, no life!" Lear cries out to a corpse that can't respond, both admitting and resisting the finality of the event by addressing his daughter as if she were alive and yet with a message that admits that her life has been inalterably spent:

> *Why should a dog, a horse, a rat have life,*
> *And thou no breath at all? Thou'lt come no more,*
> *Never, never, never, never, never!*[25]

But if Lear himself is *altogether* bereft—and he most eloquently is—must we be, too? The play, as Bloom himself aptly notes in his argument for its greatness, has one of the largest casts of fully elaborated characters in all of Shakespeare's work. It provides multiple emotional and thematic centers to attend—if, that is, we actually wish to read the play *as a whole*, in all its coherence and relations, and not just morbidly magnify its most forlorn piece: that Lear of the last scene who has lost his irreproachable daughter. And even if we focus on that moment of magnified grief, so compressed and intense that Lear dies from it, we find that in the full resonance of its meanings and feelings we have not been cast "beyond values" but carried to the very core of their authentication.

In drama as in life, meaning is cumulative and resonant, not discrete and isolate in the way that a Romantic reader like Bloom, idealizing the mind as its own place, prefers to make it. To know the whole context requires knowing the full *pre*-text. The meaning of *where* we are at the end of Act V as the king bends over the throttled body of his daughter is inseparable from *how* and *why* we arrived there, and Lear's anguish is much multiplied by his realization that his own decision to banish Cordelia has been instrumental in her death—that her *neverness* has been sired in part by his selfishness. What we have entered at this moment of magnified grief is, then, not the valueless gap of a "cosmological emptiness" but the self-initiated trap of ethical consequence—which is, in this instance, a much harder place to be.

---

25. *King Lear*: V, iii, 306–9.

If we empathetically enter this harder place, we ought to weep with Lear but cannot really wander because a series of decisions has drastically constricted the field of possible occurrences to this fixed and now unavoidable point, this physical end which is as well the play's dramatic, thematic, and ethical core: Cordelia's corpse. Many real-life deaths do seem senseless, but as in most of the great tragedies, the peculiar horror of Cordelia's death radiates from the deliberate tracking of its sensibleness. "A rat [has] life / and [she] no breath at all" because Lear himself has cracked the bond of paternal love, because he has been from the start a spiteful, selfish father and a very foolish king. In the sole instance of his patriarchal effectiveness, Lear's own enraged wish—"Better thou / Hadst not been born"—has come true in the flesh.

The fault is not his alone, of course. Just as Shakespeare's sensibility insists on the many dimensions, admixtures, and gradations of human emotion, it also relentlessly depicts the subtleties and complexities of human guilt. *Un*just supply is also the result of relations, both deliberate and careless—within which, however, one can and should discern various degrees of complicity and blame. Here as in *Hamlet*, for example, the author makes a careful distinction between the cold calculations of outright villainy and the unreflective selfishness that allows evil to reign. Edmund and Goneril are directly responsible for Cordelia's death just as Claudius is directly responsible for the murder of Hamlet's father. But as Claudius might not have become king without Gertrude's apparently glad submission to his hasty seduction, Goneril and Edmund would never have been in position to kill Cordelia were it not for, in Kent's apt words, Lear's "hideous rashness" as a king and father.

The chaos of the kingdom is thus both dramatized and analyzed, expressed and contained by a tragic coherence that helps locate the sources of anarchy in specifiable flaws in the characters—in Lear and Edmund primarily, and Regan, Goneril, and Cornwall secondarily. The compression of meaning that is the source of the play's sublime achievement depends as much on this ethical fitness—on the aptness of events as driven by decisions, on the logic that turns narrative sequence into ethical consequence and linear plot into resonant theme—as it is by the exquisite fitting of the language to the forms and rhythms of human grief.

So it is that the moral values of this canonical play, which Bloom would claim are non-existent, strongly determine and infuse the very conclusion he comes to praise. By ignoring those values here and elsewhere, Bloom actually reduces the greatness of Shakespeare's achievement, for it is precisely the architectural strength supplied by his plots (the accuracy of their narrative logic) that supports both his extensive variations in characterization and the descriptive gloss of his glorious language. Shakespeare's toughness about consequences, especially in the tragedies, allows him to indulge in an expressive and empathetic tenderness, producing a body of work that is, at once, so rich in sentiment and so immune to sentimentality.

Bloom is surely correct in assessing both the special richness of this tragedy and the deeply moving magnitude of its hero's suffering. The sheer beauty of the writing and its capacity to move us are inextricably tied, however, to Lear's own willingness to grasp the moral meaning of his plummet from rage to grief. Having lived a uniquely privileged life, Lear had fashioned a mind that, mistaking the sovereignty of the throne for the sovereignty of his self, actually believed that it could not be "changed by place or time." Only by ceding his throne, and so opening himself up to both the anxiety of others' "influence" and their outright harms, does he belatedly achieve the pain-raked clarity of a self-recognition.

By the end Lear does begin to learn the lessons of love: the moderating nature of its just supply, the necessary reciprocities of its exchange, how king and commoner alike are both vulnerable to love's harms and accountable for love's abuse. These are recognitions, however, that arrive too late and in a form far too intense to be borne. In the sort of irony that tragic drama comprehends, the worst harm that Lear has done becomes the very harm that he must suffer. His vulnerability and accountability have merged as one in the dumb and dreadful weight of his daughter's breathless body. In the bitter book of Cordelia's corpse, Lear can now read who he has been as a "deep self"—which is, finally, not separable from what he has done as a "person in society."

Inspiring Shakespeare: In Praise of Anonymity

> *They know that Hamlet and Lear are gay.*
> *Gaiety transfiguring all that dread.*
> —W. B. Yeats, "Lapis Lazuli"

It has become a cliché today to claim that the personal is political, and as each individual appetite aspires to the luster of a civil right, that equation is sometimes reduced to a self-justifying excuse for narcissistic entitlement. Yet as the plotting of Lear's demise powerfully reveals, personality and polity do remain linked, and at the deepest ontological level. Each "deep self" is as much the shadow as the source of the "person in society," and each person in society (each "piece" of the whole) remains both accountable for sustaining society's "just supply" and vulnerable to its violations. In their mastery of poetic form at every level, Shakespeare's tragedies rescue this enduring link between the personal and the political by revealing its true and interactive complexity: the ongoing influence of the one on the many, the many on the one. They dramatize again and again how the singular self can be both the site of inalienable rights and the source of alienating wrongs, the fount of elegant wondering and the forge of ugly dissembling. They insist that, just as the human voice itself radiates outward beyond its own locale, each private soliloquy has a public resonance and so, too, an accountable range of ethical and political consequences.

In his ongoing anxiety about the rise of atomistic individualism, Donne also famously warned that "no man is an island," that each of us remains a fraternal piece of the continental "main."[26] Shakespeare's tragedies accomplish something more complex and apparently contradictory: they explore the multiple islands of that era's new individualism, the unique flora and fauna of every imaginable habitat for the single human heart, even as they insist on those islands' inescapable relation to the various confederations of community. They supply, at once and paradoxically, the most eloquent expression of a "puissant" individualism *and* the most trenchant critique of its ethical and political dangers. In this they are absolutely true to the contradictory "social energies" of the historical moment in which they were composed. To read them simply as reactionary endorsements of the old medieval order or as apolitical celebrations of modernity's new "deep self" drastically reduces the scope, difficulty, and courage of their achievement, which is political *and* personal *and* poetic all at once.

Seamus Heaney, whose aesthetic opinions were tried in the fires of Northern Ireland's Troubles, defines the political function of poetry as that of metaphorical "redress" rather than literal reform. The successful political poem becomes that separate other place, that symbolic site, where the elements of public *dis*order can be made to coexist in an orderly way through aesthetic form.[27] Unlike lyric poetry, drama always has a

---

26. John Donne, "Meditation XVII," *Devotions upon Emergent Occasions.*

27. Seamus Heaney, *The Redress of Poetry* (New York: Farrar, Straus and Giroux, 1995), 190.

social dimension, and so easier access to directly political representation. Still, I know of no body of work that fulfills Heaney's subtler mission of poetic redress more completely than Shakespeare's tragedies. And of the tragedies, no other aspires to the scope of *King Lear*'s political analysis.

Even as its five acts dramatize the specific ways in which a society's center will not hold under the assault of unchecked individualism, the play's own center retains its formal shapeliness. In the course of events as driven by individual and allied ethical decisions, Lear's Britain devolves into a sphere of chaos and pain and anomie while the ur-place of the play itself remains a web of order and beauty and empathy. Not only are we given exquisitely crafted models of individual behavior from the cautionary Lear to the exemplary Cordelia—a courageous and nuanced attendance to which might indeed, contrary to Bloom's dismissive claim, make us better human beings in discernible ways; at a deeper level, the drama's own performance provides us with an ongoing model of "just supply." Scene after scene, it meets the highest standard of self-governance, that "most precious square of sense" which counterbalances the public with the private, the reality of dreadful circumstances with the redress of the poetry that expresses them.

To these I would add one last achievement, for in its unflinching projection of its own era's contradictions—its mapping of the emerging conflict between the ambitions of modernity's social atom and the loyalties that sustain the medieval social order—*King Lear* prophetically captures a tension that will haunt every subsequent would-be democracy. As such, it would seem to have a special relevance to a post-modern America caught between the decadence of a declining individualism and the crude collectivism of identity politics, a nation whose compass of relations, like that of Donne's England, has been cracking under the stress of opposing worldviews.

Those are just some of the reasons why Shakespeare should be read by today's professors, students, and regents alike, and if resentment proves precisely the wrong attitude to bring to this task, bardolatry is scarcely better. Finally we have to ask if Bloom's praise of Shakespeare is any more sincere, any less self-aggrandizing and ultimately subversive to the playwright's authority, than the unctuous verbal oozings of Lear's older daughters, whose hyperbole, after all, he more than matches. Like many a postmodernist whose smirking poses Bloom would claim to loathe, this defender of the Bard seems to assume that the irony of his self-description immunizes him from the accuracy of its implied analysis.

But Bloom *is* an idolater. And idolaters, as Isaiah knew, do not really bow down to the God they claim to honor so much as "worship the work of their own hands, that which their own fingers have made."[28]

So it is that Bloom's readings of Shakespeare—with their obsessive fears of contaminating influence, their excessive insistence on art's autonomy, their narrow fixation on single characters over narrative communities, and their allied endorsement of morbid magnitude over the squaring of sense—repeatedly obscure the richly nuanced experience of the plays with images forged by *his* mind's own place.

Like Narcissus bending close to the surface of his pool, Bloom studies the Shakespearean page only to discover there the reflection of his own pet ideas, a misreading whose scale of creativity he then tacitly allies with the potency of the divine—with "the invention of the human." In the manner of Regan's overripe regard and Goneril's oily endearments, Bloom's critical acts of excessive flattery are really masked rituals of self-promotion. On *his* watch from the heights at Thermopylae, criticism, whose crucial mission it is to explore the abundant otherness of the world, has been reduced instead to solipsism.

As such, Bloom's books do ironically reflect the "social energies" of our place and time. His "creative" misreadings are completely at home in an economy whose quantiphilia relentlessly degrades all professional callings into self-promoting careers and neighborliness into networking. Wedding Romantic egotism to rational efficiency in an unholy pursuit of vulgar magnitude, today's market economy gladly accepts Bloom's elitist aestheticism in the same way it accepts his opponents' egalitarian multiculturalism: as yet one more set of Info-Age experiences to purchase, patent, shrink-wrap, and pitch. His *discernment*, like their *diversity*, is quickly converted into a seasonal line of commercial accessories. And like the Gregorian chants, Tibetan prayers, and Shoshone myths that are now being marketed globally; like the pricey anniversary edition of Marx's *Das Kapital* and the branded memorabilia of Dr. King's martyrdom; like the packaged tours that now replace pilgrimages, ferrying spectators to and from Brazilian slums and outback oases in shows of "authenticity," Shakespeare's plays are celebrated as *pieces*, as sound-bite experiences deliberately deracinated from the robust resonance of human engagement.

Once active agents of cultural meaning, they become the passive unguents of our money culture's raw debasements. Potentially

---

28. Isaiah 2:8.

transformative experiences, they are turned instead into their own simulacra, pseudo sacraments through which cultural appreciation is made to serve the narcissistic self's constant need for confirmation. Under the tutelage of the NEA-CON crew, they supply a mirror-glance chance to feel good about one's own sensitivity: a seal of approval affirming one's status as a defender of the heights at Thermopylae. But like the antidepressants we now dose ourselves with, these hits of sublimity can't hide for long the age's actual spiritual depravity. No show of appreciation or flaunting of expertise can sate the "cosmological emptiness" that lies at the core of our era's "social energies."

Just as today's so-called celebrations of self-esteem both mask and enact an actual emasculation of America's once potent individualism by fleeing its moral and psychological rigors, Bloom's effusive praise of Shakespeare's plays weakens their effectuality by sparing us the invigorating challenge of their larger obligations. Literary greatness is, finally, not an hors d'oeuvre to savor but an opportunity for revision. As the literal meanings of both phrases attest, aesthetic discernment, like cultural diversity, *ought* to "make a difference." Which is to say that to be truly moved by the Shakespearean play is to move differently in the world beyond the theater of its staging.

The apt word for this willing embrace of influence is not contamination but inspiration. Paradoxically, it is only through this in-spiring (breathing in) of the world's circumscribing otherness—only through our willingness to observe other faces, absorb other voices, always ready to admit that they might be better than our own—that we can achieve the full potential of our individuality. To the extent that the human condition permits it, true self-genesis ironically depends more on the anonymous art of selective obedience than on the active publicity of transgressive revolt. And as William Hazlitt grasped early on, it was precisely this self-effacing readiness to become anyone or anything—this extraordinary gift for selective acts of imaginative submission—that lay at the heart of Shakespeare's greatness.[29]

That artistic immortality might be born in part out of a willing embrace of anonymity proves to be a paradox, however, that our self-promoting era cannot fathom. Ignoring the legacy of the work, we tend to pursue instead the biography of the man, and bending those few facts about him that we actually possess to our biased ends, we assert

---

29. William Hazlitt, "Shakespeare," *Selected Writings*, ed. John Cook (New York: Oxford University Press, 1991), 323–334.

that Shakespeare "really" was an aristocrat, or a closeted Catholic, or a repressed homosexual. More reliquaries for the bardolater, more opposition research for the politically correct. He becomes just one more celebrity we've exhumed to consume, to pitch or trash in the morbid marketplace of commodified gossip.

Yet the call of the work patiently survives the noisy distraction of those decadent tasks. My own return to it, after long neglect, occurred a few years back when I dipped into *Hamlet* to check a three-word phrase I planned to cite. As this five-minute errand became a three-hour immersion, my mundane commitment to accuracy took on by turns a graver tenor and a grander dimension: to live like *this*; to feel *this* keenly the full palette of emotions, to know *this* acutely the moral and psychological complexities of any given human moment.

Now as then I emerge from my reading of Shakespeare's plays charged with the sense that my own world has somehow been enlarged and enriched. Further, as if a memory rescued from the edge of oblivion, this enriching vision seems to flicker with the shapes of a founding recognition. I have the haunting sense that this deeper, defter world has been more recovered than invented. Through my willing submission to the play's influence, I'm made to feel again that, for all our differences in temper, talent, gender, and class—individuating qualities that the play itself fastidiously enacts—each of us does *not* live "elsewhere, in a time and a place of one's own." I am reawakened into the faith that we share instead a larger human place, a deeper fate, and that, even in our most divisive moments, we remain somehow together and at home.

Implicit in this faith, born in the afterglow of the reading experience, is the suggestion that its harmonies might be savored daily. This state of intense and enriched equilibrium might be ours if we could only see as clearly, hear as surely, and feel as fully as the play allows us to. If only we could meet *its* standard of self-governance, then we might return to that "most precious square of sense" in which the personal and the political can cohere.

This hint of a perpetually accessible homecoming into harmony does renew a sense of unfulfilled responsibility—to be inspired, after all, is to wish to do better—but it also supplies the most consoling gifts. Among them is the recovery of a gaiety that can transfigure all our dread. Among them, too, in the fullness of fellow-feeling from the words flowing in, is the tactile refutation of emptiness.

3

Saving the Appearances
(John Ford's Rescripting of the American Mythos)

Though rarely acknowledged in a scientific age, even the most advanced nations depend on a narrative interpretation of reality to guide their everyday decision-making. New technologies can radically empower us, but the application of those powers, whether the "shock and awe" of our smart bombs or the virtual friendship of social networking, is still shaped by the stories we tell ourselves about ourselves. Our deepest motives are animated by populist narratives, the character of a nation imprinted and sustained by our co-participation in a meaningful mythos, one whose heroic figures embody communal ideals and whose familiar plots metaphorically address the most pressing and perennial problems that we face.

Politicians grasp the implicit authority of these populist narratives, hijacking their symbols to influence opinion. So it was that when trying to drum up support for an American imperialism after 9/11, one neoconservative op-ed author evoked Cary Grant in *Gunga Din* riding to the rescue of the British Raj.[1] More effective politically, the official campaign photo for Ronald Reagan in 1980 pictured him in a cowboy shirt and hat (both white, of course), and twenty years before that, John F. Kennedy cleverly associated his presidential candidacy with the most potent American myth of all by defining the era as a New Frontier. But though those familiar tropes did generate the sort of allegiance that converted into votes, were the new sociopolitical conditions in each case really

---

1. Max Boot, "The Case for American Empire: The Most Realistic Response to Terrorism Is for America to Embrace its Imperial Role," *Weekly Standard*, 15 October, 2001.

illuminated by the old mythic metaphors, or were they obscured? And if the answer was mixed, then which aspects of the old likeness still held true and which did not? More crucially perhaps: to what degree were the leaders themselves guided or misled by the myths they borrowed to articulate their intentions and garner support?

Such questions are not unique to 1960 or 1980. Foundational myths are fashioned to fit site-specific historical conditions, and those conditions shift over time, challenging the relevance of the old story line and its central characters. And because rapid material gains can disrupt any community's inner compass, these challenges are especially frequent in a society committed to technological progress. Our engineering culture dismisses such a danger, preferring to flatter its work in utopian terms, but powerful inventions—the assembly line, radio, the birth control pill, wiki software—do undermine prevailing ethical conventions, creating confusion and contention that can destabilize the communal order. Charged with preserving social cohesion through rehearsing those stories that encode communal values and redress common problems, the mythic imagination must somehow incorporate these new facts on the ground; it must rescue coherence and consensus out of what may initially seem an incompatible mix of traditional beliefs and emergent practices.

We are well acquainted with an analogous process in the sciences: how, when new and anomalous discoveries occur, practitioners rush to render the alien familiar by subsuming it under the day's prevailing theoretical frame. In early astronomy, maps would be redrafted to include newly observed stars, but those changes were inscribed in ways that were careful to preserve the traditional geocentric model of the universe. This practice was called "saving the appearances," and what was being saved in the process was not just the unanticipated observance but also the reigning paradigm for making sense of the observable world.

As Galileo could attest, adaptations that went so far as to threaten the logic of the paradigm itself were in danger of inviting a hostile response, and the peril was far greater when the map being redrafted was not a chart of the stars but the story of human origins. As driven by the spread of the printed book—one of the most empowering and so, too, disruptive inventions in Western history—the translation of the Bible into the common tongues of the people led to contending interpretations of the foundational mythos, and these in turn helped to spur brutal bouts of revolt and repression. Scholars were burned at the stake with their own heretical manuscripts used as tinder,[2] and neighbor slaughtered neighbor as sectarian wars erupted throughout the continent and England. Akin to the vicious ethnic cleansing that took place in Rwanda, Iraq, and Myanmar, these far earlier examples from Christian Europe remind us that managing the tension between material change and moral continuity can be a life-or-death affair, and that if transformations in cultural identity are to remain peaceful, the collective imagination must somehow manage to counterbalance innovation with conservation.

As the utter failure of the past century's totalitarian regimes proved, a new identity cannot be imposed by force alone. Nor can it be imported like grain as a form of foreign aid to feed the needy minds of the global poor: a gritty lesson the avid supporters of "nation-building" have too often ignored. Instead, significant changes in communal beliefs must evolve over time and can only be achieved through a gradual reformation of the most familiar tropes and terms. Given the narrative nature of human reasoning, such changes require an artful rescripting of the traditional mythos by those intimate with the inner logic of its symbols. Here I want to examine one such instance of effective rescripting, as achieved by John Ford in his 1939 cinematic classic *Stagecoach*. First, though, we need to consider the origins of the story that Ford was amending: the myth of the old frontier that long preceded Kennedy's proclamation of the new.

From Leatherstocking to Lone Ranger

The creation of nation-states in late eighteenth- and nineteenth-century Europe required incorporating a variety of long-lived local cultures, each with its separate traditions and lore and often its own language. Modernizing armies secured borders and squelched revolts; powerful economic interests endorsed an expansion of authority that could enforce uniform rules for lending and trade; the evolution of a rationalized bureaucracy made it easier to administer the extended state; and the rapid expansion of literacy allowed the state to establish an official language and so, over time, a truly common tongue.

Still, to read the same language and obey the same laws were not sufficient in themselves to generate those ties that can bind separate clans

---

2. In 1536 William Tyndale was strangled, then burned at the stake in Vilvorde, Belgium, for translating the Bible into English. In England, Sir Thomas More, Henry VIII's Chancellor, had Tynsdale's supporters flogged or burned at the stake for not renouncing his translations: https://www.fbinstitute.com/engbible/7.html.

and tribes into a fraternal whole. Loving your neighbor is an emotional allegiance founded on actual everyday experiences, but loving your nation is an imaginative act, achieved in part through an empathetic participation in a myth of common origins, the artful conjuring of a virtual past. During the nineteenth century, the printed novel became the West's most advanced medium for mythological thinking, and the new genre that emerged to serve the urgent social purposes of nation-building was the historical romance, first established by Sir Walter Scott in 1814. Characterized by melodramatic plots based on real historical crises, these popular novels generated a series of heroes, symbols, and allegorical events that, revered by their readership, created a new and broader imaginative commons, a sense of belonging on a national scale.

The early master of this new form in America was James Fenimore Cooper, and the historical crises he utilized to advance a literary nationalism were the violent conflicts associated with settling the frontier. Born himself in a frontier town in upstate New York during the year that Washington assumed the presidency, Cooper belonged to the first generation who lived from cradle to grave under a constitutionally defined federal government. Still, cultural unity was hardly a given: the divisions of class, race, religion, and region that had characterized the colonial period, and that would eventually erupt into civil war over the question of slavery, persisted. Both the North and the South, however, possessed open borders to the West, and internal immigration (moving from the settled township to the latest frontier) remained a perpetual possibility for all Americans except the enslaved for some 260 years. Deeply engrained in the collective memory, the challenges of pioneering did provide, then, a plausible set of common experiences suitable for imagining a national identity: an American character in mythic terms that managed to transcend regional differences.

In the five volumes of his Leatherstocking saga, Cooper infused Scott's historical romance with key elements from homegrown genres, borrowing from colonial captivity narratives and from legendary accounts of actual frontiersmen like Daniel Boone to create a story line and set of character types that would calibrate the American imagination for many years to come. The saga dramatizes the adventures of the frontier scout Natty Bumppo—alternately known as Leatherstocking, Deerhunter, Pathfinder, and Hawkeye—from the French and Indian Wars in the 1740s until his death on the prairie in 1804. Four of the five volumes are set somewhere on the American frontier during that initial period when white civilization, newly arrived in the wilderness, is still threatened by the so-called savage; and borrowing the primary pattern of the captivity narrative, the plots' central events involve either protecting or rescuing their white heroines from hostile natives.

A highly idealized figure, Natty is the original fictive model for all of America's "lonesome heroes": the first in a long line of rugged individualists who, despite their self-chosen exile from civilized society, always come to its rescue in times of crisis. As a white Christian who lives in and loves the wilderness, Natty has acquired all the site-specific skills necessary for survival there. Closely allied with the noble savage Chingachgook, the last of the Mohican line, he is intimate with nature and with the crafts and customs of native ways. A master marksman and tactician, he is a formidable warrior, yet like most mythic heroes his violent ways are always applied toward virtuous ends. Those include slaying the savage kidnapper, rescuing the current damsel in distress, and selflessly leading the white settlers into the heart of the wilderness—whose forests they will then clear and fields fence in, thus ironically domesticating the very wildness that Natty most cherishes, sending him into exile again, chasing the ever westward recession of the American frontier.

The Leatherstocking saga also establishes a representative set of secondary characters, encoding through them values that clarify the proper relations between the races, social classes, and sexes, as endorsed by the actions and speeches of Leatherstocking himself. Despite his humble background and native ways, for example, Natty allies himself with the Anglo-American aristocratic class, whose traditional heroic figures, the gentleman officer and genteel lady, remain unchanged: these are the civilized roles and codes that Natty's frontier heroism formulaically saves. Meanwhile, the other races are assigned their separate "gifts," each acknowledged and praised but in ways that affirm the ultimate ascendancy of the white colonials, who, the story's climax assures, will win the war for the wilderness and safely reestablish their traditional social hierarchy there.

The noble savage can be admired, even tacitly desired in the sexual sense, but miscegenation itself, the fulfillment of that desire, is strictly prohibited. And idealized though they are, even Natty's interracial friendships and hybrid skills (the highly effective mixing of his white loyalties with his red "gifts"—his deer hunting, pathfinding, and hawkeyed marksmanship) have a limited license, restricted to the temporary phase of frontier settlement. That is why Natty must always leave the civilized scene at story's end and why too, in contrast to those many heroes who wed the damsels they save, he remains a chaste bachelor throughout. As the symbolic perfection of a transient period, Leatherstocking, too, must remain the last of his genealogical line. In Cooper's romance, the imminent passing of both the frontier scout and the noble savage is dramatized even as their roles are romantically idealized.

Their final passing, however, could easily be deferred in the American mind so long as more open territory to the west awaited settlement, supplying a new locale for a similar drama of interracial conflict and class rivalries during a period of dangerous lawlessness. Another Hawkeye could always emerge out of the wild there to save the civilized life, accompanied by another Chingachgook belonging to a different but equally doomed tribe. And beyond its literal relevance to the nation's long history of pioneering through internal immigration, the standard plot and archetypal characters of Cooper's frontier myth symbolically addressed three enduring tensions especially relevant to the American experience. Due to the ongoing impact of slavery and an unusually open immigration policy, interracial and ethnic conflicts, fear of and attraction to the cultural other, have been a perpetual feature of American life. So, too, with the tension between an equality of rights implicit in the democratic spirit and the reality of persistent class differences in wealth and power. Finally, in the most democratic culture in the world, there was, and still is, a constant tension between extolling the rights of a liberated individualism and assuring the sorts of compliant loyalty that any stable society requires.

Through crafting a hero whose mastery of violence always served the genteel, who "went native" without violating his loyalty to white civilization and who, though freed of all social restrictions, still remained true in times of real crisis to "the ties that bind," Cooper wed the raw individualism and adaptive pragmatism of frontier settlement to the conservative idealism of an established cultural order. As such, his mythic tales both acknowledged and assuaged the primary anxieties of internal immigration in a democratic society: a cluster of experiences that, despite many regional differences, supplied a common grounding for a national identity.

What happens, then, to the exquisite equilibrium of tensions that characterized Cooper's myth when its allegorical-historical frontier ceases to work as a credible metaphor for the American experience? The question proves more subtle and subdivided than it first may seem, for our myths shape as well as mind our given place. And when they change, they tend to evolve by degree, their various elements transformed unevenly and in ways that are often concealed (as in the cases of Reagan and

JFK) behind a gestural allegiance to the old symbols. A metaphor is never an exact equation, and when the metaphorical scheme in question is one as internally complex, collectively adopted, and multiply expressed as a national myth, the hope of finding a single cause or certain date for either its final devolution into irrelevancy or its radical transformation into a wholly new form is an illusory proposition.

Certainly the closing of the frontier—the practical end to the availability of land in an unsettled West still populated by native tribes—presented a formidable challenge to Cooper's original formulation. But insomuch as the mythic frontier had always stood for something more than the literal places and events it depicted, and insomuch as its plot continued to redress many of the perennial anxieties of the American experience in a highly mobile, individualistic, and multiracial society, key elements of its underlying narrative could manage to retain, with suitable adjustments in costume and setting, their unifying relevancy.

Initially, those adjustments were relatively minor as the old mythic figures were refashioned to fit that deeper, drier West whose regions would absorb, in serial fashion after Cooper's death in 1851, the characteristic conflicts of frontier settlement. Natty's fur cap and moccasins give way there to a brimmed hat and spurred boots, his graceful dash along forested trails to a masterful horse ride across a dust-plumed desert. In many cases, his rifle is replaced by a six-shooter, and the names of the native tribes and the issues dividing the contending white parties are recast to fit the historical times. Adjusting to the literary realism of the post Civil War period, this next incarnation of American virtue drops the extended sermons that Natty Bumppo favored for the terse aside, the rough verbal ore of real-guy wisdom.

But beneath the play of those new appearances and absent the native nicknames that overtly signified his character, this new version of the American hero, the now iconic "lonesome cowboy," retained the same cluster of virtues that defined Cooper's scout. Like Leatherstocking, he is at one with the wilderness he loves. Like Straight-Tongue, he never lies. Like Hawkeye, he proves to be the master of his era's most deadly weapons. And after the fashion of Pathfinder, he reliably charts a safe way through the confusion of the day, ending the martial anarchy and solving the moral complexities that characterize frontier settlement. Like Natty, too, the cowboy hero embodies the resolute independence of the outsider; he is someone who not only thinks for himself but also emerges from the literal outside of the wilderness to rescue a threatened community: that family of homesteaders, that passing wagon train or small border town whose members are imperiled by a gang of bandits or a marauding tribe.

The problem of why an outsider should prove so dedicated to saving a way of life that he himself cannot abide goes unaddressed. A counter-Hamlet in this sense, the lonesome cowboy rarely agonizes over his decision to commit; instead, he simply, reflexively, and against all odds does "the right thing," which, as in Cooper's saga, usually includes rescuing the current damsel in distress. And whatever that new hero's initial motivation, one didactic intention has been preserved: that of binding the self-reliant loner—who, after all, might be indifferent or even hostile to the welfare of the group he once gladly left behind—to the cause of civilized settlement. The potential conflict between the liberated individuality preferred by Americans and the social unity required by any communal group is thus finessed, yet the integrity of their differences is also maintained by having the hero "ride out of town" at the end of the day.

Like Leatherstocking, then, the lonesome cowboy saves the settlers only to refuse the bounded bounty of settlement itself. The temporary defender of domesticity, with its corrals and farm-field fences, mustn't ever be fenced in himself—not by a place, a permanent job, or a formal body of laws, not by any socially sanctified and rule-bound relationship such as those forged in marriage or in the military. Rather than meekly obey, in Emerson's disdainful words, "the Blue Laws of the world,"[3] his moral commitments are always spontaneous and fully voluntary. As the moral perfection of democratic individualism, the lonesome cowboy descending from Cooper must owe nothing yet give all, on a moment's notice and of his own free will.

I've been generalizing, of course. The Western assumes so many forms, involving so many separate artists of differing skills and sensibilities, and spans such an extensive period of social change (from the end of the Civil War to about 1970) that any satisfactory survey is not plausible here. To glance at just one example that clearly borrows from Cooper's model, we can turn to *The Lone Ranger*, a highly popular radio drama targeting boys that was first aired in 1933. Surviving World War II and the arrival of television, a video version was broadcast from 1949–57, its reruns lasting into 1961, and during that long run its narrative formula remained essentially unchanged.

---

3. Ralph Waldo Emerson, "Heroism," in *Selected Essays* (Chicago: Peoples Book Club), 175.

In each episode the earnest and upright Lone Ranger, dressed in his unambiguously symbolic (if utterly impractical) outfit of pure white, was accompanied by his near mute but loyal native sidekick, Tonto. And each week this ever-roving pair, riding their steady steeds Silver and Paint, would arrive from outside to save the locals' day, only to depart after that rescue, the star of the show commanding his mount: "Hi-yo, Silver... Away!" The medium had shifted from the adult novel to children's radio and teledrama, the setting from the plush Northeast during the French and Indian Wars to the arid Southwest during that second phase of frontier settlement after the Civil War, and the social subplots had been eliminated; still, the underlying story of Hawkeye and Chingachgook had been conserved. Fundamental elements drawn from the same imaginative commons had managed to survive from their first articulation as a nation-building myth in the 1820s to Kennedy's proclamation of the New Frontier.

Cooper's romances were both popular with the reading public and admired by the most sophisticated literary minds of his day. By the late 1930s, though, few believed that this later generation of frontier narratives could achieve anything like that rare marriage of the popular with the exemplary. So it was that during the same period that *The Lone Ranger* was at the peak of its popularity even a prominent director like John Ford had to struggle to get studio backing for a picture with a Western setting and adult themes. He finally succeeded, and the result proved extraordinarily influential in its own right, supplying a new template for the old mythic formula, literally and figuratively setting the stage for thirty more years of sophisticated Westerns.

From Tonto to Lordsburg

Stagecoach transformed the shape and substance of the American Western in three significant ways. It established Arizona's Monument Valley as the new archetypal stage for the mythic frontier, the area's chiseled spires, massive mesas, and dauntingly arid and empty spaces becoming the cinematic equivalent of Cooper's gorgeously described forests, lakes, and streams. It elevated John Wayne into a major movie star who would eventually replace Gary Cooper as the nation's reigning model of the virile lonesome hero. And finally this breakthrough film proved that the old genre could become relevant again, drawing on our frontier myth's standard terms to revise and, in some cases, even reverse its version of American virtue.

The overarching plot is easily summarized: the year is 1885, and we follow a stagecoach and its nine passengers and crewmen as they travel between two towns (Tonto and Lordsburg) in the Southwest during the Apache uprising led by Geronimo. To be threatened in the wilderness by hostile natives is, of course, the standard peril posed by our frontier myth, and following its well-established formula, John Wayne's character, the Ringo Kid, does arrive from outside. The last of the nine to board, he hails the stagecoach on foot and from well beyond the boundaries of the first town; with Monument Valley's silhouetted mesas framed in the background, he appears to be emerging from the wilderness itself: the natural man reentering the claustrophobic spaces of the social sphere.

And having borrowed the myth's narrative alpha, the script also mimics its standard omega; Ringo does retreat from civilization again at the story's end, riding out of town as the convention decrees: "Hi-yo, Silver... Away!"—always away. But the hero doesn't depart alone this time; nor is he accompanied by the latest reincarnation of the noble savage; nor are his heroics the sole focus of the story. In one of the many serious ironies that animate *Stagecoach*, Ford uses the generic Western's pat endorsement of the heroic individualist—that "lone ranger" descending from Leatherstocking—in order to study the possibilities for a democratic community. In doing so, he reinfuses the myth's imaginative domain with a social complexity that, over the years, had been stripped from the original myth by a highly commercialized entertainment industry.

There are three communities in *Stagecoach*: two established towns that prove to be moral mirrors of each other, and the improvisational society that evolves on the stagecoach itself when the Apache uprising isolates the group on their journey from Tonto and Lordsburg. The members of this makeshift community have been carefully selected to represent a diversity of classes and moral types. Buck, the driver (who is played primarily for comic effect) and the stalwart Curly (a marshal literally "riding shotgun" to protect the coach) constitute the working class, the crew whose job it is to serve the public. The passenger list includes Lucy Mallory, the pregnant daughter of a former Confederate officer who is traveling westward to join her husband, now a captain in the post-Civil War cavalry. Her presence in Tonto reawakens a Southern sense of honor in Hatfield, a "notorious gambler" who had once served under her father and who now, in act of spontaneous gallantry, decides to join the party as

Lucy's protector. Together, Lucy and Hatfield represent the old aristocratic class, its landed gentry and military elite, who (like Duncan Heyward and Alice Munro in *The Last of the Mohicans*) had been the co-heroes of Cooper's saga. They are the very group whose social prerogatives Hawkeye once saved but whose ascendancy is now passing and whose code of conduct can no longer prevail in a nation acutely transformed by the Civil War and the rapid industrialization that followed it.

Two members of the commercial class—which, boosted by the North's victory, has been rapidly replacing the old landed elite—are also onboard: the ironically named Samuel Peacock, a traveling whiskey salesman whose most obvious trait is his meekness, and the upscale banker, Henry Gatewood who, despite his social standing and air of pompous rectitude, is a covert criminal—an embezzler skipping town just ahead of the bank inspector. Gatewood is the one unredeemable villain on the coach, as purely bad as the Ringo Kid is purely good. Not unlike today, the symbolic association of villainy with banking was an easy equation to make at the end of the 1930s, a decade that had seen so many farms, homes, and small businesses repossessed. But inside the allegorical domain of the film, the contrast between Gatewood's high social standing and his actual moral character is just one element of a much broader critique of the established social order.

That order is indicted for its intolerance as well as its corruption. On the Noah's ark of Ford's stagecoach, those three representative pairs—the twinned members of the working class, the old aristocracy, and the new commercial bourgeoisie—are joined by two outcasts, the social dregs of Tonto: Doc Boone, a drunken physician, who has been evicted by his landlady for failure to pay his rent, and Dallas, a prostitute, who has been booted out of town by the Law and Order League, a women's society led by Gatewood's wife. In the disdainful words of the landlady, Dallas and Doc are "two of a kind."

Ford deliberately stages these banishments, though, in ways that evoke an unexpected sympathy. Though sometimes portrayed with a condescending affection, deadbeat drunks and whores were not granted anything like a true heroic status in the popular frontier narratives descending from Cooper. Yet Dallas is portrayed here as blonde-beautiful and vulnerable, not "dark and fiery," which had been the standard characterization for the type. And despite her sexual history, she is framed and lit throughout the film (including a few beatifically glowing close-ups) in the ways that traditionally signify feminine virtue. Both the visual coding and the verbal script of *Stagecoach* treat Dallas as if she were in fact the standard heroine of the American mythos: that innocent virgin who, threatened by marauding savages or bandits, must be rescued from harm by the lonesome hero. Doc, meanwhile, in a less radical deviation from type, is a cheerful and charmingly eloquent drunk, someone whose ironic temperament protects him from life's reversals, including his eviction and the social censure that accompanies it.

Character evaluations inside narratives are always relative, and so our sympathy for these two outcasts is also enhanced by the film's portrayal of their critics, Doc's landlady and the Law and Order League, whose self-righteous hectoring is made to seem mean-spirited. That these harsh judges are women, and that the Law and Order League is led by Gatewood's wife, are meaningful choices. Depending on manners and morals as well as formal laws, social authority has its feminine and masculine sides, and the corruption of Tonto's social order is efficiently signaled by the fact that it has licensed both the cruelty of Mrs. Gatewood and the criminality of her husband.

Assembled in town, the first five passengers (Gatewood and Ringo have yet to board) are suddenly confronted by a crucial decision: they've just learned about the Apache uprising, and each must choose whether to risk the ride. As the drama requires, they all elect to go, and the stagecoach departs, the absconding Gatewood joining them on the sly when they reach the edge of town. Here the setting dramatically switches from Tonto's streets, banks, saloons, and rooming houses to the open spaces of the untamed wilderness, the now iconic imagery of Monument Valley entering the nation's consciousness for the first time. The tension will soon rise in very familiar ways, but only after firmly establishing its interest in the moral dynamics of social standing does the film move into those contested spaces where the threat of violence will intensify the stakes. With just the coach itself and two isolated stations along the way as physical refuge, the makeshift society onboard must somehow survive this transitional passage through savage territory. Enter now the lonesome cowboy.

John Wayne's character seals the deal on Ford's radical revision of the generic Western, starting with his deliberate challenge to its pat equation of moral stature with social status. The Ringo Kid arrives on the scene in a manner that silently evokes the traditional frontier hero—that natural man who appears to emerge from the moral perfection of the wilderness itself. And, like Dallas, he is lit and framed throughout with a visual vocabulary that has conventionally signaled heroic status. But Ringo's backstory confounds the usual expectations. Not only has he been given a tragic past: alone in the world now, his family has been killed by the three Plummer brothers. He also has been made a social outcast of the most severe sort. Unjustly convicted of murdering the Plummers' foreman, Ringo has escaped from prison and is now on his way to Lordsburg to go after the Plummers themselves.

An official outlaw, Ford's lonesome hero is now determined to act outside the law again, and not to assist the needy but to exact a very private revenge. Unfortunately for Ringo, though, Curly is onboard. Rearrested by the marshal, he enters the coach and becomes the final member of its makeshift community. The equilibrium between its four original pairs—the working class, the old aristocracy, the new commercial bourgeoisie, and the socially disreputable—has been skewed, however. The officially scorned "two of a kind" have now become three, the deadbeat drunk and the town whore joined by a convicted murderer.

Ringo's arrival completes Ford's ironic inversion of the moral order. It's not quite true here, to borrow from the Rolling Stones song, that "every cop is a criminal / and all the sinners saints."[4] Curly, for example, as the cop onboard, displays a vigorous and empathetic moral intelligence throughout. But among the passengers, the officially designated sinners will prove themselves heroic by story's end, while the four purportedly respectable citizens will be shown as unworthy of their higher social standing. (The "notorious gambler" Hatfield can also be classified as a sinner, but given that his first act is quitting a game of cards to come to Lucy's aid, he has already reassumed the respectable role of the gallant gentleman.)

The key domestic trial for all onboard is how they treat Dallas, that fallen woman who has been recast by the film as an actual innocent. Under the standard duress the plot supplies, will she receive that chivalrous respect and allegiance, that self-sacrificial masculine protection due every damsel in distress—the same treatment, in fact, that Lucy receives? Doc, her fellow outcast and a genial social democrat, has been allied with Dallas from the opening scene. Ringo immediately addresses her as "ma'am," and then continues to offer her the formal courtesies and social deference any lady should expect. The other passengers, however, those who are not of their "kind," behave otherwise: the consistently obnoxious Gatewood

---

4. "Sympathy for the Devil," Mick Jagger and Keith Richards, © Mirage Music Int. Ltd. C/o Essex Music Int. L, Mirage Music Ltd.

scorns Dallas; Hatfield and Lucy, clinging to the inflexible judgments of the old social elite, deliberately snub her; and Peacock, the whiskey salesman, is too submissive at first to deviate from this consensus of the respectable classes.

Although we are directed to sympathize with Dallas and Doc from the start, the film's combination of the traditional visual vocabulary of the heroic and an early demonstration of their democratic manners isn't sufficient to make a convincing case that these official sinners are admirable rather than merely likeable people. The reasons behind their outcast status may have occurred off-stage, but they do still bear weight. Dallas *has* been the town whore; Doc *has* been a deadbeat drunk and, in fact, continues to drink from Peacock's supplies while on the coach. These characters can only earn our respect separate from our sympathy through taking effective action under truly trying circumstances. The opportunity arises when Lucy goes into labor at the second way station, Apache Wells. Doc sobers up there and performs like a medical professional, and, despite having been snubbed by Lucy, Dallas also comes to her aid, assisting in the delivery and then ably caring for the weakened mother and her newborn baby. Both social outcasts redeem themselves during this most crucial of domestic occasions: assuring the safe arrival of the next generation.

The fact that Dallas has passed this dramatic test of character, shown to be both competent and compassionate in the roles of nurse-companion and surrogate mother, then tests the other passengers in turn, giving each of them a chance to judge her anew. Ringo's allegiance had already been secured, but it is only after seeing Dallas with Lucy's baby that he proposes that they run away together, a fugitive couple and future parents themselves. Of those who had shunned her, Gatewood remains offensively self-centered and Hatfield obsessed with protecting Lucy alone. Lucy herself briefly acknowledges Dallas's help but will never dare to associate with her once they have returned to the civilized world with its Blue Law opinions, its fixed ranks and roles. Of the socially respectable, only Peacock, the meek salesman, passes this secondary test of moral recognition—though it's easier for him in that, as a stranger to Tonto, he seems unaware of Dallas's disreputable past. In any case, as a parent himself, he overtly admires Dallas's performance under pressure: her domestic equivalent of saving the day. So it is that, although the most submissive and silent of the men, he is the one who intervenes when, back onboard, the bickering begins again. Glancing at Dallas and the baby she holds, Peacock chastises the group with an opinion that clearly aligns with the filmmaker's own. "Let's not forget the ladies," he says, his use of the plural signaling his acceptance of Dallas as Lucy's social equal, adding then: "Can't we all show a little Christian charity one to another?"

With their overt reminder of how much the established order has deviated from its ethical heritage, those words mark the end of the first and longest movement in the film's complex narrative. During this phase, whose climax is the birth and its aftermath, Ford and his screenwriter Dudley Nichols have exploited the suspense generated by the threat of an Apache attack to focus instead on the genteel side of heroic behavior. They've utilized a standard plot device from the old genre to test the virtues of domesticity, dramatizing the ongoing tension between actual moral stature and official social status. The stagecoach has become a trope for frontier settlement itself, its diverse group of strangers forced into an alliance by their dangerous isolation in the wilderness.

Inherited status and the fixed rule of law become irrelevant in such places. Without Law and Order Leagues and armed cavalry to enforce virtuous behavior, formal rank and fixed routines must give way to meritorious improvisation. After the birth all the passengers are challenged anew to prove their domestic moral stature—that is, their true gentility—and with the exception of Peacock, the formally respectable passengers prove either inadequate or offensive, while the erstwhile social "dregs" (Dallas, Doc, and Ringo) rise to the occasion. The test of Ringo's true gentility, however, is not yet complete. In a clever touch, Ford and Nichols utilize the traditionally chaste characterization descending from Cooper, the lonesome hero as sexual innocent, to extend the suspense. Like Peacock, Ringo is unaware of Dallas's sexual history, and so his chivalrous devotion to her has yet to be tried in the full light of the truth. Enter now the hostile natives.

Once Ford finally commits to unleashing the violence he has so long delayed, he embraces and outdoes every cliché associated with this action genre. Reentering the open wilderness from the second outpost, the stagecoach is attacked by an Apache war party on horseback, and the film then depicts, with a visual flair unmatched in its day, the now standard chase scene. Once again red savages pursue white settlers who fire at them from inside and atop the coach with amazing accuracy. Once again the anarchy of frontier warfare has been carefully staged to both thrill and reassure, the scene jump-cutting between clouds of hoof-pounded dust, whistling arrows, bursts of gunfire, and astounding stunts as slain Apache warriors are hurled from their galloping horses.

Just as the domestic dimension of heroic virtue was tried by the birth and its aftermath, its virile side is now severely tested by the attack. Dallas holds and protects the baby while Lucy either leans helplessly against the door or silently prays. Ringo and Doc defend their group by aggressively and accurately shooting their attackers, as does Hatfield until he is slain. Although it is impossible to imagine Peacock as an effective fighter even if healthy, he is wounded at the very start of the battle, and for all his bullying bluster, Gatewood panics and has to be knocked out by Doc.

The various performances of the male passengers during this martial crisis are clearly differentiated, then, along the same class lines that were established in the opening scenes. The apparent sinners, Doc and Ringo, prove to be virile saints. Hatfield also fights like a warrior, but as the representative of a passing aristocracy, he and his antiquated code of honor must die. Meanwhile, the commercial class, the new postwar elite, fails this second and traditional heroic test, that of virile effectiveness. Neither the sweet but unmanly salesman nor the corrupt, cowardly banker can defend his endangered community.

The day *is* saved for white civilization as the foundational myth requires, but Ford makes sure that the rescue follows the double track he has so carefully prepared, linking the heroism of the exceptional individual to the cooperative heroics of the group. In the most thrilling single act (and the benchmark for film stunt-work for years to come), Ringo jumps on the backs of the coach's horses to redirect the runaway team after the wounded Buck has dropped their reins. But the group's survival has depended as well on Curly's shooting and leadership, Buck's driving, and Doc and Hatfield's effective fighting. And, as it turns out, this small improvisational community must also depend on the established one they have left behind. Despite their individual and collective heroics, the group runs out of ammunition and is about to be captured or killed when the U.S. cavalry arrives, just as the formula prescribes, "in the nick of time." The stagecoach, with its two damsels in distress, has been rescued not only by the lonesome hero, but also by the cooperative actions of this makeshift community and by society's most advanced form of organized virility, a professional army. In the script's complex rendering of frontier conflict, all three have been required to save the day.

Nor are we finished once the Apache have been defeated. The film immediately cuts to Lordsburg, where both the genteel and virile dimensions of heroic virtue will be tested anew. Ever the invalid, still incapable, it seems, of even holding her baby, a stretcher-borne Lucy weakly thanks Dallas but with the clear implication that she will not have the courage to continue their relationship now that they are back in society with its uncharitable biases against her kind. By contrast, the wounded Peacock invites Dallas to visit his family in Kansas City at some future date. No virile hero, he remains something of a genteel one, yet it is doubtful even now that he knows the details of Dallas's past, so that his acceptance of her, while admirable, hasn't been fully tested. Appreciative of Ringo's bravery in battle and no admirer of the Plummer brothers, Curly now weighs duty against justice and decides to honor the spirit of the law over its letter. Pledged to turn Ringo in, the marshal nevertheless allows the Kid to seek his just revenge first, even lending Ringo his own rifle.

These rapidly executed decisions and the moral evaluations they imply set the stage for the film's final and double climax. A script that, up until this point, has treated the traditional lonesome hero in a remarkably egalitarian fashion now focuses on the Ringo Kid alone, forcing him to face two tests of heroic virtue on his own. Will Ringo be able to exact his revenge on the Plummer brothers (the trial of virile prowess on behalf of blood loyalty and social justice)? And will he remain true to his damsel in distress even after learning about her sexual past (the test of chivalrous fidelity as it has been reimagined by Ford and Nichols)?

The makers of *Stagecoach* may have radically amended the ethical compass descending from Cooper on specific social subjects, but as the film's last act demonstrates, they were also committed to conserving the moral perfection of his lonesome hero. Natty Bumppo's infallible martial and moral accuracy is transcribed unchanged from eighteenth-century upstate New York to the Arizona Territory of 1885. Although the battle is three on one, and Ringo only has just that many bullets to get the job done, he successfully kills all the Plummer brothers. (Hawkeye, indeed!) Likewise, he doesn't flinch when Dallas's past becomes clear, repeating his marriage proposal instead. And just as Ringo keeps his word to Dallas, he then honors his previous promise to the marshal by turning himself in after his revenge is complete. (Straight-Tongue, indeed!) His exemplary behavior is then rewarded when, still favoring the spirit of justice over the letter of the law, Curly chooses to set him free.

Once again America's lonesome hero rides out of town at the end of the day—but this time he's on a buckboard, not a silver steed; he's accompanied by his wife to be rather than a noble native sidekick, and by a wife to be who, far from the aristocratic and virginal Alice Munro, has been a social outcast and a sexual pro. Once again, too, America's hero returns to the wilderness. They are heading for Ringo's isolated ranch "across the Border," a destination capitalized in Nichols' script to emphasize its allegorical resonance. They are fleeing to that Edenic place, beyond the reach of inept laws and unchristian snobs, where social rank can't trump moral merit—where, in Doc's wry words, they will be "saved from the blessings of civilization."

Marrying Innovation to Conservation

Although a remarkable aesthetic achievement in its own right, *Stagecoach* has merited an extended analysis here because of the adept ways in which it both revives and reforms our foundational story. Not only had the old narrative formula for frontier heroics become rote and unreflective by 1939; America itself had dramatically changed in the nearly ninety years since Cooper's death. The end of slavery, the long decline of the landed aristocracy and the associated rise of capitalism's moneyed classes, the emergence of consumerism with its antipuritanical ethos of appetitive pleasure and sexual license, the adoption of women's suffrage and allied changes in gender roles and expectations, the reinterpretation of human origins and motives posed by Darwinian evolution and Freudian psychology: facing such a radical transformation in the pace, shape, and commonsense understanding of everyday life, the nation's traditional self-conception also had to change, and in ways that were mythically imagined as well as rationally legislated. Like its judicial interpretations, America's foundational story had to somehow marry these emergent features of modern experience with the original intentions of a cultural identity that was first coalescing in the 1820s. This is precisely what *Stagecoach* achieves, "saving the appearances" of contemporary values within the old mythic frame first fashioned by Cooper.

In the most obvious change, *Stagecoach* frees feminine virtue from the traditional demands of sexual innocence. That inflexible standard was enforced by Cooper at the end of *The Deerslayer* (the last of the five novels written, though it portrays Bumppo at his earliest age). Leatherstocking rejects the beautiful Judith Hutter there because she has been too flirtatious with the officers of a nearby garrison—because she has "a reputation." Judith promises to change and has, in fact, proved valiant in resisting those attacks by hostile Huron braves that constitute the book's central drama; though not without flaws, she has behaved admirably under duress. But in Cooper's moral field, with its Romantic belief in the primacy of inner gifts and its categorical divisions of right and wrong, individuals must express their own given moral nature: character is fate. Rather than dramatize the potential for redemptive change, the Leatherstocking books enact the necessary fulfillment of individual and tribal destinies, an interpretation of human nature that is then strictly applied to women's sexual behavior. Cooper is so intent on justifying his hero's rejection of Judith that the novel ends by projecting a future in which, her fall now complete, she is rumored to have become an officer's "kept woman." As she once was, the old myth insists, so shall she ever be.

By endorsing its chaste hero's marriage to a woman with a sexually active past, *Stagecoach* boldly reverses that ending, and although that change is obviously minding significant shifts in the nation's sexual mores, it also reflects a more inclusive insistence on the possibilities for redemption. Dallas, after all, has been defined as a "kind"; she belongs to a class of social outcasts that includes Doc, whose sins against the established order are of a different sort. Where Cooper's frontier had been a sphere in which separate moral destinies, as driven by inner gifts, must play themselves out, the American wilderness in *Stagecoach* has been reconceived as a natural arena for the second chance, a new land of opportunity for remaking oneself rather than merely striking it rich. In a democratic reading of human nature, the self's Romantic destiny has been replaced by the self's moral freedom. The road between Tonto and Lordsburg is a place of self-determined transformation where the notorious gambler can become a gallant gentleman again, the whore a heroine, the deadbeat drunk a life-saving physician.

The collective result of these individual transformations inevitably challenges the class biases implicit throughout the Leatherstocking tales. Cooper was born into a pro-revolutionary but nevertheless upper-class family, his father a founder and leader of Cooperstown, New York. After the Revolution, elite families like the Coopers faced the ironic threat that the same democratic principles which had justified the overthrow of the British monarchy might be reapplied against their own authority. As one of the key anxieties of the post revolutionary period, this class conflict naturally infiltrates the Leatherstocking tales—which, like all historical romances, imagine a fictive past to address current social tensions. And unsurprisingly given their author's background, they are intent on legitimizing the reigning social hierarchy.

So it is that just as the strictly segregated good and bad Indians on Cooper's fictive frontier are defined according to their tribal affiliation (Chingachgook's Mohican tribe versus Magua's Huron), the moral stature of his white characters is determined by their attitude toward the established order. One way or another Cooper's white villains—the demagogic Sheriff in *The Pioneers*, the anarchic Bush clan in *The Prairie*—all defy the legitimacy of the social hierarchy while his white heroes are either upper-class themselves or men of lower standing who, nevertheless, gladly serve the cause of their social betters.

Even as it borrows heavily from the Leatherstocking saga's pattern of class conflicts, then, *Stagecoach* reverses the poles of Cooper's allegiances by highlighting the corruption of the established order. Curly, who is an officer of the law, would seem to be the notable exception, yet siding with justice, as heroes must, forces him to break the law by setting Ringo free. After he does, and just after Doc wryly observes that Ringo and Dallas have been "saved from the blessings of civilization," the marshal chooses to remove his badge. He is apparently resigning from office, as he indeed he must, for in Ford's revision of our frontier myth, a man cannot behave honorably and still retain his formal social status.

This deeply pessimistic reading of the social order coexists ironically with an optimistic vision of individual redemption, as powerfully exemplified by Doc and Dallas's self-transformation from Tonto's social dregs to heroes in the wilderness. As such, *Stagecoach* recalls Emerson's views on the heroic, where an overt contempt for social mediation and conformity is used to frame by contrast an enthusiastic belief in the possibility for individual greatness.

But Ford is not a Romantic transcendentalist writing secular sermons intended to inspire the educated class to spiritual self-improvement; he is a populist storyteller, thinking through imagery and narrative, drawing on a mythic legacy descending from Cooper. And in Cooper's mythic world "the blessings of civilization" *are* blessings, even if Hawkeye has to flee them at story's end. Neither Duncan Heyward nor his grandson Capt. Middleton in *The Prairie* must resign *his* high rank to do the right thing. In Cooper's fictive world, the apparently contradictory values of his co-protagonists, the hunter-scout and the gentleman officer, are endorsed alike. The two cooperate effectively during the crisis, after which, their contradictions tacitly acknowledged, they are permitted to retire to their very separate but equally admirable spheres.

That separation still occurs a century later, but the moral equality has disappeared, respectable society reconceived as debased. Such a critique was a risky enterprise in a Hollywood studio system whose industrial specifications demanded upbeat endings and effusive patriotism. But even as it appears to meet those rigid specifications—the white settlers triumphing over the red savages with the assistance of the U.S. cavalry; the white villains either punished or killed; the plucky American woman winning the affections of the West's white knight—*Stagecoach* deftly subverts their robotic optimism. It does so by simultaneously depicting an American civilization whose blessings include social snobbery, puritanical intolerance, white-collar corruption, and rank injustice; whose best women are too weak to care for their children, best men too meek to defend their community.

The new "appearances" that this artful movie "saves" within the old mythic frame are as darkly shadowed, then, as the photography of Lordsburg in its final scenes. The good cannot survive inside a social order whose honest officers are forced to resign if they want to act justly. Meritocratic egalitarianism and Christian charity, the traditional sources of American virtue, can only thrive during that dangerous journey through the wilderness between settled towns; they are most at home on the stagecoach itself, that fictive embodiment of the frontier spirit.

But the year is 1885, Geronimo's uprising is among the last of the native revolts, railroads have already replaced stagecoaches in many locales, and the Western frontier is about to close. If the moral challenges of isolation and endangerment are necessary to sustain American virtue, how can it survive the ironic success of the frontier's conquest? And if the mythic bargain between radical individualism and communal loyalty, so key to the nation's moral identity, requires that our self-reliant hero return to the wilderness after saving the day, where can he go now?

In the film he has to retreat "across the Border"—which, given its setting in the Arizona Territory, suggests an actual place as well as an allegorical one. Ringo's ranch is likely in Mexico. In a film energized by many ironies, this might be the fiercest one of all: in John Ford's revival of our frontier myth, America's foundational hero not only must ride out of town at the end of the day; he is forced to flee America itself.

As complex a work as *Stagecoach* is, saving *all* the new appearances of modern experience within the mythic frame descending from Cooper was beyond the plausible reach of any single film. Of those key tensions that animate the Leatherstocking saga and that have been so central to the dynamics of our national character—the stressful interplay between the virile and genteel dimensions of heroic virtue, between radical self-reliance and communal loyalty, and between an attraction to and a fear of the racial or ethnic other—the last receives the least attention and no real transformation in Ford's renewed Western.

In a script focused on the communal drama of moral stature versus social status in the purely white spheres of town and stagecoach, none of the major characters is Native American. Although his path is a hard one indeed, Ford's Hawkeye doesn't also have to negotiate that tricky moral and emotional boundary between admiring and abhorring "savage ways." Ringo has no Chingachgook to befriend and assist, no individualized Magua to loathe and kill. Geronimo hasn't a word in the script: he is less a character than an abstract sign for Savage Menace, his war party just the external threat necessary to test the virtues of the whites. And the explosive issue of miscegenation, so earnestly condemned in *The Deerslayer* and *The Last of the Mohicans*, has been pushed to the margins here instead, relegated to minor characters and offensively "comic" sub-plots. There are, in fact, two mixed marriages in *Stagecoach*, but both are treated with a condescending mockery that trivializes Cooper's racialist biases even as it endorses them.

Another key feature of the old myth that the film conserves is its highly idealized portrait of the lonesome hero. All the characters in Cooper's romances reflect allegorical types. Those inner conflicts that so often complicate moral choices have been segregated and externalized, so that to find the full range of human emotions and motives readers have to survey the entire cast rather than plumb the depths of any single complex soul. Unlike some other mythic tales, then, Cooper's doesn't focus on the inner transformation of the questing self into the higher plane of heroic status—no Hamlet here. Natty Bumppo doesn't *become* the exemplary American man; he simply *is* that man, expressing and enacting his innate virtues again and again.

So, too, with the Ringo Kid—which is why his character is only nominally of the same kind as his allies in the film. Although all three have been labeled as Tonto's dregs and are victims of social prejudice, Doc and Dallas at least have been judged by their community for what they have actually done. They possess flaws we sympathetically understand and then forgive, a forgiveness earned by their heroic performances in the wilderness. But Ringo has nothing to be forgiven for. Because his conviction for murder was based on perjury, the flaw to be corrected in his case resides in a corrupt judicial system—yet another blessing of civilization. And although Ford's hero has been doubly victimized—his family murdered, himself imprisoned—Ringo's moral perfection is matched by and wed to his psychological tranquility.

Unlike Doc, whose good nature is shielded by a world-weary irony, and unlike Dallas, who is visibly hurt and defensive at the start, Ringo dons no emotional armor and exhibits no woundedness. Not only are his actions always right and good, so too are his unconflicted moods: respectful of Curly's authority even though the law has "done him wrong," cheerful and polite to his fellow passengers even after being rearrested, determined to exact his just revenge but without Achilles' rage or Ahab's bitterness. Like the Lone Ranger, Ringo has been given a tragic past absent the torments of a tragic temperament. His psyche has been spared the pernicious effects of unjust violence, a danger captured by Simone Weil's arresting imagery in *Gravity and Grace*:

> *But except for souls which are fairly close to saintliness, the victims are defiled by force, just as their tormentors are. The evil which is in the handle of the sword is transmitted to its point.*[5]

Ringo has not been defiled by the force of his tormentors' swords because, more than "fairly close," he fully replicates the role of masculine saintliness that Cooper had codified in the figure of Leatherstocking. Although they are his co-protagonists and heroic in their own way, Ringo is not really of Doc and Dallas's psychological kind because he is not of their *aesthetic* type. His costume may have changed, but Ford's hero remains that "straight-tongue" who never lies, that "hawkeye" who never misses an enemy target, that "pathfinder" who unerringly discovers the right way. As someone who already and naturally *is* rather than *becomes* heroically virtuous, Ringo is a fictive figure fashioned according to the standards of early nineteenth-century Romantic idealism, even as he inhabits a new narrative environment increasingly attuned to the social criticism and psychological realism of a modernizing world.

Within the film, then, Ringo is at once a traditional and an anomalous figure. At the time of its release in 1939, he served as a kind of moral

---

5. Simone Weil, *Gravity and Grace* (University of Nebraska Press, 1997), Social Harmony chapter. See: https://theanarchistlibrary.org/library/simone-weil-gravity-and-grace#toc39.

place-holder whose familiarity reassured the era's audience by embodying a specific set of heroic qualities they knew by heart. This conservative continuity was then exploited by Ford to introduce selected elements of significant change—those new appearances, ethical and aesthetic, that he wished to save. In the film Ringo remains as morally perfect as Natty Bumppo, but perfection itself has been redefined in crucial ways, reversing both Cooper's endorsement of the social hierarchy and his condemnation of Judith Hutter.

That America's white knight now accepts as his bride a woman who can't wear white, a woman with "a reputation," represents a significant shift in the moral compass of our foundational myth, and because the action is allegorical as well as literal, this change has implications beyond the sexual sphere. By marrying Dallas, Ringo is not just accepting her sexual past but also embracing a different conception of the heroic character. He is freely choosing to wed the heroism of the wounded, the damaged, the socially rejected; *his* story of moral perfection and psychological immunity is joining *her* story of self-transformation through the democratic drama of the second chance.

Obsolescence

Many children would be born from this cinematic marriage of Romantic idealism to social and psychological realism. John Ford repeatedly returned to America's lonesome hero in a Western setting, finding new angles for exploration and saving other new appearances from contemporary life within the old mythic frame. The most remarkable example of that would be his 1956 film *The Searchers,* where the very features he conserved in *Stagecoach*—Cooper's contempt for miscegenation and the moral infallibility of his lonesome hero—were the ones now targeted for reformation. And the success of *Stagecoach* inspired other talented directors, including Howard Hawks, Anthony Mann, and John Huston, to work within the genre, creating an impressive body of Western films for adults and leading as well to a twenty year domination of primetime television.

But by 1975, when CBS's *Gunsmoke* went off the air, the adult Western had been exhausted as a meaningful form and was being replaced in popularity by police and law procedurals, modern medical dramas, and—after the first of *The Godfather* films—by the surprising revival of the gangster story in the new guise of the mafia mythos. Even in their most updated versions, the carefully crafted character types and repetitive plots of Cooper's myth were ceasing to work as credible metaphors for the primary tensions of everyday life. Not only had the frontier been closed for nearly a century; our fully industrialized economy had made the challenges of a liberated individualism increasingly irrelevant. In a nation of wage employees subsumed by corporate and governmental bureaucracies, the lonesome hero was becoming, at best, a figure of nostalgic denial. The once crucial mythic mission of civilizing the rugged outsider had been reduced to a moot issue when the outside itself was disappearing.

In a narrative equivalent to the shift from an earth- to a sun-centered universe, "saving the appearances" of contemporary experience now required a categorical revision of the mythic template. So it was that in the new novels, films, and TV shows both the good cop and the bad mafioso found themselves entangled within social hierarchies. After saving the day the crime-solving police detective still had to type up his bureaucratic reports, the daring surgeon defend his actions before a review board. Even the American spy now worked for the so-called Company, while the brutal hit man had to submissively kiss the cheek of his don, who was himself weighed down by multiple "family" obligations. The relationship of Hawkeye and Chingachgook did faintly survive in the form of the buddy film, but its white and black co-protagonists were also forced to operate within the System. And as if tacitly confessing their decline into anachronism, these works often assumed a tone of light self-mockery that was incompatible with the old hero's story. In the day's most popular narratives, as in post-modern life itself, there was no liberating Border to flee across, no riding out of town at the end of the day. Now that the open spaces between the new Tonto and Lordsburg had been paved over with strip malls and apartment complexes, the "blessings of civilization" were everywhere.

In retrospect, then, Kennedy's proclamation of the New Frontier was only accurate in the crudest sense. Insomuch as the phrase was predicting the imminent challenges of substantial change, it did hold true for an era that would be characterized by a dramatic revision in our collective understanding of the good and the true. But the very nature of that transformation was also one that would render the specific terms and tropes of our frontier myth obsolete.

Where Cooper had preached sexual innocence and, even while praising the noble savage's alliance with the frontier scout, had insisted on the ultimate separation of the races, the sixties would bring an end to legally sanctioned segregation and (completing Ford's revision) destigmatize sexual license for women as well as men. While *alienation* was a common experience in the postwar years, the serene *isolation* that Natty Bumppo cherished was becoming less and less possible in an age of pervasive cameras and invasive news: a shift in the nature of everyday life that first became evident in the events surrounding Kennedy's own death, when the murder of Lee Harvey Oswald was broadcast live, witnessed in real time by millions of Americans. And these actual features of the ironically named New Frontier only intensified in the ensuing years, so that today—when the wilderness itself, in order to be saved, has to be fenced in; and when the old celebration of lonesomeness has been superseded by the new imperative of social networking—the specific images and actions of Cooper's once powerful narrative have ceased to resonate in any meaningful way.

The exploration of outer space might seem to be the one exception, yet even the moon program launched by JFK proved detrimental in the end to the commonsense conceptions enfolded within America's foundational myth. For our entry into this latest untamed wilderness, so inhospitable to all races and nations, didn't really provide a new land of opportunity for plausible settlement. The most meaningful product gained so far has not been NASA's collection of lunar rocks but the iconic image of the Earth itself—that lovely yet all too lonely pearl surrounded by airless and icy space. Through projecting ourselves outward, we had unexpectedly acquired a new perspective on our point of origin. For the first time then, we could see our planetary home as a discrete unit, an indivisible whole, its perpetual spinning an acute reminder that what goes around does come around, and so, too, a tacit refutation of the linear logic of endless expansion that had characterized our original romance with frontier settlement.

The patriotic pride that accompanied winning the race to the moon was oddly undermined by an image which, so self-contained and isolated, seemed to render commonsensical the necessity of viewing *all* nations, and indeed all living creatures, as belonging to, and dependent on, the same circumscribing biosphere. On the verge of its apparent realization, the escapist dream of colonizing space had spurred a counter recognition: that we were all passengers alike on a planetary stagecoach, one whose fragile enclosure was our only refuge in a truly hostile wild. To save *this* unexpected appearance would require of us, then, a categorical reconception of the meaning of community. From family to clan to linguistic tribe to formal kingdoms and modern nation-states, here was the next necessary phase in the transformation of our self-understanding: the admission of our kinship on a fully global scale.

For all our international treaties and trade, we have yet to come close to fulfilling *that* difficult mission. As the post-modern equivalent of the printing press, our digitized media do supply the means for a transnational participation in events. But to be made collectively memorable—which is to say, meaningful—the news of the day must be mythologized, and we still await the next generation of foundational stories: a new mythos which, *e pluribus unum,* can artfully rescript the space-age contentions of a polyglot humanity into the campfire consensus of the old fraternal tribe.

4

Two Sides of a Tortoise
(On Herman Melville and Charles Dickens)

> *Dollars damn me. And the malicious Devil is forever grinning in upon me, holding the door ajar. My Dear Sir, a presentiment is upon me.—I shall at last be worn out and perish, like an old nutmeg-grater. . . . What I feel most moved to write, that is banned,— it will not pay. Yet altogether write the other way I cannot. So the product is a final hash; and all my books are botches . . . Though I wrote the Gospels in this century, I should die in the gutter.*
>
> —Melville writing to Hawthorne in June, 1851[1]

Genial Misanthropy: A Story of Wall Street

Few events in the history of American letters have so seemed to confirm the romantic notion of "the misunderstood artist" as Herman Melville's rapid descent from respected best-seller to neglected genius. After publishing at the tender age of twenty-six the eloquent, semi-fictionalized travelogue *Typee*, which even as it won public favor established its author as a serious literary mind-in-the-making, the prolific Melville grew less popular and acclaimed with each succeeding book. Following the perverse romantic formula with disturbing exactitude, the evolution of his art seemed to chart as well his steep decline into social estrangement, as his greatest works, stretching from *Moby Dick*

---

1. Excerpt from a letter Melville wrote to Hawthorne in June 1851, when they were neighbors in Western Massachusetts and he was writing *Moby Dick*: http://www.melville.org/hawthrne.htm.

in 1851 through *The Piazza Tales* and *The Confidence-Man* in 1856 and '57, were greeted with a mix of critical contempt and public indifference. No respect, no sales, the double-blow of disdain and debt, neither his ego nor his family fed.

Adding to the retrospective allure of this tale of unjust neglect (sometimes called the Melville Eclipse) is the mystery of its dramatic ending. At the age of thirty-seven, after publishing for little more than a decade and still at the very peak of his powers, Melville simply stopped writing fiction. (He did take up poetry, but in a very private way and with less masterful results.) Contrary to the tragic cases of Mozart, Schubert, Shelley, and Keats, whose abbreviated careers fueled the romantic mystique, death by disease or accident was not the malicious agent who stole from us the genius artist in his prime—this silence was self-imposed, *this* extinction of the great mind a deliberate abstention.

The obscure meaning of that abstention, the degree to which it was principled or cowardly, carefully plotted or merely resigned, has come to haunt me in recent years. It's not the private life behind the great mind that obsesses me so. Unlike many contemporary biographers, I'm not in hot pursuit of that sordid secret, usually sexual, which is thought, reductively, to explain "it" all. I'm far more interested in the potential parable than the hidden peccadillo. I'm haunted by the act as possible evidence of the great mind still at work, as if Melville's withdrawal were itself the final plot turn to his entire body of fiction, the thematic climax of his imaginative engagement with the industrial age. Because we live in a transitional era that seems to echo Melville's—a time when technology once again confounds the patterns of community and when incorporated commerce has, once again, been left unchecked to methodically raze the precious covenants of democratic practice—his refusal to write suggests a scary relevance to our immediate lives. In questioning the meaning of Melville's silence, I am also asking, by implication, whether any serious author or artist can engage the political economy of our privatizing age without suffering an equivalent eclipse of influence. For though we may have digitized the money economy that Melville so surgically satirized in the 1850s, we dance anew to its soul-numbing beat. Our lives, no less than Bartleby the Scrivener's, have come to merit his tale's subtitle: "A Story of Wall Street."[2]

---

2. Herman Melville, "Bartleby the Scrivener," in *Fiction 100*, ed. James Pickering (New York: Macmillan, 1984), 1028–52. Oddly, this anthology leaves out the original subtitle: "A Story of Wall Street."

To see Melville's self-extinction as imbued with a kind of grander fictive meaning merely reflects in reverse the autobiographical significance of his later fiction. "Bartleby" especially seems designed, in part, to allegorize its author's desperate aesthetic predicament, as that predicament was plaintively captured in the letter to Hawthorne cited at the start. In "Bartleby," it could be argued, Melville plots out with a comedic ferocity the higher moral logic behind his own ensuing suicide as a public author. And unlike most suicide notes, which tend to inscribe the very private wounds of the lunatic mind, this letter, if carefully read and courageously attended to, can still supply us with the sanest reflections on the meaning of our own place and time. As context for such a reading, I'll begin, however, with a few summary observations about the origins of the industrial economy and its impact on Melville's America.

Although greed is ancient, a perennial potential in human nature, the rationalization of greed, the recalibration of an entire society to the goads and lures of its abstract imperative that *more* (production, consumption, acquisition, efficiency) *must equal better*, is an historically unique phenomenon. It emerged out of the philosophical turn toward rational materialism in seventeenth- and eighteenth-century Europe, and its radical effects on the body politic first became manifest in early nineteenth century England.

The key historical marker in America was the Civil War, that great divide after which our country's transformation from a provincial, agricultural republic into an urban, industrial nation-state accelerated unchecked. Formal political independence did expand gradually after the war as first blacks and then women won the right to vote. Material prosperity also surged, with at least some of that unprecedented wealth eventually shared, if only after decades of organized struggle by workers themselves. But these gains concealed considerable moral, spiritual, and political costs, and ones that the most conspicuous beneficiaries of the new system were loath to acknowledge.

The terrible irony of this postwar period, and the one that best captures the mixed legacy of our rational materialist economy more generally, is that the moral victory which attended the end of legal slavery was simultaneous with a broader (if less overtly political) erosion of liberty's native grounds. Key features of this erosion included: the practical emasculation of democracy's "economic man," as independent farmers, artisans, and shopkeepers were converted into subservient wage employees; the subsequent division of the population into widely divergent economic classes; the degradation of work itself as production was fully rationalized and employees were reduced to cogs in a mammoth productivity machine; the enclosure of the natural landscape through industrialization and urbanization, changing the basic pace and shape of social interaction; and the ongoing corruption of American plain speaking into either technocratic jargon or glad-handing salesmanship. Suffusing all these changes, at once their spur and their spawn, was a gradual recalculation of value away from two deeply rooted strands of American idealism: an abstemious Protestant spirituality that first arrived with the Puritans and (for its day) an egalitarian secular politics that resulted in the reinvention of Western democracy after the Revolution.

Oh, the images of Jesus and Jefferson retained their symbolic luster in industrializing America, as indeed they do today, for a system so rooted in sheer avidity cannot easily generate its own moral heroes. But in practical fact the rational efficiencies of technological progress (know-how) and the material profits of mass-market commerce (money) were becoming the primary measures of both communal improvement and personal betterment—of "value" and "virtue" in everyday America. That pursuing *that* so-called good life, as calibrated by ever niftier gadgets and fatter bottom lines, might require a violation of the good life as defined by either the spiritual parables of the New Testament or the political principles of the American Revolution became an observation that was, at once, nakedly obvious and socially unspeakable.

Contrary to the standard bohemian critique of mainstream bourgeois America, the primary "repressions" in American life since the mid-nineteenth century have not been sexual and emotional but spiritual and political. Both the characteristic means and the reductive ends of the economy we have been practicing for nearly two centuries are inherently contrary to the ideals prescribed by our spiritual and political heritages. The more triumphant that economy in any given period, the greater the need to repress its incompatibility with these our oldest conceptions of virtue and value. And any public figure who dares to shine the light of his intelligence on the fault line of that hypocrisy is likely to have his message "eclipsed."

Although it was published in 1853, eight years prior to the start of the Civil War, "Bartleby, the Scrivener: A Story of Wall Street" foresaw (in the words of Lewis Mumford, an early Melville biographer) "all the sordid developments" of this new political economy "while they were still in their germ."[3] In this one story, Melville supplied his contemporaries with a cryptic yet highly prophetic map of both the newly evolving American workplace and the disingenuous moral mindset required to justify its dehumanizing practices.

As the title character, Bartleby has been crafted as a highly stylized victim of, and then rebel against, such practices. Recently hired as a scrivener for the small and grimly appointed office of a nevertheless successful Wall Street lawyer, he has been reduced to a word-machine, forced to mindlessly recopy legalistic jargon for minimal pay, six days a week. For him and his two co-workers the very medium most responsible for the democratic revolution (written language) has been converted perversely into an instrumental imprisonment. America's self-reliant citizen has been reassigned, in practical effect, to a scribal chain gang, democracy's independent thinker reductively rationalized into a verbal robot. Melville's narrative charts his scrivener's staged refusal of this degrading job and supplies, by allegorical implication, a scathing rejection of both the broader economy that would prescribe such work and the moral character of the new managerial class who would most profit from its ruthless tactics.

At first Bartleby applies himself dutifully, doing an "extraordinary quantity of writing,"[4] but even then his silent, pale, and mournful affect—his refusal to be cheerful as well as industrious—disturbs the working atmosphere of the office, bothering especially the lawyer who has hired him.[5] And soon enough Bartleby ceases to be industrious as well. The plot accelerates through a comic yet highly revealing sequence of graduated refusals. He won't assist with proofreading his own copies, and then with those of his fellow scriveners; he won't run errands for his boss, nor for his boss's customers, and eventually abstains from all copying as well. As it turns out, his boss discovers one Sunday afternoon, Bartleby is refusing even to leave the premises; he has turned the grim office (which,

---

3. Lewis Mumford, *Herman Melville* (New York: Harcourt Brace, 1929), 327.

4. Pickering, 1033.

5. Even this early in American history, long prior to the nation's Disneyfication via mass-market entertainment, the new managerial class is expecting that its disenfranchised worker should be pleased with his lot—a cheerful mouse à la Mickey or Minnie. Surely the moral logic of such an attitude bears some relation to the plantation owner's fantastic reinvention of his slaves as members of a "happy-go-lucky" race. In America it is not sufficient that one's oppressed underlings prove industrious and obedient—they also must sustain a masquerade of enjoying their fate. They are expected, in the words of the Broadway show tune, to "put on a happy face."

sparely furnished and devoid of sunlight, is the white-collar equivalent of an urban factory) into his makeshift home. He has become a permanent, *un*cheerful, *non*-industrious Wall Street resident: a fly of the forlorn in the unctuous ointment of its moneyed contentment. An immovable *won't-do* in the fervent flow of its unstoppable *can-do*.

Each of these refusals is expressed in the same way: quietly, mechanically. Using a retiring tone for the most rebellious of employee activities (refusing to work), he responds to each assignment with the same apparently timid and tactful demurral: "I would prefer not to." "You *will* not?" his boss eventually exclaims in irritation. "I *prefer* not," Bartleby corrects him,[6] and the stress here, along with the word's repetitious use throughout the story, emphasize both a politeness of tone and a freedom of choice, a temperamental passivity paradoxically wed to an aggressive willfulness.

In Bartleby, Melville has fashioned the ultimate irritant to the moral duplicity of the new money economy, a character who quickly becomes both a mocking mirror of and a provocative prod to the dubious presumptions which justify that economy's practices. Those presumptions are embodied, with equally exquisite authorial care, in Bartleby's turn-a-blind-eye and "make-nice" boss, who is also the story's nameless narrator, and Melville captures through his disingenuous voice a new species of American identity. In *The Confidence-Man*, he will dub this newly evolving moral character "the genial misanthrope," predicting a time when "the whole world will be genialised" and when even the most hateful schemes shall be hidden beneath "an affable air." As an early version of this "new kind of monster,"[7] the narrator is portrayed not as an overtly ruthless robber baron but as a faux humanitarian. A nice guy, with middling ambitions, *this* captain of industry is the maestro of the half-gesture: someone who will offer one of his scriveners a coat while failing to raise the man's pitiful wages; a tea-time Christian whose grin of propriety reliably evades the grit of the crucifixion.

Nameless, he has been crafted by Melville as a comic incarnation of the age's new managerial class: a figure whose purblind mind has evolved to hide the darker side of an industrial economy that is rapidly co-opting the American experiment. As someone who vaguely accepts the new rational materialist optimism, who wants to believe that know-how and

---

6. Pickering, 1037.

7. Herman Melville, *The Confidence-Man: His Masquerade* (New York: Grove Press, 1995), 208-10.

money (science and capital) can somehow solve the perpetual problem of human unhappiness, Bartleby's boss can't quite accept the obvious fact of his scrivener's melancholy, with its uncongenial endorsement of the tragic sense of life. And as someone whose own social and financial standing depends on the new economy's rank inequalities, the narrator can't admit, as Bartleby's protest repeatedly insists, that the very system enriching him is one source of the man's manifest misery.

Given these biases, the narrator's own refusals, no less than Bartleby's, are the ones that drive the story to its tragicomic conclusion. For while the scrivener *would prefer not to* work or live in such dehumanizing conditions, his boss *would prefer not to* recognize those conditions, political and spiritual, for what they really are. Beneath the passive glaze of his geniality, the narrator aggressively resists acknowledging what the facts of the story relentlessly if tacitly convey: that the office he commands and the economy it represents are, at their very core, both undemocratic and anti-Christian.

The narrator *is* tempted toward such a radical admission, however, and that temptation provides the story's comic tension. But his true investment is in maintaining appearances, not reforming practices. And when, near the end, he is asked of Bartleby "In mercy's name, who is he?," the narrator's answer confirms the final totality of his refusal to learn. "I know nothing about him," he insists,[8] and this ignorance, we understand once we penetrate the haze of his "affable air," has been a feat of avoidance arduously earned. In the story's own terms, knowing nothing is what he has preferred.

The preference not to know is entirely one-sided. His nemesis Bartleby insists on the opposite. "I know you" are among his final words to his boss, in an exchange that occurs in the prison yard where the scrivener has been jailed for vagrancy: "I know you . . . and I want nothing to say to you." Only to add, when the narrator attempts to cheer him up: "I know where I am."[9]

Unlike the narrator's protestations of ignorance, Bartleby asserts an unblinking knowledge of the people around him and the place where he has lived—which is, of course, literally and figuratively on Wall Street. He now comprehends both the new economic regimen and its representative man. Penetrating the show of geniality to grasp the ruling misanthropy,

---

8. Pickering, 1048.
9. Ibid., 1050.

he knows that the narrator will never see who he really is or read "in mercy's name" the message of protest he repeatedly brings. Intimate with a system that forbids intimacy, the scrivener has come to understand that, whether actually in jail or "gainfully employed," he will always be imprisoned, forever walled off from the reach of true mercy and the realm of real preference: that is, from both the spiritual solace and the political empowerment that had once constituted the double promise of the good life as defined by America's traditional values.

And so the logic of rejection as an expression of personal preference reaches its ultimate end: the freely chosen rejection of life itself. The man who has preferred not to smile or obey, to explain or to change, to take money or advice, now prefers not to take food. First refusing to *produce*, Bartleby now refuses to *consume* and, huddled against the prison wall that has literally and metaphorically enclosed his life, he quietly dies.

For Melville, the accuracy of this allegorical map proved personal in precisely those ways suggested at the start: as an imaginative rehearsal, three or so years before the fact, of his own aesthetic suicide. For Melville was also refusing at that time to be a mindless scrivener. Trying to resist both the explicit suggestion of condescending critics and the market's own so-called wisdom, he *preferred not to* recopy his early successes—no more of *Typee's* "life among the cannibals" to titillate the public's romantic obsessions. (To borrow from the brilliant metaphor used in his letter to Hawthorne, he preferred *not* to become the aesthetic equivalent of a nutmeg-grater: that is, an industrial machine repeatedly "grinding out" the exotic spice of the romanticized prose favored by that day's literary marketplace.)

Melville, like Bartleby, tried again and again in the 1850s to convey his serious message, but that message was addressed to the deliberately obtuse and so remained either misapprehended or entirely unread. Finally, as his later works show, Melville also knew exactly *where* he was—the deepest implications of the West's new adventure in a fully rationalized political economy. He knew its dehumanizing place, grasped its antidemocratic character, and rather than heed the Devil of the dollar its advocates worshipped, he soon would, like Bartleby, "want nothing [more] to say to [them]."

So it is that Melville's aesthetic self-extinction, like the scrivener's physical one, can be read as a principled decision, a credible if extreme preference, enacted in response to the best available evidence. Such a preference seems to confirm the prediction that the great artist—at least if stuck in an age of stupefying geniality—will be shunned by his contemporaries.

It is also a prediction often reconfirmed when I teach this story. I'm not someone who frequently complains about his students. Fortunate in my profession, I find them on the whole to be uncommonly smart and hard-working; and, having selected "creative writing" as a concentration, they can hardly be accused of mercenary ambition. Yet when I assign this story blind, more than a few of my aspiring undergraduate authors either overtly side with the narrator or recapitulate his convenient cluelessness. They, too, "know nothing" about Bartleby or his protest, and they tend to accept at face value the narrator's self-congratulatory account, one that casts himself as a would-be humanitarian stymied by Bartleby's rejection of his help.

Even when I frame the story as a prime example of unreliable narration, many of my students are largely baffled as to the exact nature of the man's biases as I have described them here. "Do you not see?"[10] Bartleby asks his boss (and, through him, Melville his readership) in 1853. A hundred-and-seventy years later, the answer appears too often to be the same. The author's reputation may have been revived, but too much of his message remains eclipsed.

Two explanations occur to me when I ask myself why so many of this story's vital truths often remain inaccessible to what ought to be, after all, Melville's most appreciative audience. The more obvious explanation appears, at first anyway, to be rooted in the mere vagaries of literary fashion. Both comedically and allegorically exaggerated, Bartleby is, by design, a one-dimensional figure. He has been crafted as a cryptic message, the animated principle of astute rebellion against an entire political economy, and, until very recently, the literary taste of our age has not been congenial to such abstract characterizations. What my students often *prefer* instead is what Melville refuses to give: a psychologically deep character they might identify with. They want someone whose motives and moods plausibly emerge from a detailed backstory. In this case, given Bartleby's misery, they want or expect some form of personal tragedy: an abusive childhood, a lost love, a broken family, a long descent (associated, perhaps, with drink or drugs) into mental illness.

That this bias toward psychological or (perhaps more accurately) therapeutic realism might be indicative of something other than a purely

10. Ibid., 1042.

literary fashion begins to become clear, however, when I reflect on the following coincidence: such a personalized backstory is precisely what Bartleby's boss, our unreliable narrator, also wants. He's so desperate for a biographical explanation for his scrivener's suicidal melancholy that he supplies a conjectural one at the end. As is the case throughout his narration, this comic-pathetic conclusion, based on a rumor—the inhumane circumstances of *another* job, no less—tells us more about the narrator himself than it reveals about his now long deceased employee. It supplies the climactic seal to the man's unreliability, proof that his preference "not to know" remains unchecked.

If, after all, Bartleby's story is merely yet one more personal tragedy and not also "a Story of Wall Street," then the narrator can maintain the same self-exonerating masquerade of sympathy: the temperamental lie that allows him to repress any sense of complicity in the man's demise. He can remain a "nice guy" in his mind's eye, a small-scale philanthropist who would, literally, "give the coat off his back" to a needy employee, and not someone who has grown rich off the very economy that is creating a whole class of such needy workers.

The second explanation for some of my students' failure to "see," then, proves more disturbing than the first—which it, in fact, enfolds, the literary fashion but one expression of the broader ethos. Their reading can be opaque at times because they unconsciously share some of the narrator's biases, the very blind spots that are the source of his unreliability. They, too, tend to prefer a show of "cheerful industry" to a stubbornly melancholic refusal to work. Though not without sympathy for the downtrodden, they, too, tend to accept on some level the increasingly delusional but nevertheless commonly held presumption that America is a classless society, where the primary causes of despair and social failure are individually based.

Let me be clear on this last point. I don't believe these students of mine are self-consciously "blaming the victim," but they do scale their explanations toward the individualistic. And on that scale, they have tended, until very recently, to presume personal causes for human unhappiness (a history of family abuse, a genetic predisposition) to the exclusion of political or metaphysical ones (an unjust economy, a cruel universe)—sources whose scope can't be addressed by some regimen of therapeutic analysis, psychoactive drugs, romantic recovery, or savvy self-help. Although my students are, by any plausible assessment, more socially tolerant, aesthetically engaged, and commercially skeptical than the population at large, they still partake of the age's moral common sense.

As in fact, dismounting my high horse, do I. The difficulty my students have decoding the narrator's unreliability (their inability to see through the virtual geniality of the man to the essential misanthropy of the office he runs) is akin to *my* difficulty seeing through the bright packaging of the athletic shoes that I buy twice a year to the "melancholy" of the Indonesian laborers who have stitched them. The cheap price, the cushy feel and bright colors, the heroic marketing narrative that flatters my childhood fantasies of sinking that corner jumper to win the game—all these pleasing qualities are immediately, almost mindlessly accessible, while the misery inherent in their distant manufacture requires a comparatively abstract and self-generated act of imaginative projection. I'd love to claim that, "in mercy's name," I sustain such an act of projected sympathy—and, having spent two years of my working life in a factory, I'm certainly better qualified to do that than most of my students—but I can't.

In one of the story's most revealing passages, the narrator, contemplating the fact of his scrivener's mysterious unhappiness, observes that "misery hides aloof."[11] That single phrase captures, in meaty miniature, the strategic character of the man's moral dissembling, the way he repeatedly transforms every temptation toward genuine fellow-feeling into formulaic acts of moral evasion. And the key to parsing this pattern of deceit and self-deception lies in the phony agency of that phrase's active verb. Does "misery," after all, "hide" itself? And is "misery" (that stuffily abstract personification) really the agent who remains "aloof"? The narrator conveniently forgets that, as soon as Bartleby was hired, *he* was the one who hid his new employee behind a folding screen—a work station where he could be summoned by voice at will but where his gloomy countenance and inhumane duties would otherwise remain hidden from view.

Such a tactic is completely consonant with a worldview that was redesigning the West's economic regime in the 1850s. A philosophy that believes in mechanized causality, and that proceeds through reduction, division, and specialization to "manufacture" its scientific truths, logically produces an economy that organizes wealth-producing labor after it own metaphysical and methodological images. Because its ends are material and its means mechanical, such an economy cannot accept a workplace conducive to individual preferences; nor can it abide a managerial class

11. Ibid., 1039.

whose workplace decisions are routinely made "in mercy's name." To indulge in understatement: the ruling ethos of rational materialist manufacture constantly presents a public relations problem for its American advocates, addressing, as they must, a nation whose primary moral traditions have been a Christian spirituality (centered on compassion) and a democratic politics (rooted in honoring individual preferences).

More than any writer of his age, Melville foresaw the special species of self-deception that would be necessary to sell this system on American shores.[12] He grasped the affable air and willful opacity that would have to be mustered to conceal its political and spiritual deficiencies. And, in just one of a score of brilliant allegorical touches that animate this story, he captured in a single action, concealing Bartleby behind a folding screen, a key feature of that strategy, as operative today as it was in 1853.

Nor do we have to transport ourselves to low-wage factories on Asian shores, where the misery of workers is conveniently removed by an ocean or two from the plush precincts of our executive "campuses" and tony malls, to confirm the lasting accuracy of Melville's vision. Summon to mind the faceless "organization man" of the 1950's and -60's, or today's Dilbert confined to his keyboard cubicle; visualize the robotic routines and habitual humiliations of either the postwar paper pusher or the post-millennial cyber serf, and we should recognize that each is little more than a recapitulation in "upgraded" terms of Melville's deranged and dehumanized scriveners.

Likewise, consider the discrepancy between the generous posture of some of today's nouveau philanthropists and the tactics by which they have earned their billions: monopolistic cheating, radical downsizing, slashing employee benefits, extorting local governments and exploiting offshore havens for tax "relief" or sheer evasion, buying off politicians through campaign contributions, exporting jobs to the foreign poor. In such a combination we can recognize a moral character cut to the same genial misanthropy initially satirized in Bartleby's boss. These *are* the

---

12. The double-bind that the narrator faces, his desire to be both a "nice guy" and still profit from the grim conditions of the workplace he runs, might seem at first the stuff of tragedy, but Melville had the good sense to cast his diagnosis in the form of a comedy instead. The formulaic denial of others' misery on behalf of one's own moneyed contentment—that is, the moral masquerade of consumerism exemplified in Bartleby's boss—does not bear the characteristic grandeur of a heroic flaw, to say the least. To cast his belief that "the easiest way of life is the best" as "a profound conviction," as the narrator does at the start, is just the sort of gassy self-delusion that satires fuel on. See Pickering, 1028.

sorts of jobs that our economy, if left unchecked, characteristically creates. This is just the sort of moral disingenuousness that its division of mind exploits to hide its multiple miseries.

Art surely is, as Ezra Pound insisted, "news that STAYS news."[13] But though I know of no story written in the 1850s that has remained more newsworthy than "Bartleby," the very ongoing accuracy of its prophetic message about the special character of American self-deception would seem to guarantee its continued eclipse.

Yet the obscurity of Melville provides an incomplete and so, too, unfair picture of the industrial West's receptivity to social criticism in the nineteenth century. That the unmasking of the moral masquerade of success could, in more moderate forms, actually be applauded was repeatedly proven by Charles Dickens, who, although Melville's contemporary and rough artistic equal, remained phenomenally popular on both sides of the Atlantic from his first book to his last.

Two more vital sensibilities cannot be imagined; among many other gifts, each bequeathed to us an acute critique of scientific capitalism's moral deficiencies. Still, the core natures of these equally formidable minds were, in key ways, as profoundly different as their fates in the literary marketplace. By plumbing those differences we can both locate the deeper causes of the Melville Eclipse and gain a truer gauge on the specific sorts of self-criticism that our own age might be willing to accept. We can also clarify two very distinct but complementary roles the literary artist can assume in transitional times: the poet as parish priest and the poet as wilderness prophet.

Secular Priest: The Author of Ritual Reintegration

The Irish poet, Seamus Heaney, has written eloquently in *The Redress of Poetry* on the political importance of the poetic imagination, which arises, he insists, not from simply voicing a grievance or vetting an agenda but from a recovery of "sense" in poetry's own terms. The artist's act of imagination precedes the treaty authors' compromise, the jury's verdict, the convention's new conception of the governing order. In its precedence, though, the poem doesn't dictate the precise codicils of political reform (as in, say, the abstract list of the Ten Commandments) but provides instead a metaphorical model of the mind's sheer capacity for

---

13. Ezra Pound, *ABC of Reading* (New York: New Directions, 1960), 29.

imaginative reformation (as in the concrete narrative of the Moses story). Rather than "legislate" the world, as Shelley suggested in his "Defence of Poetry," the poet "redresses" it through creating a separate, parallel space, one reflective of, yet different from, the social world.

That separate realm of the poem is, paradoxically, the one place where the elements of contemporary disorder can be made to coexist in an orderly way through aesthetic form. By unifying the as yet irresolvable social "facts" through its rhythms and rhymes, images and ironies, by enacting its "principle of integration in . . . context[s] of division and contradiction,"[14] poetry can evoke harmony in the very act of articulating divisiveness. It can generate hope even while bearing witness to inconsolable despair. To borrow from Yeats: the artful poem or story allows us to hold both truth and justice, the intractable real and the perdurable ideal, in the same mind at the same moment.[15]

In the essay just cited, Heaney was referring to the dilemmas of multicultural conflict, specifically to the problems of a Catholic citizenry in a Northern Ireland that has a dual and divisive political identity, at once Irish and English—a citizenry whose every utterance of protest must be spoken in a cultural language heavy with the history of its own oppression. But such a collision of cultures and conflicting allegiances can be internally driven as well as imposed, and Heaney's model of poetic redress helps explain, I believe, the extraordinary appeal of Dickens' novels to his contemporary audience, which was, after all, caught up in its own revolution, buffeted and baffled by all the stresses, contradictions, and radical revisions of the new industrial economy.

In truth, of course, Dickens' appeal was multidimensional. There can be, finally, no reductive accounting for an artist of his order. He was from the start a keen student of manners and professions whose early jobs in an attorney's office and as a parliamentary reporter gave him access to the full range of English society: its aspiring clerks and declining lords, its felons and fops and reformist zealots, its arriviste merchantry and oppressed urban poor. To this handy combination of social intelligence and on-the-job knowledge, the author added a host of rhetorical skills, including an actor's ear for accents, a cartoonist's gift for comic exaggeration, and an unmatched capacity to convert, through a sudden spurt of eloquent empathy, one of his comic caricatures into a figure of

---

14. Seamus Heaney, *The Redress of Poetry* (New York: Farrar, Straus and Giroux, 1993), 190.

15. Ibid., Heaney citing Yeats, 150.

miraculous depth. (See the moral revival of Sir Leicester Dedlock in *Bleak House*.) An enthusiast and optimist with a complementary gift for indignation, Dickens also possessed the necessary descriptive intelligence to evoke his own extremities of allegiance and revulsion—the rare verbal reach to convey his heart's extreme leaps. Yet for all his expressive intensity, this was an author who aimed, finally, toward an artful moderation, a compositional containment—of both his own passions and his age's complexities—through a mastery of the novel's form.

It is just this aspect of Dickens' talent, his formal mastery of the novel's deeper rhythms, that best suggests the special redress his fiction supplied. Industrialism's pace of change and organizational complexity, its stunning busyness, directly challenged the traditional story's ability to organize experience and inform identity. The Victorian novel evolved in response to that challenge, and Dickens, in particular, found the artful means to make narrative plot enact Heaney's "principle of integration" in the age's new and ever-more baffling "contexts of division and contradiction."

Dombey and Son, Little Dorrit, Bleak House, David Copperfield: few authors (and certainly not Melville whose one consistent weakness as a novelist was his inability to sustain dramatic unity) could manipulate so many vivid and varied characters in so many subplots with such ease, and all while submitting them to larger thematic ends. Through the artful orchestration of these rococo plots, with their diverse social venues and large casts of characters, Dickens provided a deeply reassuring experience of unity and continuity to a society beset with change on all sides. He addressed nearly all of the elements of industrial England's new and unprecedented social complexity—the explosion of wealth and knowledge; the division of classes, sexes, and professions; the conversion to rational materialist values with the subsequent conflict between domestic harmony and commercial productivity, Christian charity and capitalist ambition—while making those elements coalesce into a single, interactive narrative whole.

The graceful management of complexity in literature will always supply an aesthetic pleasure, but the satisfactions to be found in Dickens' mature works had deeper psychic and communal dimensions. In that the high-born and the low, the urban and the rural, the practice of the office and the ritual of the home were all woven together inside that separate place of the novel's imagination, Dickens' fiction "made sense," in the richest meaning of that phrase, of the West's new order. By both expressing and domesticating all the frenzy and complexity of the industrial age, his work instilled in his readership a faith that this new England was still a conceivable place. And so compelling was his particular articulation of that one imaginable place—let's call it the parish of Dickensia—that our own conception of Anglo-American culture was long shaped by its vision. (What would Christmas be today without the sentimental modeling and ritualistic template of *A Christmas Carol*?)

Traditionally, it is the function of the priest in any society to maintain those rituals that both express and enforce communal identity. Like Heaney's poem, those rituals carve out a separate parallel space, one reflective of yet different from the social world. Entering that space, all of a society's members—however unique their talents or unequal their achievements, however immediate their alienation or fierce their intramural rivalries—are literally "reminded" of their commonality through their co-participation in the rhythmic recitations and symbolic reenactments the ritual prescribes. By calling Dickens the parish priest of his age, I am referring specifically to this ritual-like experience his novels supplied: the redress of their reintegration of the diverse population of industrial England into a single vision of community.

Dickens was a special priest in that he didn't merely maintain a set of traditional rituals but invented new ones necessary to accommodate past beliefs to present circumstances. He was a *secular* priest because the present circumstances were precisely those ones that were enacting the final conversion of Anglo-American culture from agricultural Christendom to scientific capitalism. (The symbolic climax of that conversion occurred at the height of Dickens' career in 1859 with Darwin's publication of *Origin of Species*—science's retelling of the Genesis story.) And the accommodation this secular priest achieved was one that reinfused the capitalist province with the Christian ethic. One might say that Dickens' work constituted a kind of retelling of the New Testament's social gospel, updated to the size, pace, and plenitude of industrial England, and complete with a new set of exemplary and cautionary characters—Gradgrind, Fagan, Pip, Scrooge, Micawber—"types" whose stories became the pole stars and watchwords to guide his readers through the moral labyrinth of modern life.

The will to guide was both intentional and unavoidable. Cultural identities, after all, serve as directive maps as well as decorative badges, so that any re-envisioning of a nation's identity becomes inseparable from a reformulation of its sense of justice. Which is to say that, in his own and far more artful way, Dickens was as didactic as Horatio Alger. The artfulness mattered. Unlike the shallow preachments of Alger's work, Dickens' novels were ethical and political acts both in the narrower sense of giving voice to specific grievances *and* in the grander sense of Heaney's definition. For beyond the issues they addressed (debtors prisons, orphanages, cruel country schools, a corrupt and callous justice system), his plots labored to show that, even in this age of mass mechanization, individual decisions mattered—the ground belief out of which every ethical system must emerge. And they did that by tracing the trail of consequences across all boundaries, so that the moral effects of decision-making were made visible and palpable.

In a Dickens novel, the death of the lowliest unwed mother years before can affect the current happiness of the highest lord (*Bleak House*); an orphan's benefactor might prove to be an escaped murderer (*Great Expectations*); the rich can torment, ignore, or assist the less fortunate while the poor can scheme their way into villainy, stoically endure, or even rise to the rescue of their social betters. Resentment is an equal opportunity corrupter, infecting the heiress Havisham and the underling Heep alike. In the parish of Dickensia, neither the assignments of class nor the accidents of talent can exempt one from the universal problems of accountability and vulnerability.

This "principle of *moral* integration" was Dickens' perennial deeper message, the way he rescued unity, continuity, and compassionate connection within a political economy whose machine-like schemes were producing intellectual disruption, social division, and emotional alienation. The very ideas whose dangerous effects John Donne had lamented two centuries before in "An Anatomy of the World"—"Tis all in pieces, all coherence gone / All just supply, and all Relation"—had become institutionalized, and Dickens' fiction responded by harnessing that same new system's industriousness to the compensatory tasks of recovering coherence and insisting on relation.

Through his mastery of plot and his expressive intensity, Dickens dramatized again and again John Donne's countervailing message that "no man is an Island," that each is an accountable and vulnerable "part of the main." The English became one again ethically as well as aesthetically inside his richly imagined fictive domain, for all the characters, whether rich or poor, were adjudged alike by the plenitude of their loyalty, generosity, and joy—by the degree to which they loved or loathed their neighbors. Redressing the inherent indifference and selfishness of rational materialism, Dickens, in essence, reinvented the Christian message of brotherhood for his money-mad age.

This reinvention was as much a secularization of Christianity as it was a reformation of capitalism. Dickens' "special place" of redress was never really a spiritual domain. His were society novels with a difference—in part, of course, because society itself was so radically changing—but they were society novels nonetheless. For even as they dramatize the manners and morals of the day, Dickens' novels, like Jane Austen's, never really question the ultimate basis of society's values. On the ur-subjects of sex, death, and religion, Dickens toes his culture's party line instinctively, almost aggressively, his native intensity mostly reduced to sentimentalizing the conventional Victorian attitude—as in, say, his repeated endorsement of the age's desexualized vision of ideal womanhood. The restless intensity of his imagination ranges up and down the entire stretch of the social hierarchy and partakes of nearly the total palette of social emotions, but he shies away from the philosophical, the spiritual, those problems and sentiments that tend to arise in solitude yet address the universal.

Although this avoidance marks the most serious limit to his achievement, it was indispensable to his appeal, which was extraordinary by any measure. Indeed, if we were to include all scales of achievement, no author in the history of the language, with the exception of Shakespeare, has been so successful. Dickens was a bestseller from his first publication to his last; widely admired by the best minds of his own time, his fiction inspired political reform as well as artistic imitation. And not only did his reputation survive his death, his novels continued to recalibrate the very consciousness of the industrial West for decades to come: buck-making, muckraking, and myth-making, immediate fame and artistic immortality all in one.

Finally, though, Dickens could never have been so popular and influential without being complicit to some degree with the foundational dreams of the new social order. The parish priest could reach so many of his parishioners precisely because he spoke the language of their hopes, tacitly endorsing the new emphases on material ambition and upward social mobility, even while attempting to reform their application.

This endorsement was what I meant when I noted earlier that Dickens secularized Christianity as much as he moralized capitalism in Christian terms. Indeed, most of Horatio Alger's crude rationalizations of the money economy had their more artful origins in Dickens' own work. In particular, the hope for a sudden stroke of monetary fortune and the idealizing of the patron who could effect that intervention—the whole secular reinvention of grace—arose first in Dickens' fertile imagination. Perhaps because his own vaulting out of poverty had depended on an unexpected legacy, Dickens simply accepted that money could make a difference, that social and material ambition were permissible, even commendable, so long as generosity and sociability attended one's ascension.

That the compensatory generosity he espoused might still be funded by an ultimately corrupting, systematic selfishness; that the geniality he so valued might actually mask a deeper misanthropy; that, in short, Dickens' ritual integration of Christian charity with materialist ambition might remain at heart a contradiction, one that he had less resolved than concealed with his own appeal to a disingenuous sentimentality—these were features of a disturbing critique that only a more severe and estranged sensibility could admit.

Secular Prophet: The Author of Mythic Disintegration

While the priest resides at the very center of the tribe, tending its stories of origin and restorative rituals, the prophet moves to the margins. His is a mind that seeks out the extremities of isolation and whose meditative trances, as empty as the deserts of their chosen setting, are fitfully struck by a comprehensive clarity—the sort of lightning-like vision whose sudden forking can illuminate and frame the entire plain of human activity. A priest supplies the stately rhythms of integration, a prophet the raw stutterings of inspiration. A priest officiates and adjudicates to assure continuity; a prophet disrupts and disturbs, bringing back from the boundaries of perception a message of often apocalyptic discrepancy: something is wrong, terribly wrong. While the priest regulates the internal relations of the tribal fold, the prophet judges the tribe as a whole and from a God's eye view with all the intemperance of revelation, and he does so in the strange and often anguished language of the new. Given their respective missions, the priest is generally revered and obeyed in his own time and place, while the prophet is feared and misunderstood and must await justification in a later age.

To call Melville a secular prophet is to recognize not just the severity, unpopularity, and ultimate clarity of his vision but also the fitful nature of its articulation, the sudden seizures of insight amidst pages of obscurity, and too its founding angle of perception—a view from the edges that emerged in part from biographical circumstances. Melville's early life, however, paralleled Dickens' in one very crucial way. Both were raised in a family that lost its social standing due to economic failure, the surety of a funded education and a respectable job suddenly withdrawn. For Dickens, the formative traumatic experiences of this period were his father's stay in debtors prison and his own time spent as an involuntary child laborer, memories that would spark his reformist indignation. His life's journey, like those of the boys in Alger's stories, was within and between the very separate realms of England's new industrial hierarchy, and the mapping of those internal boundaries and the drama of their crossing became central obsessions of his fictional domain.

After *his* father's business failure and early death, Melville's formative experiences were, by contrast, his journeys to sea—first as a teen, and then later and more importantly at the age of twenty, when he joined the crew of a whaler and sailed to the South Pacific. Melville was away from America for four self-defining years, the pivot point of a young man's maturity, and his experiences aboard ship not only supplied the setting and metaphorical dressing for much of his best fiction; they also shaped a sensibility trained to the solitary contemplation of elemental things.

His interactions with Polynesian natives—especially in the Typee valley where he was held captive for a month after jumping ship in the Marquesas Islands—were no less important. As the aphorism has it, *No one knows England who only England knows*, and Melville's vision of Anglo-American culture was deepened and darkened by this early immersion in a preliterate tribe whose contrasting values showed him that modern "civilization [did] not engross all the virtues of humanity: she had not even her full share of them."[16]

While Dickens' childhood experiences drove him to redress the injustices of class relations, Melville's multicultural adventures were leading him to question the ultimate foundation of any culture or civilization, and so to question the very possibility of justice itself. His view from the edge of the wilderness and from the lip of our preliterate past shook his allegiance to the idea of the West without supplying a substitute he could honestly accept. It brought him to the very brink of nihilism. And staring into the abyss of potential meaninglessness for the seven years of his highest achievement, the man neither jumped nor blinked.

---

16. Cited by Mumford, 49.

It would be unfair to the depth and difficulty of Melville's search, then, to limit our reading of a story like "Bartleby" to its astute critique of scientific capitalism. We are given both more and less than a socioeconomic analysis if we dare to look—more clarity, less certainty. The scrivener is not a Dickensian intruder, that mysterious benefactor or malefactor whose social mask hides his moral essence: the gruff philanthropist with a secret heart of gold; the fawning servant whose very obsequiousness conceals an agenda of ruthless resentment. Melville is not Dickens. We wait in vain for the recovery of insight and the restoration of the moral order that proceeds from the revelation of the true nature behind the falsifying front. We never get to savor the piquant flavor of the heart's eventual reformation, as in the ethical coming-of-age of a Pip or a David Copperfield or a finally generous Ebeneezer Scrooge; nor are we favored with the belated reward of injustice redressed, as in the unveiling of Heep and the drowning of the seducer Steerforth.

If Dickens had written "Bartleby"—and its oppressive work environment was just the sort of venue he liked to expose—we can easily imagine how the plot might have differed. Converted like Scrooge, awakened to that "misery [that] hides aloof," the narrator would have suspended the inhumane work rules. He would have happily hosted a communal feast for his employee "family," one larded with a thick pudding and a rich roast and liberally interrupted with toddy toasts of fellow-feeling, all to climax, in a favorite Dickensian touch, with the baptismal bestowal of an affectionate nickname for the now adopted scrivener: the priestly confirmation of his initiation into the genial fold of the Pickwickian club.

Against the mechanism of the market and the dry abstraction of money, Dickens supplies the ritual of the feast, the juicy sustenance of gravied meat and brandy-soaked pies served within the globe of the hearth's warming light. Against the division and alienation of the rationalist scheme, he founds the club of fraternal belonging and bestows the favor of a personalized name. Contrast this rich vision of social redemption with the stark severity of Melville's actual ending—the pale figure of Bartleby fasting to death against a prison wall; the narrator's geniality more a strategy of avoidance than a means for recalling the estranged individual back to the fold—and the radical divergence between these two sensibilities becomes clear.

The source of that divergence can be defined in precisely those terms that Seamus Heaney used in his exploration of poetry's political nature, for if the ultimate aim for every artist is to find the means, in Yeats's words again, "to hold in a single thought reality and justice," few authors can sustain a perfect balance in their principled attempts at integration. And though they share an eloquence of nearly Shakespearean stature, Dickens and Melville are clearly divided as to which of those two poles, in the tension of their opposition, one ought to favor.

Justice prevails in the parish of Dickensia. Not only does the author, in glad agreement with his mass audience, favor the happy ending; he actually believes in the ethical grounding that makes human happiness both credible and prescribable. Dickens never seems to question that there *is* a moral order, a foundational compass of right and wrong behavior essentially Christian in nature, and, if need be, truth will be distorted (through sentimental excess or narrative coincidence) to insist on that order's reality.

In Melville, however, the grounds of justice, those deeper assumptions that Dickens never questions, are constantly being plumbed and investigated. His own fictive vessel—properly named the *Truthful* not the *Faithful*, the valiant *Veritable* replacing the foolish *Fidèle*—keeps searching for some credible source for humankind's faith in a just and orderly universe, a source that can support the diverse worldviews of both the Polynesian native and the Pittsfield farmer. Like any treasure map, this plotted path of hope must pass the test of experience but in Melville's eyes can't. His later fiction spies in all such belief a seductive self-hypnosis from which we must awake.

Gazing into the rare calm of the sun-gilded sea, even *Moby Dick's* cautious Starbuck can say "I look deep down and do believe," but in order to do so he must first "let faith oust fact, let fancy oust memory." He must deny that beneath the golden surface lurk "teeth-tiered sharks," a Nature calibrated to "kidnaping, cannibal ways." The ease of optimism, in Melville's view, always requires the labor of repression; the idyll of innocence demands the erasure of memory, and so the evasion of maturity's chastening lessons. Beneath life's "velvet paw," there always waits, curled, "a remorseless fang," and consequently "the mortal man who hath more of joy than sorrow in him, that mortal man cannot be true—not true, or undeveloped." In Melville's fictive world, truth must prevail, and when truth does the gauzy fog of faith evaporates beneath its scorching light. There can be no happy ending on the voyage of the *Veritable* because the pilot can't forget that all endings point to death. There is no finally fruitful spiritual quest because beyond nature's "remorseless fang" and "cannibal ways" lies an impenetrable blackness that no human idea can comprehend.[17]

This insistence on the ultimate inscrutability of the universe is completely opposed to the hubris of an age that actually believed all mysteries would soon yield, happily and profitably, to the scientific method. It presages a postmodern writer like Don DeLillo in its suggestion that the West's avid manufacture of rational knowledge shall end in exhaustion, a coagulation into nonsense. On Melville's allegorical voyage, the Enlightenment results, ironically, in a self-generated darkness. The extreme pursuit of abstract rationality ends in concrete unintelligibility, the self-cancellation of systems so baroque that they become opaque.

So it is with the Counterfeit Detector at the end of *The Confidence Man*, the rococo details of which generate more doubt than certainty in the attempt to distinguish real money from the fake. As a bonus supplied by the scam-artist child, the Detector is counterfeit itself, of course, a cynical device perversely designed to magnify doubt in the very guise of supplying surety. "Free," it becomes a gratuitously cruel means to extend the con man's mystifying power past the moment of the sale by exploiting the new economic man's over-dependence on expertise to ascertain value. As such, it stands as a mocking emblem to mark the systematic erosion of American self-reliance under scientific capitalism.

But on this subject, too, Melville's critique extends beyond the economic instant to the human condition. For even the most earnest instruments for discerning value fail in Melville's world, and not even tribal culture, untouched as yet by the cynicism of salesmanship, is immune to the fate of knowledge turned opaque. Such is the case with the tattoos on *Moby Dick*'s Queequeg, whose "hieroglyphic marks," inscribed by some long-departed native seer and covering his entire body, constitute "a complete theory of heaven and earth, and a mystical treatise on the art of attaining truth"—a theory and a treatise whose mysteries, however, not even Queequeg can read any longer.[18] The pattern remains but not the original code that translates shape into sense. Literally wearing a cosmology that he cannot comprehend, Queequeg becomes a walking emblem of humankind's alienation from metaphysical sense. Even this most heroic of Melville's characters has been cut off from any culturally

---

17. Herman Melville, *Moby Dick* (Norwalk: Easton Press, 1977), 524–25.
18. Ibid., 514.

defined "principle of integration" that might link his behavior to some ultimate meaning or divine intent.

In such a life—where Nature's cruelties are the limit of the truth we can reliably assay and where knowledge's "progress" only serves to disguise, as in the Counterfeit Detector, the reassertion of "cannibal ways"—in such a life, "the truest of all men is the Man of Sorrows, and the truest of all books is Solomon's, and Ecclesiastes is the fine hammered steel of woe. 'All is Vanity.' ALL." Even as he asserts the totality of this stoic truth, the author—speaking through his fictional alter ego, Ishmael in *Moby Dick*—understands that "this wilful world hath not got hold of unchristian Solomon's wisdom yet,"[19] and he uses this world's resistance to spur his own artistic intent.

For it is just this sort of "unchristian wisdom" that Melville aspires to reinvent: a new song of Solomonic sorrow but one dressed in the trim and tackle of the industrial age, all the better to sing of that age's particular forms of Vanity, including the folly of colonial conversion, the collateral cruelties of capitalist progress, and, not least, the cataclysmic danger inherent in the rationalist dream of total control. (As the over-pursuit of knowledge only generates darkness, the unchecked drive to conquer Nature invites instead a self-annihilation—the monstrous redress of the Great White Whale.) And when the new age refuses to "get hold" of this wisdom he would bring, Melville turns, in alternating moods of satirical rage and wry despair, to a penetrating study of the self-deceptions that fund its "wilful" rejection.

This sorrowful wisdom is *un-* rather than *anti-*Christian because Melville regrets the darkness of the message. As Hawthorne observes in his moving record of their last meeting in 1856, Melville still suffers the great religious questions up to the very point when he quits writing fiction; he still seeks "a definite belief" that can withstand his rigorous scrutiny but cannot find it.[20] And so where the Christian, against all the

---

19. Ibid., 454–55.

20. In 1856 Melville visited Hawthorne in Liverpool, England; it would be their last meeting. In an excerpt from the older author's journal, dated November 20, Hawthorne offers the following observation: "Melville, as he always does, began to reason of Providence and futurity, and of everything that lies beyond human ken, and informed me that he had "pretty much made up his mind to be annihilated"; but still he does not seem to rest in that anticipation; and, I think, will never rest until he gets hold of a definite belief. It is strange how he persists—and has persisted ever since I knew him, and probably long before—in wondering to-and-fro over these deserts, as dismal and monotonous as the sand hills amid which we were sitting. He can neither believe, nor be comfortable in his unbelief; and he is too honest and courageous not to try to do one

invasive evidence of sin, can still summon joy as life's ruling temper, Melville, against all the gravity of human hope, can uncover only woe. Not the woe of individual self-pity but the deep communal woe that admits the agonizingly unbridgeable gap between the most profound of human wishes and the most persistent of earthly facts.

Rather than merely reject the Christian's version of the happy ending, Melville plumbs the existential depths for the basis of any and all happy endings, and he fails to find it. In the seven years of his highest achievement, Melville's work repeatedly insists that truth and justice, honesty and optimism cannot be integrated—not at least by human consciousness as he has come to know it in the age of rational materialism. The honest seeker cannot, after all, as Chesterton insisted, "find a way [to love] the world without trusting it."[21] He cannot cultivate such an unblinking love because the world is, finally, at its self-defining core, unlovable. Consequently, those who do love the world in Melville's fiction—like the chipper dying family in "Cock-A-Doodle-Doo!"; like Captain Amasa Delano, in "Benito Cereno"; like that genial lawyer, Bartleby's boss—can only do so by trusting it. And they can trust the world only through a "wilful" refusal to "get hold" of its multiform sorrows: by deliberately keeping "misery aloof."

So it is that at the very moment Dickens is striving to revive Christian ethics for the new society of scientific capitalism, Melville, diving deep into the heart of that society's contradictions, is questioning the ultimate basis of Christian metaphysics. While the parish priest struggles to reform the moral intelligence and restore a social order based on generosity and joy, the wilderness prophet portrays the enclosure of that intelligence and the masking of misery through a false generosity and a self-centered joy, both of which are serving the "profound conviction that the easiest life is the best." Trafficking on the social boundaries between morals, manners, and economic methods, the Englishman seeks to integrate the old morality with the new economy and to domesticate its industrial complexity through newly intricate narrative forms. Probing instead the outer boundaries of the human imagination where ethics must emerge from metaphysical facts, the American questions the

---

or the other. If he were a religious man, he would be one of the most truly religious and reverential; he has a very high and noble nature, and better worth immortality than most of us." See: http://www.melville.org/hawthrne.htm.

21. G.K. Chesterton, *Orthodoxy* (New York: Doubleday, 1936), 79.

possibility of any principle of integration—any final shapeliness to our doings and our makings.

As a consequence Melville proves to be the less effective moralist but the more arresting ethicist; the less polished artist—someone who, with the notable exception of "Bartleby," cannot reliably sustain the larger integrations of aesthetic order—but the greater visionary. Because Melville suffers as well as sees the consequences of his revolutionary age, his fiction proves prophetic in so many ways.

- *Philosophically*, he anticipates the threat of nihilism which the combination of scientific skepticism and cultural relativism will soon bring to the Western intellect.

- *Artistically*, he mixes the genres of fiction and nonfiction, appropriating news accounts for his narratives ("Benito Cereno," *Israel Potter*); advertising fact while supplying invention (*Typee, Omoo*); filling his pages with technical information (*Moby Dick*) and even metafictional commentary (*The Confidence Man*). And he does in distinctly modern, even postmodern ways. He practices a style that flirts with the very opacity (through complexity or "duplicity") that he so often warns against, the medium risking the diagnosis of its message.

- *Politically and economically*, he manages to prefigure, in the character of Bartleby, the temper and nearly all the tactics of political and economic protest to come. Not only does he invent the very archetype of the passive aggressive personality; he predicts in the parable of the scrivener's rebellion the work slow down, the work stoppage, the sit in (occupying the office), the principled suicide of the hunger strike.

- *Ethically and psychologically*, he examines nearly every dimension of the emerging society of self-deception, unveiling the hidden cruelties and pervasive lies that, under the new regime of "progress," are corrupting America's native traditions of religious and political idealism. In Bartleby's boss, Amasa Delano, and the whole "ship of fools" in *The Confidence Man*, he dissects that new American identity—technically savvy and materially productive but morally obtuse and spiritually empty—which I have elsewhere dubbed the Idiot Savant.

Even as the priest strove urgently to make the best of times out of the worst of times, the prophet saw visions and dreamed dreams. Like the "obscure bird" in *Macbeth* who "clamored the live-long night," Melville prophesied "with accents terrible / Of dire combustion and confus'd events / New-hatch'd to the woeful time."[22] But that seven-year night ended, no one attended, and his vision of dire confusion rapidly became the moral venue of everyday life.

Apocalypse Now: The Immortality of Preferring Not to Be

> ... It is the dead,
> Not the living, who make the longest demands:
> We die for ever ...
>
> —*Antigone*

When comparing Dickens to Melville, we mustn't make the reductionist mistake of presuming our appreciation of one's view should preclude an admiration for the other's. Unlike Thomas Carlyle's Quack and Dupe, this priest and prophet are not "convertible personages," but, in their separate attempts to redress the multiple degradations of modern progress, they are "upper-side and under" of the best of the Anglo-American intelligence at this pivotal moment in Western history.[23] Ever the allegorist, Melville supplies an apt image for the necessary coexistence of two such divergent truth-seeking temperaments. In a sketch entitled "Two Sides of a Tortoise" in *The Encantadas*, the author reminds us that the tortoise shell has both a "dark and melancholy" side facing the sky and a brighter breast

---

22. Shakespeare, *Macbeth*: II, iii, 59–60.

23. *We are governed, very infallibly, by the 'sham-hero'—whose name is Quack, whose work and governance is Plausibility, and also is Falsity and Fatuity ... And Quack and Dupe, as we must ever keep in mind, are upper-side and under of the selfsame substance; convertible personages: turn up your dupe into the proper fostering element, and he himself can become a quack; there is in him the due prurient insincerity, open voracity for profit, and closed sense for truth, whereof quacks too, in all their kinds are made.* This concise ethical/psychological diagnosis by Thomas Carlyle, one of the earliest and most astute critics of the new industrial economy, sums up Melville's central subject in *The Confidence Man*. The complementary relationship of Quack and Dupe can be seen as the inverse of the relationship between poetic prophet and priest, as I have been defining them here—the former pair allied in their pursuit of deceit, the latter in their commitment to truth-seeking. See *Past and Present* (Boston: Houghton Mifflin, 1965), 30–31.

plate underneath, and that we should "enjoy the bright, keep it turned up perpetually if [we] can, but be honest and don't deny the black."[24]

The increasingly armored enclosure of industrial progress had, like the self-protecting shell of the tortoise, two sides, and, as with the tortoise, it was becoming ever more difficult to envision both upperside and under in a single thought, a unified mind. Yet in attempting to understand this age when the mind and the place of the modern West were firmly forged and when, out of those new values and venues, our own postindustrial selves were already being formed, we still must strive to find some principle of integration that will allow us to hold in mind both the priest's redemptive joy and the prophet's reluctant woe. Now as then, however, the ease of such an integration proves uneven. Insomuch as we do naturally prefer "the bright side" of this two-sided tortoise and have entered, as Melville so clearly foresaw, an age of adamant affability when "fancy ousts memory" and "faith ousts fact," we must work that much harder to "be honest and not deny the black." Which is why I will end this examination of two authors I greatly admire by emphasizing the prophecy of the darker side.

And dark it is. There can be no honest diminishing, no softening or spinning, of the bleakness of Melville's sense of things. In his prophetic vision, the lights *do* go out, the ship *does* go down; the virtual asphyxiates the actual as even the Word—the saving, sacred Word—is swallowed within the well of its own articulations. On his prophetic stage, the rotten state of Denmark reinvents itself in the hold of the *Pequod,* on the decks of the *Fidèle,* in the workaday warren of Wall Street's lightless cells. But now, although the time again is "out of joint," no hero arises—no hero can arise—to "set it right."

In Hamlet we are given the most eloquent expression of an accountable individuality: a new Western self whose anxious inwardness can be used to redress the duplicities of evil and the dulling divisions of human indifference. The powers of privacy, self-reflection, and independent thought that characterize the newly literate post-Renaissance mind have been reinvested in the individualized conscience so that society acquires a new and counter intelligence to that of the Machiavellian schemer— someone equally effective but devoted to the good.

But on Melville's stage, the possibility for such lonely heroism has evaporated. The rescuing prince has become instead a Capt. Delano

---

24. "Two Sides of a Tortoise," *Great Short Works of Herman Melville* (New York: Harper & Row, 1969), 103–4.

whose survival depends not on brave introspection but on the idiocy of unreflective optimism. Hamlet's father, that wise but suffering ghost come to advise of evil unredressed, has been reduced to a ghostly scrivener whose repeated protests remain unread. "Mark me," he says again and again like the ghost of Hamlet's father, but now there is no loving son like Hamlet to say "I will."[25] Now instead, converted to the "profound conviction that the easiest way of life is the best," the new American prince of success "would prefer not to."

That plea, though, persists. Like a beached and bottled S.O.S., Melville's story perpetually awaits a mind willing to comprehend who, in mercy's name, Bartleby is. Antigone was right: the dead, dying "for ever," do "make the longest demands," their memorial requiring our constant and careful participation. But they also can supply the longest-lived rewards. For even as the dead depend on us to revive the memory and so the meaning of their individual lives, we depend on them to advise us as to what is real and lasting in human nature.

The great irony of Bartleby's (and Melville's) self-annihilation is that, in the care of its composition, it perpetually invites a paradoxical resuscitation. Like those two other martyrs whose deaths have calibrated the best of Western progress—Socrates who preferred truth over life and Jesus who preferred love—Bartleby lives (and dies) "for ever" whenever the meaning of his preference is carefully attended. The story of his eclipse is born again when to his ghostly "Mark me," we consent: "I will."

For the message in his bottle—"do you not see?"—is that something has gone wrong, terribly wrong. Although long dead, both the author and his character still "know who [we] are"—what we in America have increasingly become—and unless we reawaken "in mercy's name" and for the sake of real preference, they will continue to have "nothing to say to [us]." As the true prophets of our current confusion, both Melville and Bartleby have mapped exactly where we are, and, reversing the finally hopeful tragedy of *Hamlet*'s plot, each in response, now and forever, prefers "not to be."

---

25. *Hamlet*, I, 5, 2.

5

In the Beginning[1]
(Adam and Eve Reconsidered)

Evidence of the dissolution of American modernity's once potent cultural order multiplies daily. The rancor of our political scene, so rife now with racial and regional tribalism, is mirrored relentlessly in a new civic sphere dominated by social media. There, in an anxious pursuit of likes, retweets, and viral links, American individualism has been surrendering to an often crude collectivism, its virtual spaces haunted by ranters, hackers, click-bait bots, corporate eavesdroppers, and self-selecting "communities" of conformity. And as smartphone addiction spreads throughout the body politic, the dubious ethos of an online behavior too often defined by scolds and trolls has been infecting every domain, undermining norms long in the making. We can hear its ugly echoes ricocheting now from the statehouse, the White House, evangelical pulpits, and progressive podiums.

Although recently exploited by external enemies, this assault on our democratic character was not initiated by some foreign intelligence service, much less by the many illegal immigrants we tacitly invite into our country to mow our lawns, pick our food, and care for our children. It is instead entirely homegrown, an unintended consequence of our reckless drive for progress, narrowly defined. The globalization of the economy and the digitizing of public and private communications have together

---

1. The two books reviewed in detail in this chapter are: *The First Love Story: Adam, Eve, and Us*, Bruce Feiler (Penguin Group USA, 2017) and *The Rise and Fall of Adam and Eve*, Stephen Greenblatt (New York: W.W. Norton, 2017).

been destroying the very logic of liberal modernity, its default habits and commonsense presumptions. We can build a border wall a mile high on every side and we wouldn't be safe from the anarchic forces now set loose.

The West last suffered a self-generated "identity crisis" on this scale during the seventeenth century, when the radical empowerment of print technology was eviscerating Europe's hierarchical societies. Eventually, after much confusion, strife, and internecine violence, a new cultural order was established, including a Protestant spirituality, a free market economy, and a democratic government, each licensing in its own sphere a new individualism rooted in literacy. Such an historical comparison raises the question of how a people go about successfully reconfiguring their identity. A total rejection of the old system is bound to fail. The utter erasure of old ideas usually means a ruthless extermination of those who still believe in them, and the regimes that have attempted such a scheme, including the French, Soviet, and Cambodian revolutions, have themselves proven to be, in Thomas Hobbes's oft-cited critique of precivilized life, "nasty, brutish, and short."

Ex nihilo nihil fit: out of nothing comes nothing. Or, as William Faulkner insisted: "The past is not dead. It is not even past."[2] If, in the tidal turns of history, "all things fall / and are built again,"[3] they are built again from the remnants of the cultural order preceding them—they are reformations in the literal sense. Rebellious Protestants in the seventeenth century returned to the Bible, reinterpreting its meaning, emphasizing those passages and doctrines that best fit their era's new social and intellectual environment. They were vociferous opponents of the reigning ecclesiastical order, even as they stressed core elements of traditional belief, including the stories of Adam and Eve, Cain and Abel.

When a once vital cultural identity is breaking down, as ours is now, the emerging confusion about how we should behave inevitably leads to reconsiderations of who we truly are. And insomuch as those default conceptions have a narrative base, that often means returning to our myths of origin for reorientation. However crude its actions, the so-called Tea Party's protests of 2010 supply an obvious example of such an attempt. Other people, however, need to probe deeper into the substrate of meaning and being. For them, as for the earliest Protestants in their own divisive era, any reformulation of who we should become has to be

2. William Faulkner, *Requiem for a Nun* (New York: Random House, 1951), 73.
3. William Butler Yeats, "Lapis Lazuli," *Selected Poems and Two Plays of William Butler Yeats*, ed. M.L. Rosenthal (New York: Collier Books, 1962), 159–60.

rooted in a renewed understanding of who we once were, not just as a nation but "in the beginning," the *very* beginning. Which is why it seems more symptomatic than coincidental that two recent books revisit in detail the Judeo-Christian West's aboriginal story: the creation and fall of Adam and Eve.

1

Much of the lore recorded in Genesis likely predates literacy and exhibits, therefore, the features of oral storytelling: its brevity, repetitive phrasing, and simple symbolic plots. Such stories were composed to be easily recalled, becoming a sort of portable wisdom in metaphorical form for an oral tribe. The biblical account of the first man and woman, including their expulsion from their once idyllic home, certainly fits that mold. With one divinity, three archetypal characters, and a linear plot in which a sequence of choices, actions, and reactions has dramatic consequences for all the characters, Genesis 2 and 3 are less than a thousand words long.

Brevity doesn't guarantee certainty of meaning, however—nor is it intended to. Effective parables, like adjustable lenses, supply a range of possible interpretations, allowing the inherited wisdom of the tribe to interact with and adjust to changing times. And because this parable sits at the start of the West's most influential book, its skeletal narrative has been reassessed multiple times, creating in the words of James Grantham Turner "a vast ramshackle edifice of interpretation."[4] In looking back to Genesis, we might ask ourselves, then, whose previous reading might be coloring our own: Augustine's? Freud's? some Neo-Darwinian atheist's? Are we returning to those thousand words alone and rereading them closely, as a New Critic might? Or, in a kind of narcissistic presentism, are we projecting our self-conception onto the ancient story in an anxious search for scriptural endorsement?

The title of *New York Times* columnist Bruce Feiler's book *The First Love Story: Adam, Eve, and Us* succinctly defines his narrow approach, which strives to turn the West's first couple into a romantic model for our post-millennial selves. Hyperbolic praise for the biblical story prevails throughout. The Old Testament is not only "the greatest chronicle of human life in the ancient Near East"; it also "introduced love into the

---

4. James Grantham Turner, *One Flesh: Paradisal Marriage and Sexual Relations in the Age of Milton* (New York: Oxford University Press, 1987), 10.

world."[5] The author's biblical boosterism extends to chastising the usual grimmer interpretations of Genesis 3, the orthodox doctrine of original sin recast instead as "the greatest case of character assassination in the history of the world."[6] Indeed, the Fall, in Feiler's view, was not such a bad thing, after all, for "only after falling from grace can Adam and Eve fully fall in love with each other." When Adam defies God by accepting the forbidden fruit from his mate, he "chooses love over obedience," and "who among us," the author wonders, "cannot relate to that?"[7]

The verb in that rhetorical question captures a second theme of *The First Love Story*: the Old Testament narrative is not only wonderful, it is *relatable*. Like today's youth-oriented mega-churches, with their informal dress, pop music, hip sermons, and digital apps, Feiler clothes his analysis with contemporary references, supplying, for example, twee chapter titles like "Chore Wars" and "Meet Cute," the saccharine rhetoric intent on sweetening earnest advice of the self-help sort, such as "What Adam and Eve Can Teach Us About Relationships."

Whom exactly is *The First Love Story* aiming to teach? For which segment of the population is *its* version of this ancient story especially relatable? Feiler's position as a *Times* columnist and, too, his past role as the host for two biblically themed PBS documentaries suggest a familiar demographic: an urbane, reasonably well-educated middle class of mating age that tends to reside in progressive silos like Brooklyn and Seattle (Feiler's and my hometowns); well-meaning men and women who consider themselves "spiritual" rather than "religious," and who are, like many today, anxious about the state of their romantic relationships.

Beyond its biblical boosterism, which quickly trespasses into inaccuracy—the Hebrews did not "introduce love into the world"; even a cursory glance at scholarship on ancient Egypt would have revealed that, and the presumption that all preliterate peoples lacked love is arrogant on the face of it—Feiler's analysis is predictably in tune with his target audience. Loneliness is harmful; healthy relationships require caring, commitment, and an equality of roles, including the co-creation of a shared narrative. Sound biblically-based advice about love is now available, but in a new and better way, where "commandments are being replaced by recommendations," and "guidance" is given instead of "mandates."[8]

5. Feiler, 16.
6. Ibid., 11.
7. Ibid., 99–100.
8. Ibid., 251.

Rather than "blunt messengers of the consequences of disobedience," Adam and Eve are "ambassadors of equality, transgression, forgiveness, and reconciliation."[9] Feiler sees in them "what [he] believes they saw in themselves: that what will endure of their union is their togetherness. What will survive of them is love."[10]

Such an array of platitudes is indistinguishable, really, from the many bulleted lists in the how-to titles that lard our current bookshelves with relationship advice. Its sole distinguishing feature is the author's strenuous effort to anchor the authority of those assertions in the cultural bedrock of our oldest myth of origins: his attempt to authenticate who *we should become* (as couples and lovers) with *who we once were* "in the beginning." If, after all, the first couple on earth could earn the Hallmark Hall of Fame happy ending to their story that Feiler discerns, then so can we.

Unfortunately, no such ending exists in the original story. Other than listing their offspring, Genesis supplies almost no information about Adam and Eve after their expulsion from paradise. Starkly allegorical figures from the start, their compatibility as a couple, their happiness alone or combined, however defined, are not subjects for dramatic enactment or homiletic advice. At that point in the Old Testament's serial narrative, their sole function, it seems, is to produce the next generation of allegorical figures, Cain and Abel. The reconfiguring of Adam and Eve into three-dimensional characters, whose attitudes and behaviors might prove instructive, comes later, through the multiple if often contradictory commentaries that constitute our ever-expanding "ramshackle edifice." After acknowledging an ugly misogyny that taints some of that interpretive tradition, Feiler turns instead to more hopeful texts. Key among those is *Paradise Lost*, whose intricate portrait of the first couple resolved a central struggle in John Milton's own life, depicting in the end a potential model for the successful marriage of sexual passion with Puritan piety.

Fair enough, and as Voltaire slyly observed: given the myth's brevity, "every commentator" *is* more or less forced to "make his own Eden."[11] Still, like Thomas Jefferson, the Enlightenment rationalist who excised all references to Christ's miracles to fashion his own cut-and-paste version of the New Testament, Feiler's curated version of Genesis is defined as much by what it omits as what it includes. Conspicuous among the missing is that awesome and often jealous God who does command, rather

9. Ibid., 248–49
10. Ibid., 269.
11. Cited by Turner, 39.

than recommend, and whose response to those who reject his mandates includes fire, pestilence, and obliterating floods—that *deus absconditus* whose power is felt and feared but whose ultimate intentions can never be plumbed. Indeed, there is almost no God-talk at all in Feiler's account. The old Jehovah, like original sin, is shown the back door; both are treated as antiquated concepts that today's believer has progressed beyond.

Fair enough again, but if so, Feiler fails to supply any alternative explanation for the pandemic suffering of humankind, or for the viciousness that we have inflicted on each other in every age and place, yea even unto today in Brooklyn's lofts and Seattle's coffee shops. Nor does he address our perennial estrangement from the rest of creation, that deeper sense of lonely homelessness that seems woven into the human condition, and that was beautifully expressed by Milton's contemporary Henry Vaughan. "Man is the shuttle, to whose winding quest / And passage through these looms / God ordered motion, but ordained no rest."[12] Along with the shame in Eden's shadows, the simmering sense of something precious lost has been pithed from Feiler's version of the myth. In *his* new Old Testament, spiritual practice has progressed or devolved, depending on your perspective, into something more like a therapeutic regimen: one whose simple central theme, "all you need is love," was composed by John Lennon for the Summer of Love in 1967.

Is that all we need, though? (We might recall, by way of context, that 1967's Summer of Love was quickly followed by 1968's spring and summer of assassinations, riots, and violently suppressed war protests.) And is Feiler's progressive reading of our origins any more helpful to reimagining a renewed America than the Tea Party's reactionary nostalgia? Or, rephrasing that question to fit the narrower scope of his book's ambition, are his teachings really sufficient to assuage the agonies and uncertainties of those seeking romantic love today?

Living in an era when traditional roles have been collapsing all around us—an age of degrading dating apps, online porn addiction, gender warfare, viral sexting, ghosting, "slut shaming," and a fully commodified wedding industry—I don't doubt that we need new civilizing models for how to make and sustain meaningful relationships. I do doubt, though, that converting the profound ambiguities of our ancient scriptures into the banal positivity of self-help literature is equal to that task.

12. Henry Vaughan, "Man," *George Herbert and Henry Vaughan*, ed. Louis L. Martz (New York: Oxford University Press, 1986), 336.

2

Worldviews can pass, and when they do, the relevance of the wisdom literature that expressed their core values may fade too. The interpretive lens of a once revered myth can only adjust so far before it more skews than clarifies the new cultural circumstance. In those instances the once authoritative parable, out of scale and out of touch, becomes ripe for parody, as in 1605 when the heroic chivalry of the questing knight was reduced to the tragicomic delusions of Don Quixote. Stephen Greenblatt's *The Rise and Fall of Adam and Eve* argues that our myth of origins has been suffering just such a decline, even as the pun in its title announces a significant shift in authorial tone. In this return to our scriptural beginning, the refined ironies of the literary scholar have replaced the earnest homilies of the spiritually-inclined advice columnist.

Greenblatt first achieved scholarly renown as a founder of the New Historicism, an approach to analyzing literature that stresses its cultural and historical contexts. And though he has left behind the academic monograph lately to seek a wider audience, his writing has remained largely true to its original premise, emphasizing how "certain remarkable works of art are at once embedded in a highly specific life-world and seem to pull free of that life-world."[13] And so Greenblatt naturally begins his study of Adam and Eve's story *before* "the beginning," analyzing the historical origins of Genesis itself.

Judaism, as we now know it, emerged in the aftermath of a tribal catastrophe: Nebuchadnezzar II's conquest of Judah, his subsequent deportation of many of its Hebrew residents to Babylonia, and the destruction of their holy Temple ten years later in a failed revolt. The trauma of that period, the fight to retain their tribal identity during a sixty year captivity where they were exposed to a cosmopolitan diversity of myths, customs, and deities, eventually led to a fierce reformation of their own beliefs and practices. Once they regained their freedom and returned to Judah, mixed marriages were banned and the worship of foreign gods strictly proscribed. In a now familiar reactionary attempt to assert a doctrinal purity, an unknown group of priests and scribes began selecting a set of approved chronicles, myths, and ritual instructions from the wide array available. Just as a single all-powerful God would now be strictly worshipped, His doctrine would be contained in a single sacred text. Despite

---

13. "Greenblatt Named University Professor of the Humanities," Harvard University Gazette, 21 September, 2000.

IN THE BEGINNING

the urge to purge alien influences, portions of that text, including the story of a catastrophic flood, did borrow from other tribes. As Greenblatt aptly notes, though, the Hebrews applied their own interpretive lens to the stories they retold. "To [their] way of thinking there had to be a moral reason for the disasters that humans encounter,"[14] and this obsession with ethical causation begins in the beginning, with the story of the Fall.

The plot is simple, and given the discrepancy between its minimal facts and the elaborate interpretations later educed from them, it bears repeating. The first man and woman, "naked and unashamed," were placed by God within an abundant garden, whose bounty they were allowed to freely forage, with a single exception: upon threat of death, they must not eat from "the tree of the knowledge of good and evil." Enter the serpent, "more subtle than any beast of the field," who tempts Eve into disobeying that command by denying she will die and insisting instead that her "eyes shall be opened" and that, "knowing good and evil," she'll then become "as gods" herself.

Without any hesitation, first Eve, then Adam eat the forbidden fruit. Their eyes are opened, but rather than achieve any blissful sense of divine entitlement, their first reactions to the new knowledge gained are shame and fear: they become aware they are naked and cower in the trees when they hear their Lord approach. Although they aren't killed, God's punishment proves severe. The first couple is banished forever from Eden's garden of ease. Eve's "sorrows" are "multiplied," as from then on she will suffer in childbirth and need to submit to "the rule" of her man. The ground beyond Eden will be "cursed," made full of "thorns and thistles," and only "by the sweat of his brow" will Adam now be able to eke out a living.

Plot, as I define it for my writing classes, is "a sequence with consequences." The sequence here, from prohibition to temptation to disobedience, is quick and clear, and its consequences grave: first shame and fear, followed by perennial exile, sorrow, suffering, and labor. In just 694 words, Genesis 3 (KJV) depicts how paradise was lost by Adam and Eve, a fate then inherited by all their progeny. No one knows the deeper history of this myth, and whether it too was borrowed by the Jews. But placed at the start of their sacred text, it does establish a moral severity characteristic of the rest, and which then became a central theme of the Judeo-Christian West. "In the beginning," the darker aspects of the human condition, its sense of loss and longing, its suffering and labor, were

---

14. Greenblatt, 48.

earned through transgression. The common state and shape of the lives we live now are, in part, the "wages of sin."

After he summarizes the origins of Genesis, the plot that interests Greenblatt the most—the "rise and fall" he traces—is the struggle to codify an orthodox interpretation of Adam and Eve's story, followed by that version's gradual decline in cultural authority. Although determined in part by the wider audience he seeks, his tactical approach of focusing on just a few key thinkers has other justifications as well. Insomuch as history is written by polemical as well as military victors, some opinions on this topic have mattered more than most, and none so much as those of Augustine of Hippo (354–430 AD), whose impact on Christian doctrine has been second only to its first great evangelist, the apostle Paul.

Augustine was a brilliant thinker, a prolific author, and, just as importantly, a fiercely committed polemicist, adept at ecclesiastical politics even when living apart from Rome. His interpretation of the Fall evolved over time and was hardened in response to a series of theological opponents, including Origen, who preceded him, and his contemporaries Pelagius and Julian of Eclanum. In Augustine's reading, the story revealed in Genesis 2 and 3 wasn't an allegorical tale but the literal, historical truth. Adam and Eve *were* the first man and woman, made in the flesh in God's own image; the serpent was a living "beast," and "the tree of the knowledge of good and evil" an actual tree. "Determined to save the divine creation from any imputation of injustice,"[15] the Bishop of Hippo insisted that every baneful feature of the human condition was a punishment earned, that "the human race got what it deserved."[16] In their prelapsarian state, for example, the first couple not only enjoyed the material ease of Eden's bounty; they were immortal as well, so that along with exile, suffering, and ceaseless labor, their disobedience brought death itself into the world.

For those who wonder at the source of Christianity's frequent fear and loathing of sexuality, a plausible answer can be found in Augustine's erotophobic reading of Genesis 3. In *The Literal Meaning of Genesis*, he asserted that what Adam and Eve first saw when their eyes were "opened" after eating the forbidden fruit were "their own genitals, and they lusted after them with that stirring movement they had not previously known."[17] That "stirring movement" points to Augustine's bizarre obsession with erections, which, as involuntary physical reactions, he presumed to be

15. Ibid., 101.
16. Ibid., 104.
17. Ibid., 114.

deeply sinful and the first tangible proof of Adam's fallen state. He regarded all postlapsarian sex, then, as both corrupted and corrupting. Conceived through the sinful "stirring movements" of sexual desire, even a newborn baby was inherently fallen and condemned to damnation unless saved by the Lord. In Augustine's version of the Judaic fixation on ethical causation, "human sinfulness" was, in Greenblatt's dry rendering, "a sexually transmitted disease."[18]

None of these assertions—that the myth was meant to be literal; that prior to the Fall the first couple were immortal; that sexual desire is, without fail, corrupted and corrupting; that newborns are damned prior to even making a free choice of their own—is self-evident in the original 694 words themselves. And all were opposed by other theologians of the day. But with the zeal of a convert, the charisma of preacher, and tactics worthy, at times, of a D.C. lobbyist, Augustine defeated each of his rivals. In the case of Pelagius, who argued that death was natural, rather than a moral consequence of the first couple's failure, and that people possessed the free will to escape a sinful state, the Bishop of Hippo rallied his contacts in Rome to accuse his rival of heresy. In the sort of novelistic detail that makes *The Rise and Fall* so frequently compelling, we learn: "fearing that treatises alone might not secure the condemnation of his doctrinal enemy, Augustine was careful to send, through an ally, a magnificent gift of eighty Numidian stallions to the papal court."[19] Like Euripides' Medea, the theologian seemed to believe that "gifts . . . persuade even the Gods; / with mortals, gold outweighs a thousand arguments"[20]—in this case arguments about the source and substance of human nature. With his hopeful stance on those subjects "outweighed," Pelagius was convicted, excommunicated, and exiled in Egypt.

After summarizing some of the aftereffects of adopting the Augustinian account, including the later emergence of a virulent strain of misogyny, *The Rise and Fall* leaps ahead to the Renaissance, focusing on Milton, who is given three full chapters, the last of which bears the revealing title "Becoming Real." According to Greenblatt, the "fall" of the orthodox reading of the Fall ironically began in the very era when it seemed to be gaining intellectual rigor. As Renaissance artists and thinkers strove to render "real" the psychology, physiology, and history of the

---

18. Ibid., 108.
19. Ibid., 106.
20. Euripides, *Medea*, line 941.

first couple, they sought out the exact location of the Garden of Eden, calculated the precise number of years since the expulsion, and so forth.

The ambition to authenticate Augustine's reading inevitably led, though, to disturbing anomalies. Just as the geocentric conception of the heavens was challenged in this era by a host of new astronomical observations, the insistence that Adam and Eve had been literal figures was undermined by multiple discoveries in paleontology. Gradually, the accumulation of scientific facts undermined faith in the orthodox fable. For if the Augustinian account was not physically true, as the new sciences appeared to show, then all the related moral and spiritual features long associated with it (the invention of death, the inheritance of sin, sex as corrupted and corrupting) might be called into doubt as well.

The obvious pivotal moment in this long process of disenchantment occurred with the arrival of Darwin's theory. In its account of human origins, "paradise wasn't lost; it never existed,"[21] and rather than the result of some original sin, our nature as a species was the slowly evolving product of natural selection. After some 2500 years, the West's characteristic causal link between moral decisions and natural consequences was being severed, and as a result, "for many people today," including Greenblatt, Adam and Eve's "story is a myth." After some darker turns, including the distortion of Darwin's theory in racist terms, "the Enlightenment has done its work, and our understanding of human origins has been freed from the grip of a once potent delusion."[22]

Unlike Feiler's, however, this happy ending is shaded by regret: the vestigial loyalty of a literary scholar who remains intrigued by the stories whose fall he has been tracing. Genesis 2 and 3 may be just "myths," but Greenblatt still insists that they continue to "have the life—the peculiar, intense, magical reality—of literature."[23] And he ends his book with this curious pledge of allegiance to them: "Millions of people in the world, including those who grasp the underlying assumptions of modern science, continue to cling to the peculiar satisfaction that ancient story provides. I do."[24]

---

21. Greenblatt, 269.
22. Ibid., 284.
23. Ibid., 284.
24. Ibid., 299.

3

But after proclaiming that we've "been freed from the grip of [their] once potent delusion," does Greenblatt truly believe that labeling these myths as "literature" and praising them as "magical" are sufficient endorsements to support their enduring value? To this reader, his final "I do" sounds less like a marriage vow than an embarrassed confession of nostalgic affection, an antiquarian's indulgence in a now obsolescent mode of mind. And as with his omega, so too with his alpha. When, in its prologue, *The Rise and Fall* describes the Genesis account as "fiction at its most fictional, a story that revels in the delights of make-believe,"[25] the masquerade of praise barely conceals the condescension implied, myth-making viewed as a charming but also childish pastime, its form of make-believe an early mental stage that a mature modernity has progressed beyond.

For a self-proclaimed lover of literature, Greenblatt has a strangely constrained view of what reality means. Exhibiting the "physics envy" that has long afflicted some humanities' scholars, he tends to narrow reality's primary range to the material plane, even choosing to end his study by visiting Uganda's Kibale Chimpanzee Project, where he imagines he may be viewing the closest we can come to the aboriginal Adam and Eve. (That such a trip ironically repeats the failed attempts by Renaissance scholars to find the "real"—that is, physical—Garden of Eden doesn't seem to occur to him.) Such a vision, however, discounts by omission those other dimensions of our lived reality traditionally explored by the mythic mind.

This bias becomes evident early in Greenblatt's analysis when he focuses on Origen of Alexandria, whose insistence that Genesis should be read allegorically was overthrown by Augustine. If that earlier theologian's "approach had triumphed," he predicts, "Adam and Eve would gradually have faded into arcane symbols, interesting perhaps for the ways in which they pointed to subtle philosophical problems but not otherwise compelling."[26] Whether he's referring here to a specific interpretation of Origen's isn't clear, but as a categorical "approach," surely the opposite is true. Many allegories and their close cousins (parables, and aphorisms) have been fashioned to last, and they succeed in doing so because, in part, their standards of accuracy when measuring reality aren't literal but analogical.

25. Ibid., 3.
26. Ibid., 79.

Lasting myths are elaborated forms of metaphorical reasoning, proven true through their usefulness—the poetic mind's version of "the survival of the fittest." But if assessed by the standards of literal truth alone, every metaphor—keen or clumsy, archaic or current—will necessarily seem false, and a person who relies on such a mode of thinking (as I routinely do) might even be accused of living "in the grip of a potent delusion," someone whose worldview is *just* "a myth." Given that most of the words we use are metaphorical in origin, that would suggest, however, that all our language-based thought is inherently delusional, a stance that seems less the work of the Enlightenment than the trendy turn toward a postmodern nihilism. You can't begin to grasp, for example, the comic truth captured by the aphorism "acorns arguing / which is the tallest" with a literal mindset, which would want to insist that such a statement is nonsensical—that acorns, after all, can't possibly speak, much less argue.

The enduring attraction of certain myths is not that they seem "magical" but that they prove meaningful, and they prove meaningful because the metaphors they use, if adeptly read, continue to supply a clarifying lens on human experience. The importance of reading them correctly—that is, of mastering the intricacies of their metaphorical reasoning—was powerfully expressed by Robert Frost in "Education by Poetry."

> *Unless you are at home in metaphor . . . you are not safe anywhere. Because you are not at ease with figurative values, you don't know the metaphor in its strength and its weakness. You don't know how far you may expect to ride it and when it may break down with you. You are not safe with science; you are not safe in history.*[27]

The "satisfactions" that lead us to "cling," then, to certain myths aren't "peculiar" but profound. Insomuch as we are cultural as well as physical beings and *our* reality, as a result, contains vital ethical, political, and psychological dimensions, such stories can prove essential to our very survival: we aren't safe without them.

Greenblatt understands this on one level at least. He realizes we need stories of origin, and that though the Darwinian account "happens to be true," that "does not in itself make it good to think with"—that is, good to address the moral and metaphysical issues encoded in these myths. And even as he harbors the hope that a story incorporating the science

---

27. Robert Frost, "Education by Poetry," *Amherst Graduates' Quarterly*, February, 1931.

of evolution will be found, he admits that the theory's current "resistance to narrative coherence makes it one of the great challenges of our age."[28]

As it turns out, Darwin himself suffered a similar crisis, confessing to his children that, over time, he had lost his earlier love of poetry to the point where he found Shakespeare's work "so intolerably dull that it nauseated" him. He worried about this unexpected change, suspecting that it was "injurious to the intellect, and more probably to the moral character." He even recognized that it might be associated with the nature of his work. But while acknowledging that his "mind had become a kind of machine for grinding general laws," he couldn't grasp "why this should have caused the atrophy" of his "higher tastes."[29]

Neither can Greenblatt, who has "no solution to what baffled Darwin," an admission which, given the breadth of his reading and his affection for literature, seems odd indeed. He could have turned, for example, to William Hazlitt's *Lectures on the English Poets*, which in 1818, when Darwin was still a boy, supplied the following diagnosis of the dangers inherent in the over-specialized mind:

> whenever an intense activity is given to any one faculty, it necessarily prevents the due and natural exercise of others. Hence all those professions or pursuits where the mind is exclusively occupied with the ideas of things . . . and not as they are connected with practical good or evil, must check the genial expansion of the moral sentiments and social affections.[30]

Or surely Greenblatt could have recalled instead that the incompatibility, to the point of rivalry, between mythical and rational ways of thinking is a very old story in the Western canon, nearly as old as the Torah itself. In the *Republic*, noting that the "quarrel between philosophy and poetry [was] ancient"[31] even then, Plato chose to expel the Homeric epics from his ideal society. Like all the many censors who would follow him, he recognized the pedagogical power of dramatic narratives but abhorred their purportedly immoral influence and sought to supplant their emotion-laden imagery and ambivalent plots with the unequivocal principles of his rational philosophy.

---

28. Greenblatt, 281–82.

29. Ibid., 283.

30. William Hazlitt, "On Mr. Wordsworth's 'Excursion,'" *Lectures on the English Poets* (Russell and Russell, 1841), 356–57.

31. Greenblatt, 302.

Yet even Plato reluctantly acknowledged the social utility of mythical thinking. Near the end of Book III, he has Socrates propose that his republic will have its own myth of origins: a story which, although admittedly untrue, would be broadly believed and so unify the city's diverse population by linking them all to a shared beginning. The normally confident Socrates is, however, so chagrined by the necessity of this proposition—which he calls both a "noble lie" and an "audacious fiction"—that he hesitates to state it and, when he does, he can barely meet the gaze his interlocutor.

This rare moment of embarrassment for the wisest man in Athens supplies a key, perhaps, to grasping Greenblatt's own uneasy allegiance to the Genesis myths. Although his lifelong subject has been literature, his method for addressing it, rational analysis, has naturally influenced the credo underlying his ultimate message. Just as Plato frequently cited Homer's "charms," even while insisting such charms were dangerous, Greenblatt praises the old myths as "magical" and the "most fictional" of fictions, even as he details their gradual debunking. He recognizes that these creations of the mythic mind are "potent," but as a committed rational materialist, he still believes at some level that its stories are "delusional," that however fascinating or even noble, they are, at heart, lies.

In any case, the vague hope he harbors for a new story of origin that will incorporate the facts of evolutionary theory is not a feasible solution to our current confusion. Human beings are natively, it seems, "of two minds" (and maybe more), and no alchemy available can plausibly convert the statistical into the lyrical or, vice versa, narrative plot into logical proof. Given their persistence over time, we surely need both these modes of mind. But as a technological society we have radically favored the authority of the "one faculty" over the other, and that mental "machine for grinding general laws" can never fully fathom the ambivalent truths of metaphorical reasoning, much less fashion the mythical meanings that can cultivate "the genial expansion of [our] moral sentiments and social affections."

The folly of assuming otherwise was captured long ago by these four words, orally composed by the mythic mind: "Jelly / in a vise."[32]

---

32. W.S. Merwin, *Asian Figures* (New York: Atheneum, 1973), 59. The "figures" are anonymous Asian aphorisms translated by Merwin, and the one cited here is Japanese in origin.

IN THE BEGINNING

4

Greenblatt seems at times to forget that what his argument has traced, and with impressive efficiency, is the fall of a particular interpretation of Genesis. But if that orthodox account has been shown to be false, does that mean all other readings must be as well? Rather than condescend to the "make-believe" of our ancient ancestors, can we now return to *their* beginning—the original myth, freed of the "ramshackle edifice" obscuring it—and rediscover there some clarifying guidance for our own troubled times? *Is* Genesis still "good to think with"? More specifically: returning to Origen's approach, and so "at ease [again] with figurative values," can we "ride" its mythic metaphors to the promised land of moral and metaphysical understanding? Or, more nags now than Numidian stallions, will they "break down" as fully and fatally as Augustine's literal reading has?

In fact, religious opposition to the literalist position has existed all along. Reinhold Niebuhr, one of the great theologians of the mid-twentieth century, defined the truest form of Christianity as mythic at its core. "Myth alone," he insisted, "is capable of picturing the world as a realm of coherence and meaning without defying the facts of incoherence."[33] Literal readings, however, missed the ambivalent wisdom implicit in the mythic method. The orthodox approach mistakenly transformed "the myth of the Fall . . . into an account of the origin of evil, when it is really a description of [evil's] nature." "Original sin is not an inherited corruption," much less a sexually transmitted one. But it *is* "an inevitable fact of human history . . . true in every moment of existence."[34] The "genius" of mythic religion, in Niebuhr's view, is that—unlike today's techno-utopians, who believe we can invent our way into a state of social perfection—it recognizes the natural limits placed on both our virtue and our wisdom. And insomuch as it encourages moral vigilance without inducing metaphysical despair, it proves more relevant to and realistic about our everyday ethical decision-making than either evolutionary theory or utopian rationalism.

Secular thinkers have also continued to find Genesis "good to think with"—not magical but meaningful, not peculiar but profound. In his 2010 essay "Agrarian Anxieties," historian Steven Stoll[35] recovers from its

---

33. Reinhold Niebuhr, *An Interpretation of Christian Ethics* (New York: Harper & Row, 1935), 16.

34. Ibid., 55.

35. "Agrarian Anxieties," Steven Stoll, Harper's Magazine, July 2010, 6–9.

myths an accurate history of our species' development and even a possible template for current reform. In Adam and Eve's "abrupt expulsion from [Eden's] kindly wilderness," he sees "an allegory of the Neolithic transition." Then, in Genesis 4, the first couple "beget the material and political archetypes of the Bronze Age: Cain the farmer and Abel the herder," with the former "emerg[ing] as an ambiguous symbol of the victory of farming," whose insatiable need for arable land will induce more violence. Later, Stoll praises the "remarkable innovation" of the Hebrew sabbatical, which not only saved their farmlands from depletion by decreeing they lay fallow every seventh year; it also made the agrarian economy's wars of expansion less necessary, peace allied with prosperity again. And in the jubilee, the ritual law that periodically reversed all land sales, relieved all debts, and released all slaves, he sees a savvy solution to the sort of class divisions and economic inequalities that dog us now. Which, on that issue at least, poses the question as to whose system of thought is caught "in the grip of a potent delusion."

For me, however, the chapter most relevant to our current predicament remains Genesis 3, the story of the Fall of Adam and Eve. In returning to that beginning, I see within its plot a profound depiction of our abiding nature: the qualities that make us not only unique as a species but also uniquely dangerous to ourselves. In his spiritual meditations, Pascal divided the human propensity to sin into three categories: *libido sentiendi, libido sciendi, libido dominandi*—our "lusts," respectively, for sensual pleasure, for knowledge, and for power. Contrary to Augustine's later fixation on carnal desire, it's a hunger for knowledge and, secondarily, for the godlike powers that new knowledge might supply that first tempt Eve. In this at least, the mythic and the scientific seem to agree. We haven't chosen, after all, to call ourselves *homo sexualis* but *homo sapiens*; though the distinction between knowledge (*scientia*) and wisdom (*sapientia*) remains contentious, we do identify ourselves as the *thinking* creature. Our most unique feature has been our capacity to name and number, to reflect and project, to accumulate knowledge and, with it, power.

Rapid infusions of new knowledge, however, are not only creatively "disruptive"; they can be socially destructive. When the powers gained through such surges of new knowledge are set loose in a cultural garden not designed to contain them—as, for example, the capacity to manipulate public opinion via today's largely unregulated social media—the checks and balances of the old order are rapidly undermined in dangerous ways. The commonsense presumptions of a whole way of life, its rituals and customs and unifying myths, are called into question: losses that then spur fear, confusion, dissension, and despair.

Such is the pattern of self-punishment concisely enacted in Genesis 3, after our primordial parents "eat of" the tree. For if paradise is not merely a site on a map but a harmonious relationship between mind and place, then as Adam and Eve cower behind the trees in shame and fear, they have *already* been expelled from their once happy home. Before their Lord can speak, the very knowledge they have gained has, summarily, cast them out of Eden, that garden whose Hebrew name also means *delight*. They were never immortal (all gardens have death folded into their cycles), but now, due to the dawn of their self-consciousness, Adam and Eve are afraid to die. Made aware of the possibilities of both good and evil, they've been stripped of their innocence and now feel naked. No longer at home in their first garden, they will have to craft a new one, built from knowledge rather than instinct—a difficult mission "east of Eden" whose struggles are recorded in the rest of the Torah.

According to Genesis 3 our original sin wasn't *libido sentiendi* but *libido sciendi*—a lust for knowledge, whose acquisition made us more godlike in our powers but also estranged us from the rest of creation. For today's rational materialists, this reading reeks of oppressive superstition; they see in it the censorious preaching of a priestly caste who, in full flight from Enlightenment progress, would keep us in the dark and under their ecclesiastical thumb. But, as the *Republic* demonstrated, rationalists too can be inclined toward censorship to enforce their beliefs, either strictly banning the mythic mindset or demeaning its findings as "make-believe."

And if we want to be safe with the science we now practice, a sober glance in the rearview mirror would warn us that history is cyclical as well as progressive, and that *"all* things fall," not only the superstitions of religion but whole societies, along with their orthodox conceptions of reality. Looking back might remind us, too, that the invention of printing sparked an information explosion that not only led to the amazing achievements of the Renaissance but also to the anarchy of the seventeenth century—a period when Europe was torn apart by assassinations, revolutions, and sectarian violence that resembled nothing so much as today's Middle East. "Tis all in pieces," John Donne lamented then, "all coherence gone."[36]

---

36. John Donne, "An Anatomy of the World": https://www.bartleby.com/lit-hub/the-poems-of-john-donne/the-first-anniversary/.

Now, as we are both feasting on and cringing from a new information explosion, that cycle is repeating itself, and the cultural innovations that finally civilized the forces set loose in Donne's era are themselves corroding. The capitalist economy that once helped liberate the middle class from an oppressive aristocracy has become a threat in itself, aggressively asserting plutocratic control over our lives at work and at home and generating inequalities that have little to do with actual merit. A Protestantism that arose, in part, to morally discipline the individualism associated with the spread of literacy, and that periodically has restrained our nation's lust for monetary gain (*libido pecunia*), has now become instead Mammon's apologist and political enabler. Its most popular churches have adopted the "[ig]noble lie" of a prosperity theology whose grace panders greed, and embraced a president whose cupidity was without precedent.

The fruits of the computer age *are* impressive. I benefit as an author nearly every day from my instant access to its "tree of knowledge," and I recognize its exciting potential for scientific discovery and artistic innovation. But can the political institutions and social conditions necessary for any form of lasting progress survive the constant disruptions that now characterize our everyday lives?

Spend an hour online following links, reading blogs, viewing YouTube videos, imbibing their swirling stew of beauty and bile, old truths and fake news, and it's hard not to conclude that in our era, too, "all coherence [is] gone." That we can stream the nightly news while drifting in a remote canoe doesn't dim the suspicion that the digital revolution that was supposed to unite us into a global village is complicit in the divisive xenophobia that news conveys. In times of social chaos and intellectual confusion, "the best lack all conviction, while the worst / are filled with passionate intensity,"[37] and those conditions then invite authoritarian solutions, as in the pseudo elections and "presidents for life" that now threaten the demise of democratic rule.

In a nation where a TED talk passes for prophetic utterance, the presumption has been that each challenge we confront can soon be solved by a technical fix: a software patch or app, a hardware upgrade or new set of "best practices." But cleverness is not wisdom, method not meaning, and productivity alone is never sufficient for true prosperity: *homo sciens* cannot do the work of *homo sapiens*. Google's driverless car and Amazon's

---

37. W. B. Yeats, "The Second Coming," *Selected Poems and Two Plays of William Butler Yeats*, ed. M.L. Rosenthal (New York: Collier Books, 1962), 91.

cashierless grocery store may be technical marvels that soon will provide a categorical leap in commercial efficiency. But once they "scale up," they are also likely to cast millions of citizens out of work. By then, drones may be dropping packages atop our front steps, but how will the unemployed pay for them? In their despair, how will they spend their idle time? In their likely fear and anger, who will *they* vote for?

The self-generated crisis we now face is being driven not just by the pace of the new knowledge gained, nor by our disingenuous faith that *more (data, profit) must equal better*—a potent delusion that I call *quantiphilia*. As Hazlitt knew, our problem also lies in the narrow nature of the knowledge we pursue to the exclusion of other kinds. In the heady days following the fall of the Wall and during the dawn of the PC revolution, who could we have turned to capture a hint of the perilous conditions that actually lurked within such signs of apparent progress? Bill Clinton, with his oily optimism about "growing the economy for the twenty-first century"? His neoconservative opponents, with their self-congratulatory boasts about the "end of history" and final triumph of the democratic project? The techno-utopians whose columns in *Wired* were promising our imminent liberation from scarcity, labor, loneliness, and death—more Eden 2.0s to sell their IPOs? From our perspective, whose narratives now seem to have been spun from the sugar-plum visions of make-believe?

Instead, choosing prudence over pride, we could've turned back then to the West's first story, which, rather than pitching the imminent arrival of paradise, narrates how the good life can be lost. Some myths, after all, have been crafted to last—their past is never dead; it's not even past. They remain relatable to anyone who, schooled in figurative values, can ride their sequence of images to their necessary consequences. If, as Ezra Pound insisted, "literature is news that STAYS news,"[38] then Genesis 3 remains a literary gem. We don't need to fly to Uganda to spy its tragic Fall in action. We are reliving it here. In fear, if not yet shame, and from Brooklyn to Seattle, we are suffering through it now.

---

38. Ezra Pound, *ABC of Reading* (New York: New Directions, 1960), 29.

6

A Prescription for Contemporary Fiction

INCLUDING:
A Sermonette on Aesthetics
A Psalm to the Senses
And an Ethical Sucker Punch
(To Arrive Disguised by a Political Joke)

Wanted: a fiction whose fundamental design and worldview, therefore, is not a mindless (or even mindful) projection of nineteenth century mechanistic science: characters with no more spirit or will than the naïve materialist's conception of the atom, the ruling forces of their world always external and often merely random, their life stories reduced to a ricocheting action. Enough of the entropic soap opera, of the hero as pinball. In their place, a fiction whose organization is ecological in nature, that gathers and conserves energy, that regulates and moderates and multiplies possibilities of meaningful interaction through symbiosis, allowing in a small space a complexity of life forms and a depth of perception. There are rules in this sort of fiction—not abstract but concrete and adaptive, with some features unique for each new environment. And just as we can't pollute at will or introduce alien species into an ecological niche without threatening the health of the whole, so an author can't violate the separate orders of these fictional worlds without serious consequences. In this fiction, decisions, both by the authors and their characters, *matter*. In this fiction, unlike so much that is published today, not just anything can happen.

A PRESCRIPTION FOR CONTEMPORARY FICTION

A fiction, therefore, that doesn't condescend to its own characters, that allows them the possibility of a complex inner life, a chance at perspective, and an opportunity to be held at least partially accountable for their own confusion, pain, and fear. If about the oppressed, a fiction that doesn't sentimentalize their state with the sort of secret snobbery that presumes a fifty-word vocabulary and a hundred-proof liver, and that doesn't always cast them into the role of the passive victim, more "symbols" sacrificed to tout a moral lesson. Who says that wealthy heirs like Thoreau are the only ones allowed to revolt by retreating to a pond? That other Lincolns can't emerge from the shambles of a ghetto or the margins of a farm to change the world?

A fiction whose rhetoric isn't pellet-sized; whose tab button isn't stuck "on," paragraphing automatically every second declarative sentence; whose model of engagement isn't a tweet or a TikTok video, presuming a readership with the attention span of a gerbil on speed; whose vocabulary is diverse, intelligent, lively, allowing itself moments of clarity yea-even-unto eloquence; and whose style, when reticent, has the power of stoicism, of great passion contained by a fierce self-discipline, as in the prose of Yasunari Kawabata or the best of Hemingway.

A fiction, therefore, that is not tone deaf, that understands that music is not just a decoration but an essential quality of the place we share. This, too, is a philosophical question. I pose it as follows: given that a realistic attitude toward the human condition embodies a certain necessary sadness whose range can stretch from the high tragedy of Shakespeare to the feculent farce of Beckett's solipsistic cave, how do we respond to the non-human setting in which we live? The world *I* experience is, however ugly or despairing its human element, astonishingly beautiful. And I don't just mean snow-capped mountains and crescent-carved shores but also the play of light on ice in a glass, the hitch and skip of a boy entering a class, the profusion of colors from books on a shelf. Pay attention, please! Everywhere the extraordinary beckons from within the bounds of the ordinary; in every second, small harmonies can be heard, subtle rhymes if you will, sensory rather than thematic epiphanies. (The wonder of John Updike was his rare ability to rescue for us those small harmonic moments.) Whether you find a momentary consolation in all this splendor or, as I do, sense within it a hint of something more profound, to denude our fictive stories of its presence seems a violation akin to strip-mining: the unconscionable devastation of a living world.

Wanted, too: a shift away from parody, pastiche, and urbane irony toward forms more serious, passionate, and profound. I could assert that parody is essentially parasitical and, therefore, a lower art form, but the more telling argument is strategic in nature. In a culture that actually conceived a *drive-through* funeral parlor (a grief-burger and large fries to go?), in a country that was once led by a president who trained for the job playing second banana to a chimp in a film, by another whose penis became the focus of an obscenely sanctimonious Senate trial, and by a vulgar third whose so-called credentials were earned on reality TV; in such a place can a literary parody have any bite at all? Can a cartoon be cartooned? In our current environment, better an allegory, parable, serious fairy tale, better a new Book of Job than another in-joke.

Wanted, finally: a fiction that matters, whose existence poses a serious challenge, that reorients, clarifies, vivifies, chastens. A fiction that is useful, a fiction pragmatic. My life is different. I'm a better man because of certain stories and novels I have been privileged to read. I understand the irrational ritual of passion far better for having read Marguerite Duras's *Moderato Cantabile*, the pathos of adolescence for having read and reread John Barth's "Lost in the Funhouse." The abstract aphorism "character is fate" was brought to life for me with stunning potency by Yukio Mishima's very short story "Swaddling Clothes." Want to feel the possibility of art as communion sacrament?—read Updike's beautiful "The Music School." Want to experience in riveting if repulsive detail the psychology of evil?—spend a few days with Pär Lagerkvist's *The Dwarf*.

In an age (as I edit these pages) of rising authoritarianism, pandemic panic, and racial and ethnic hostility, every man and woman could benefit from reading that novel and, too, Faulkner's lynching story "Dry September": the world might be, marginally at least, a safer place if they did. Wendell Berry's essays in *Standing By Words*. John Gardner's story "John Napper Sailing Through the Universe," which is so much more nuanced than the nonfictional jeremiads he is better known for these days. Graham Greene's *The Quiet American* and *The Heart of the Matter*. All of Josef Conrad and Alice Munro.

I *use* these works—not just to write or teach but to live, to navigate my way through our difficult world day to day. Watchwords, examples, vivid symbols. *Remember Major Scobie!* I admonish myself when my compassion begins to turn egocentrically imperial. *Remember Marlow, and steer the boat toward the spears!* I remind myself when, to avoid a momentary trial, I let my life drift toward a much more consequential

A PRESCRIPTION FOR CONTEMPORARY FICTION

disaster. I actually met the Dwarf once. I didn't recognize him soon enough, but I'm convinced that the disguise would've been prolonged, the wreckage far worse, if I hadn't been instructed first by a terrifyingly accurate fictional world.

I won't pretend that all, or even any, of the authors I have mentioned would subscribe to my beliefs. There are many paths but only one Way. Behind the diversity of style, content, and philosophy, there lies, I believe, a quality they share, a harmony of accomplishment we long to hear. And what would that quality be? The rarest thing of all, I think, a gift whose value never changes, whose standards, seeing through the vagaries of fashion, are fixed to the everlasting. What these great works share is a concrete wisdom about how we think and feel, behave and misbehave, the limits and imperfections of our native state and place.

What should contemporary fiction be like? Who, as an author, do I want to become? I could say this, that I want to become Don DeLillo wed to Wendell Berry, to marry former's relentlessly contemporary wit with the latter's sanity, clarity, sense of natural history. I could say that I want to merge the passion of Duras with the intelligence of Barth, the inventive zest of Paul West with the laconic sagacity of Lagerkvist. And more, of course. I could go on and on; there's no end to one's appetite when perusing the buffet of literary delights. The hard truth is, though, that art isn't made by mere addition, that too many ingredients, like too many cooks, can spoil the savory soup of any fiction. A single name, then—one writer to serve as the arch exemplar of what fiction at its best has been for me.

Although Flannery O'Connor only lived thirty-nine years, and was seriously ill too much of that time, teaching her stories to my writing students has been among the most humbling experiences of my professional life. I found, for example, that in order to do justice to them, I had to bring to class, by way of introduction to the content of the work, a copy of the Bible and a volume of Aeschylus. A weighty armload, that one: in twenty-five pages, the usual length of her stories, the revivified essence of 2500 years of Western civilization. Now *that* is the real prescription for any age's fiction. I want to read and to write stories like that. I want to enter new worlds which, whatever their accent, have that potency, that clarity, that honesty, that depth.

. . . which brings me, believe it or not, (*Here it comes—duck!*) to my favorite joke about Ronald Reagan, one gleaned from an article long ago when citizen Reagan, trying to win the nomination, was speaking to caucuses across the nation. After one such talk, a Southern Republican, when asked to assess the candidate's performance, conceded that Mr. Reagan was exceedingly smooth. But then he added (I can almost hear the honeyed drawl, see the wry wrinkling of eyes and lips) that behind the practiced gestures and smiling face, the man was, in his considered opinion, "about as deep as piss on slate." A good one, no? Oh the power of a pungent simile. Serious people all, we readers and writers of literature, our political sympathies carefully attuned, our powers of observation safely removed from the vulgarity and superficiality of our age, we smile as one, cynically amused, in our dens across America.

Wait a minute, though. Isn't it time we took an accounting, too, asked our own constituency to provide a review? Would it be any more odiferous, any less contemptuous? And I'm not speaking of the usual contempt the public is wont to show us when we venture beyond the ambit of our books to comment on issues of public policy (the old Jane Fonda syndrome), but their response on matters closer to home, their assessment of our stewardship of the very profession we call our own. We, after all, are looked to for leadership, too. However remote, we canvass for support and are, in our own odd way, soliciting votes.

So look to your desks, then, pretenders to the throne of Dickinson and Melville, Hawthorne and Thoreau. Is the fiction that appears in your favorite glossy magazine or trendy website, that is assigned in your classes and praised in your blurbs, that is bought and borrowed and lent to your friends, is the fiction right now scrolling down your screens or filling up your pads in our book-lined dens made to last? Is *our* performance, it seems only fair to ask, any deeper than that of Bonzo's friend?

Another prediction of decline unto Doom, then? Not exactly. Yes, we do live in a vulgar and superficial age and, yes, much of what passes for serious fiction is insubstantial, the literary equivalent of bleached white bread. But has it ever been different? Dickinson wasn't published at all, Melville harassed out of fiction writing at the peak of his powers by hostile reviews. Only Hawthorne of the four luminaries mentioned above was an indisputable success in his own lifetime, and that percentage, one out of four, might well be predictive for our or any subsequent literary generation.

Whatever the numbers prove to be, we can assume this: much of the best in contemporary letters won't be recognized as such until our time has passed, the authors themselves old or dead. Nevertheless, sustained by other rewards, the good work goes on in unexpected places, discretely and ignored. And now, when more people are writing than ever before, the possibilities for quality fiction would seem to abound. Surely even as I write these words down, someone is inventing a new fictional world whose habitat will house those nuanced truths we need to hear and feel. Decades may dissolve before its value is noted, its cause promoted, but the fiction that is made to last will last, the merely fashionable eventually pass. So let a hundred thousand stories bloom. Time, relentless as ever, will ruthlessly prune.

A Coda

In Which the Author is Upended,
His Ending Amended

The ending seemed smooth, don't you think? An aphoristic couplet, assonantly rhymed, suggesting completion, an organic design. That's what *I* thought anyway—I had been aiming to arrive there since the second page. But now that my destination has been reached, the design complete, I find it offensive (slate-deep?) in a number of ways. The political reference, the revised Maoism, given the ongoing oppression of Chinese artists and authors, seems to me now inexcusably flip. And the sucker punch I had so carefully planned seems instead to have been a roundhouse hook which, circling back, has sent me flying on my own derriere. For doesn't the couplet, in an unplanned irony, seem to suggest those very points of view—neoliberal politics and mechanistic science—which are targets of this piece? Isn't relying on "Time," that stuffy abstraction, to provide for our children a literature that matters something akin to trickle-down economics where, eventually, the theory goes, the needy will be fed by the drippings left behind by the crapulence of the rich? And doesn't the passivity of the statement suggest as well a process driven by forces, "external and random," providing results indifferent to our will and beyond our control?

Someone, I'm reminded belatedly, discovered Dickinson at last; *someone*, and not Time, resurrected Melville from critical contempt. And what would have happened if in the year Lagerkvist was awarded the Nobel prize, another Pearl Buck had been named in his place? Would *The Dwarf* have ever ended up in my hands?

Sobering questions. They beckon action. They remind me once again that we mustn't be passive, that we ought to embrace every chance we have to hound the poseur and herald the substantial. The prescription, then, is this: promote the books you love, defend their achievement. If the authors are living, send them money, food, and bouquets of praise in honest letters of appreciation. Don't let the apparent but transient triumph of bad taste, the cant of the age, depress you into acquiescence, for silence, too, is a kind of ratification—more applause for the fake.

Take faith instead in the discipline we love, the wisdom of its craft. For we have an advantage over the economist, the scientist. We know that *once upon a time* can be a better beginning, a more fruitful way of thinking, than *recent studies show* or $x=y$; we know that the history we are living is best understood neither as a marketplace nor as a mechanism but as a story—a complex, interactive, ongoing novel. And in this chapter, to be entitled "The Living Word," you and I—lovers of literature, the guardians of fiction—*we* are the characters whose choices matter, who are shaping even now the plot's direction. A second ending, then. A reformation of a sort, the first born again.

Yes, Time will prune. But we are her agents: be responsible when you choose.

7

Real and Fake Accounts[1]
(Fiction in the Age of the Internet)

That we often aren't the masters of our own machines, and can even become their witless lackeys, are cautionary claims as old as Isaiah and as urgent as those bogus newsfeeds "pushing" the latest conspiracy theory into our smartphones and laptops. As a species gifted with inventive minds and opposable thumbs, we are ever about the business of generating new tools and techniques that will, we're certain, better our lives. Time after time, though, those new methods and machines also prove to change our public spaces and private selves in radical ways we fail to foresee and come to regret.

The pace of such progress with its hidden discontents increased exponentially in the twentieth century. Take radio as a useful example. Although the nation's first local newscast occurred in 1920, two years later there were already over five hundred licensed broadcasters in America. Just four years after that, the first national network was created, allowing millions of citizens coast to coast to hear simultaneously a single program: a mighty megaphone inevitably co-opted throughout the West by the era's chief propagandists, first its admen and then its politicians. On February 1, 1933, two days after he had been appointed chancellor, Adolf Hitler addressed the entire German nation via radio; some forty days later, a week after he was sworn into office, Franklin Roosevelt gave his first

---

[1]. The three books reviewed in this chapter are: Lauren Oyler, *Fake Accounts* (New York: Catapult, 2021), Patricia Lockwood's memoir *Priestdaddy* (New York: Riverhead, 2017) and her novel *No One Is Talking About This* (Riverhead, 2021).

fireside chat. In England, Churchill; in Italy, Mussolini: oratory had gone electronic and was quickly exploited by statesmen and demagogues alike.

Despite that well-documented history and a plethora of excellent research on the disruptive impact of new communications technologies, American leaders, in journalism as well as government, were shocked to discover that the most effective exploiter of our new social media in the political sphere was yet another narcissistic hate-monger. Just twelve years after Facebook was launched as a site restricted to Harvard students, it had over a billion active users and was being manipulated by both campaign officials and hostile foreign powers to spread lies, sow dissension, and promote the candidacy of Donald Trump: a strategy whose success has done more damage to our democracy than the physical attack on Pearl Harbor or the Twin Towers.

The political dangers of these largely unregulated sites and devices are now widely acknowledged and debated, if to little practical effect so far. Two very different recent novels, Lauren Oyler's *Fake Accounts* and Patricia Lockwood's *Nobody Is Talking About This*—both written and set during the Trump presidency—are also centered on the impact of social media on our lives, but as literature is wont to do, their focus instead is on the personal consequences of our nation's addictive submission to its latest round of miraculous machinery. Written by women who came of age during the social media phase of the digital revolution, these novels explore the social and psychological costs of a life increasingly lived online.

Fake Accounts

Oyler first made her name as controversial critic for the online site *Bookslut* and then as a blogger for *Vice,* where she established a persona allergic to the pieties of her generation and to its emerging literary stars, such as Sally Rooney and Jia Tolentino. In her debut novel, the same oppositional temperament and sardonic voice that has characterized her criticism prevails, this time via a nameless narrator whose background closely resembles Oyler's.

The novel opens in Brooklyn (the hub of the woke hip) just prior to Trump's inauguration when the narrator hacks into her lover Felix's smartphone and is shocked to discover he's opened a secret account on Instagram. There, à la the Donald, he has attracted a following by promoting conspiracy theories: the initial fake account among the many that will be satirized, including the fraudulent self-presentations common on dating apps. Disturbed by Felix's deception, she resolves to break up with him after she gets back from the women's protest march at Trump's inauguration. Before she returns, however, she learns that he has been killed in an accident. At a loss as to how or even whether to grieve for him, she is reduced to googling the topic but can "find no example of the way to react to the death of a semi-serious boyfriend about whom you felt ambivalent at best,"[2] and she soon decides to flee back to Berlin, where they first met. There, an aimless and alienated expatriate who doesn't speak the native language, she spends a lot of time online where she had "gotten used to using people [she'd] never met, or met a few times, to muffle the sound of time passing without transcendence or joy."[3]

That's about it for plot; with the exception of the last few pages, not much of consequence happens after the narrator returns to Berlin. Though the novel's events are largely chronological, its author is not really interested in probing the narrative consequences of individual decision-making; the characters, settings, and events have been staged instead as occasions for acerbic social commentary. Oyler may have exploited the new opportunities the Internet era has provided for writers to launch her career, but the novel is here to let us know she has not been fooled by the self-congratulatory delusions of today's digerati, or anyone else of her age and class.

Note the commentary of her autofictional narrator on the topic of her fellow workers at a digital site very much like *Vice*: how they had tricked "themselves into thinking that because our office was cool, not like other offices, we were not really working, and that being at work was in some ways actually more fun than being at home, alone, streaming a TV show we pretend is good while eating delivery we pretend to afford."[4] Or on her yoga classmates, who were "primarily white women living in Brooklyn, and although [she] too was a white woman living in Brooklyn, [she] of course did not identify as such, since the description usually signified someone selfish, lazy, and in possession of superficial understandings of complex topics such as racism and literature."[5] Or on the shallow outrage sparked by Trump's election: "for a few months the political catastrophe seemed so dire that one's music and movie preferences

2. *Fake Accounts*, 93.
3. Ibid., 117.
4. Ibid., 64–5.
5. Ibid., 59.

were no longer considered the ultimate markers of one's fitness to fight fascism."[6] Or on how her own "high-level search-engine excavation skills were knavish and petty; they marked [her] as a member of a generation that grew up watching reality TV, without respect for fundamental principles of a functional society and the human soul."[7] Or on her dismay with Felix's inattentiveness: "he refused to see the advantages of certain relationship best practices, like ignoring your friends and surroundings in order to text your partner constantly."[8] Or on the conveniently passive pessimism of her generation: "consensus was the world was ending and we were too late to do much about it; we [didn't] want to die but also [didn't] want to do anything challenging."[9]

Stylistically as well as culturally, Oyler resists the fads and fashions of her age. Rather than a fragmentary, aphoristic prose delivered in pellet-sized paragraphs surrounded by space, demanding that the reader intuit the themes and emotions meant to connect them—a style popular in the boutique literary marketplace for the last twenty years—this author prefers elaboration over concision, sardonic explanation over coy implication. And despite the syntactical complexity of the prose, a reader never gets lost in her lengthy sentences; the diction is almost always apt, often inventive, and sufficiently varied to avoid predictable patterns.

But if the vocabulary is variable, its tone is not. The snark is relentless and, after a point, begins to seem suffocating, the novel trapped in a compulsive need to debunk. As the narrator moves from Brooklyn to D.C. to Berlin, her acerbic attitude becomes indistinguishable from cynicism: a mental machine programmed to reshape every person and occasion to fit its own expectations of cowardly conformity and bad faith. This is a problem for the novel dramatically, too. The other characters don't get much of a chance to speak or act on their own, and so to earn our contempt, but are mostly summarized (and therefore preclassified) by this very witty but also jaundiced voice.

The problem is compounded by Oyler's solipsistic reliance on self-conscious commentary and metafictional devices. Periodically, her narrator holds up a mirror to the content or the process of her prose. She either addresses her readers directly, anticipating our objections and interpretations to show that she already knows what we're thinking

6. Ibid., 59.
7. Ibid., 42.
8. Ibid., 73.
9. Ibid., 5.

(she first! she first!), or cites a chorus of undepicted ex-boyfriends whose comments and criticisms remain tightly under her own control. Even the structure of the novel is self-conscious, its six sections labeled "Beginning," "Backstory," "Middle (Something Happens)," "Middle (Nothing Happens)," "Climax," and "End." The combined effect of these tics and tricks is to make the reader feel as if he were trapped inside a graduate student lounge with a very smart but equally insecure PhD student in English literature.

Adding statements like "to be clear: I know this is boring"[10] doesn't make the preceding content any less boring. The purpose of self-criticism, after all, isn't to provide a preening display of our own discernment, but to prod us into actively changing our ways. In the instance just cited, it would spur the author to cut the boring passage—advice that, frankly, could've been applied to a number of passages in the last two-thirds of the novel, which, however articulate, become repetitive. Rather than drive the narrative, test the main character, or contextualize the theme, they seem to exist because Oyler herself has been there, done that in her second home Berlin, or because the novel needs to bide time until its abbreviated climax arrives. There is, finally, a plot turn at the very end of *Fake Accounts*, and our narrator, who so relentlessly mocks her contemporaries, gets her comeuppance. But there's little emotional kick or thematic news sparked by that event.

Three very brief lines from William Carlos Williams' *Paterson* capture a fundamental feature of both artistic and scientific achievement: "Dissonance / (if you are interested) / leads to discovery."[11] (The same principle is expressed in cyberneticist Gregory Bateson's widely cited definition of information as "a difference that makes a difference.") What's most missing from Oyler's fictional account of our era is any dissonance, any difference. Unlike many social satires, her novel provides no island of innocence against which to measure the depredations of our digital age. Nor do we witness in stages the corruption of any particular character or institution because, as prejudged by our narrator, they are already corrupt, inauthentic by default. When one of the ex-boyfriends wonders, "Aren't all personalities false?," the narrator insists he's "missing the point."[12] But he isn't missing the larger point, one the novel makes again and again.

10. Ibid., 164.

11. "William Carlos Williams, from Book Four of *Paterson*: https://archive.org/stream/PatersonWCW/Paterson-William_Carlos_Williams_djvu.txt.

12. *Fake Accounts*, 161.

Every generation needs its oppositional voices, writers brave enough to expose its hypocrisies and self-delusions, the old human flaws in their new and shiny guise. Oyler clearly has the smarts, wit, and writerly chops to assume that role. Whether she is emotionally brave enough, though, remains open to question. In a fictional world where all personalities are shown to be false, all accounts fake and emotions inauthentic, the dissonance of satire quickly devolves into the rote rehearsals of cynicism; there are no discoveries, just repeated confirmations of the same scathing bias. Jonathan Swift, when writing his own mock obituary, defended his work by asserting "His satire points at no defect, / But what all mortals may correct."[13] In *Fake Accounts*, though, we are given no sense that correction is possible. Rather than oppose the pat consensus that "the world was ending and we were too late," Oyler's account of our digital age exemplifies its pessimism.

Nobody Is Talking About This

The poet Patricia Lockwood's engagement with the online life has been far more thorough, complex, and, as was detailed in her powerful memoir *Priestdaddy*, deeply personal. That book's oxymoronic title is, in her case, literally true. Her father Greg, a domineering narcissist into heavy metal, Tom Clancy novels, and anti-abortion protests, was also a Lutheran pastor who successfully petitioned the Vatican to become a Roman Catholic priest. Lockwood and her siblings, then, had the rare experience of being raised as a priest's kids in two Midwestern rectories, where they had to dodge their dad's wrath, wrestle with his rules, and suffer his disharmonious guitar riffs.

Two weeks before Lockwood was supposed to enter college, he ambushed her with the news they couldn't afford the expense. (To catch a flavor of the man's self-centeredness: not long thereafter he bought himself a pricey guitar originally made for Paul McCartney). Forced to stay at home during what should have been her freshman year, she slept in an abandoned convent next to their rectory. Alone in that suggestive setting at the turn of the century when the Internet was young, she went online, where she discovered (and how quaint this term sounds today) "a

---

13. Jonathan Swift, "Verses on the Death of Dr. Swift": https://www.poetryfoundation.org/poems/45272/verses-on-the-death-of-dr-swift-dspd.

bulletin board devoted to the discussion of poetry.[14] That digital space became Lockwood's substitute schooling in life as well as letters, the site where she found not just her calling as a poet but also her future husband Jason, with whom she ran away at the age of nineteen. At that point, their entire relationship had been conducted online or by phone and might have easily fallen apart once they met in the flesh. It didn't, though; they married two years later, and Jason proved to be a downhome version of Leonard Woolf, financially and emotionally supporting his poet wife's calling, allowing her to focus entirely on her writing.

Later, when Jason needed an eye operation they couldn't afford, friends and admirers of Lockwood's poetry raised the money for it online. Shortly thereafter she posted an autobiographical poem, "The Rape Joke," that went viral, and, abracadabra, within a day or two, the poetry manuscript that had been sitting unread on a Penguin editor's desk for months was accepted. Joining Twitter in 2011, she rapidly developed a large following there for her bizarre and bawdy tweets, leading to multiple invitations to give talks and participate in panels on the topic of social media.

Unlike Oyler, then, whose mastery of the new media seems at once successfully transactional and very skeptical, Lockwood has had multiple reasons to be profoundly grateful that the Internet was available to her. A fortunate Rapunzel, she was rescued from the tower of *her* confinement by connecting with others via its "portal" (her preferred term). Through it she found her prince and her profession, and while one of its sites helped save her husband's vision, others became the means to establish her career as a poet, prose writer, and commentator. Unsurprisingly, then, her appreciation of those early days online has the glow at times of a second Eden before the Fall. "The feeling of getting an email! As if the ghost of a passenger pigeon had flown into your home and delivered it directly into your head, so swooping and unexpected and feathered was the feeling."[15]

In the memoir, Lockwood was revisiting her childhood and reassessing her complicated relationship with her impossible priestdaddy and his stultifying religion. Though it won the Thurber Prize for American Humor and is frequently hilarious, the book's ambitions are serious, and its final recognition of the ways in which Lockwood has and has not liberated herself from her domestic and religious heritage is both wise

14. *Priestdaddy,* 19.
15. Ibid., 19.

and moving. "People accuse me of blasphemy . . . which is their right. But to me, it is not blasphemy, it is my idiom. It's my way of participating in the language I was raised inside, which despite all renunciation will always be mine."[16] And even after exposing the hypocrisy of her dad and his often intolerant version of Catholicism, she still finds and retains the pearl concealed within that pigsty. "But faith and my father taught me the same lesson: to live in the mystery, even to love it."[17] The absence of bitterness, the inclination to love, the acknowledgement that there are mysteries beyond our capacity to classify or satirize: these are the emotional and spiritual resources that sharply distinguish Lockwood's sensibility from Oyler's.

In *Nobody Is Talking About This*, Lockwood's debut novel, the thematic focus initially shifts away from her birth family to the portal itself and the ways it has changed since the early days when she discovered it alone in that abandoned convent. Again we have a nameless female central character whose background closely mirrors the author's, but this time the voice is in third person, as if to gain a wedge of perspective on herself as well as on the evolving character of our social media. Though the sensibility of the author remains the same, the structure of this book has shifted from longer chapters organized by topic to short and discontinuous probes, meditations, and jokes, little islands of observation separated by space, in the manner of today's tweets and posts—the very style that Oyler scorns as "trendy . . . and melodramatic, insinuating utmost meaning where there was only hollow prose."[18]

The novel's first brief section is representative of the whole. "She opened the portal, and the mind [that is, the collective online mind] met her more than half-way. Inside, it was tropical and snowing, and the first flake of the blizzard of everything landed on her tongue and melted."[19] In just two sentences, the poet-author captures the portal's surreal contradictions (both "tropical and snowing") and its blinding abundance ("the blizzard of everything"), even as its imagery suggests, ironically or not, *her* experience of it as sacramental. (If you know Lockwood's upbringing, that single flake of snow can't help but evoke the transformative crux of Christian ritual: a communion wafer melting on the tongue.) The meditative voice then begins to question the nature of the online life—"Why

16. Ibid., 312.
17. Ibid., 6.
18. *Fake Accounts*, 164.
19. *No One Is Talking About This*, 3.

did the portal feel so private when you only entered it when you needed to be everywhere?"[20]—and then to balk against the ugliness of its emerging temper during the Trump administration. "Every day their attention must turn, like the shine of a school of fish, all at once, toward a new person to hate. Sometimes the subject was a war criminal, but other times it was someone who made a heinous substitution in guacamole."[21]

A month after the election, our nameless hero gets caught up in the initial outrage in her own unique way and is "banned from the portal for forty-eight hours for posting a picture of herself crouched down and having her period on a small sculpture of twisted pipe cleaners that was labeled TREE OF LIBERTY."[22] But like Oyler's narrator, she soon begins to scorn the authenticity of such gestures. "We were being radicalized, and how did that feel? Like we had just stepped into a Girl Scout uniform made of fire? Like the skies had abruptly shifted to the stripes of an old Soviet poster, and the cookies we carried through green and well-watered neighborhoods had been cut by the guillotine?"[23] And she can't help but contrast the current climate online to the past she fondly recalls. "The [collective] mind we were in was obsessive . . . it swam with superstition and half-remembered facts pertaining to how many spiders we ate in a year and the rate at which dentists killed themselves. . . . But worth remembering: the mind had been, in its childhood, a place of play. . . . It had also been the place where you once sounded like yourself. Gradually it had become a place where we sounded like each other."[24] The impact of her own obsessive behavior within the portal begins to bother her. "Already it was becoming impossible to explain things she had even done the year before, why she had spent hypnotized hours of her life, say, photoshopping bags of frozen peas into pictures of historical atrocities."[25] And she recognizes that though the value of such efforts may be illusory, their allure remains addictive. "When she set the portal down, the Thread tugged her back toward it. She could not help following it. This might be the one that connected everything, that would knit her to an indestructible coherence."[26]

20. Ibid., 3.
21. Ibid., 9.
22. Ibid., 40.
23. Ibid., 65.
24. Ibid., 71–72.
25. Ibid., 90.
26. Ibid., 99.

Then, just past midway in the book, while in Europe speechifying about the Twitter-verse, our hero receives a text from her mother: "Something has gone wrong... How soon can you get here?"[27] What has gone wrong is the pregnancy of the younger sister she adores, the one who is "living a life 200 percent less ironic than hers."[28] The fetus she's carrying has a fatal birth defect, the Proteus syndrome, its head growing at ten times the normal rate, placing its mother's life in danger. For their very Catholic parents, abortion is an abomination, and the state of Ohio has just passed a law making it illegal to induce labor before thirty-seven weeks. The shock of the news and intimacy of sharing its dilemma changes everything, for now "the question that was the pure liquid element of the portal—who am I failing to protect?—had found its stopped clock answer."[29] And the playful speculation that has characterized the book acquires a wholly new dramatic urgency. "What did we have a right to expect from this life? What were the terms of the contract? ... Could we sue? ... Could we ... could we post about it?"[30]

The sister does receive special permission to induce an earlier labor. Despite the doctors' best guesses, the baby girl, Lena, is born alive, and the final sections of the book portray their caring for this infant, who is blind and they know cannot survive for long. The commitment undertaken is complete, unstinting. "'I want a year,' her sister said fiercely. 'I want one year,' when for so long the rest of us had been thinking only how to skip ahead until the dictator was gone."[31] Named as Lena's godmother, our central character is just as devoted; she can't resist the call: "'Touch me!' the baby demanded at all times. 'Touch me, I am in the dark!'"[32] She talks and sings to Lena too, savoring "the great gift of the baby knowing their voices, contentless entirely except for love."[33]

The emotional intensity of the experience shows in two contrasting ways. "She found herself so excited by the baby that she could hardly stand it. [Lena] was stupendous.... That every person on earth might be watched in that way, given a party whenever she waved and raised her

27. Ibid., 119.
28. Ibid., 30.
29. Ibid., 120.
30. Ibid., 155.
31. Ibid., 157.
32. Ibid., 173.
33. Ibid., 156.

little arms, breathed just like the rest of us."[34] And later, when the source of the novel's title is revealed: "she wanted to stop people on the street and say, 'Do you know about this? You should know about this. No one is talking about this!'"[35] But when away from Lena and behind her bedroom door at night, "she exploded into a white mist of tears and strange gasping sounds that were a million years before or after language."[36] The profundity of the emergency calls into question our hero's previous commitments, including those online: "If all she was was funny, and none of this was funny, where did that leave her?"[37] And when she explains to her husband why she keeps flying back to help with the baby, the self-accusations become more acute. "'A minute means something to her, more than it means to us. We don't know how long she has—I can give them to her, I can give her my minutes.' Then, almost angrily, 'What was I doing with them before?'"[38]

Those minutes pass, and as Lena nears the end "her face was luminous, as if someone had put flesh on the bone of the moon, and her beautiful eyes were larger than ever, as if coming to the end of what there was to see."[39] She survives six months, and for the family gathered to witness her death "it was like nothing any of them had ever seen. There was nothing trivial left in the room—not the clearing of a throat, not an itch on the arch of a foot."[40] Afterward, no one involved has to google how to grieve. Lena's exhausted mother intones: "'I would have done it for a million years . . . I would have gotten up every morning and given her thirteen medicines. There is no relief. I would have done it forever.'"[41] Our hero finds herself "cry[ing] uncontrollably in cafes, taxis, grocery stores, bars,"[42] but her pain also becomes the means for a moral awakening into a broader empathy. "The doors of bland suburban houses now looked possible, outlined, pulsing—for behind any one of them could be hidden a bright and private glory."[43]

34. Ibid., 145.
35. Ibid., 145.
36. Ibid., 146.
37. Ibid., 125.
38. Ibid., 171.
39. Ibid., 184.
40. Ibid., 186–87.
41. Ibid., 200.
42. Ibid., 196.
43. Ibid., 197.

Patricia Lockwood is an abundantly gifted author; her metaphorical intelligence, musical ear, and capacity for invention routinely delight and surprise. Some of her humor, as evident especially in her online posts, is not to my taste and can seem adolescent. But what's most impressive about both *Priestdaddy* and this autofictional sequel are the ways she employs those poetic gifts: the intensity and variety of the emotions evoked, the honesty of her self-scrutiny, the willingness to shed irony when the occasion requires an earnest approach. The question she poses to herself—who is she failing to protect while devoting herself to her online life?—is one many of us might ask when lost in "the blizzard of everything," scrolling through posts, streaming sports highlights, idly shopping for this or for that. And when her antic meditation on the portal's changing nature shifts midstream to memorializing the autobiographical tragedy of a sister's anguish and an infant niece's demise, not a word feels fake.

8

Toward a Literature of Awe

Every word is a sound, every sound has a meaning, and its meaning is what it does.

—*Shantanand Saraswati*[1]

1

As a writer and reader of serious fiction, I'm about to ask a very basic question, aware, however, that all such questions are also philosophical in nature, that the choices we make when crafting of our fictional worlds are reflective of decisions we have made, self-consciously or not, about our actual world—that literary techniques imply, though do not preach, deeply held beliefs. Prefaced that way, the question I ask is more easily phrased than patly answered: *where* does a fictional story take place? In probing the problem, I see two related realms of inquiry.

The first and most obvious is that of setting in the traditional sense: those analogue social and geographical spaces, whether fantasized, romanticized, or realistically rendered, within which a story's

---

1. Saraswati was an Indian spiritual leader, the quotation supplied to me by a member of the School of Practical Philosophy which follows his teachings. His series of observations linking word to sound, sound to meaning, and meaning to practical activity acutely captures a key difference between oral and literate traditions of thought. For Saraswati, working out of a religious tradition that still emphasizes face-to-face teaching, language spoken *is* action taken, with all the social, political, ethical, and spiritual resonance that implies.

characters labor and love, wonder and worry, frequently struggle, more rarely thrive. It includes the economy of actions and network of customs that orchestrate their days with incentives and restraints, and it describes both the natural habitat (forest, field, or shoreline) and the sorts of settlements (from tribal encampments to urban skylines) whose site-specific mix of shapes and sounds calibrate its residents' everyday perceptions. Unlike lyric poetry, which has other artful options, stories almost always create a physical place, lush or spare, and trace their characters' lives through it over time.

That span can range from the epochal transformation of seven generations of the Buendia family in Gabriel Marquez's fictional Macondo to a fatal summer season for the shady social climber Jay Gatsby, down to the milliseconds that transpire as a bullet passes through the brain of Tobias Wolff's indignant literary critic, Anders. But even in Wolff's brief story, external settings remain essential—both in the present, when a bank heist is in progress and the critic's arrogant comments provoke a thief to shoot him in the head, and in the past, as the dying man's final memory recalls the playfield of his boyhood, when language was still more a wonder to savor than a performance to scorn. Often the setting can become a central feature, a character even, in an author's work. The Shire in Tolkien. Hawthorne's mythologized New England. Wendell Berry's rural Port William. Sandra Cisneros's urban Mango Street. Faulkner's history-haunted Yoknapatawpha County, which lies adjacent to but differs from Flannery O'Connor's Christ-crazed, race-damned South.

What concerns me most in this realm of my inquiry, though, is the shifting ratio over time between the natural and the social in the depiction of place; how the evolution of fiction, following the history of our species, has lost touch first with the wilderness and then with the agricultural garden—how self-enclosed, how *interior* it is in danger of becoming. And lately, with a frequency that's only bound to increase as our daily habits change, those settings have begun to shift from physical spaces of any sort to virtual domains where lives are conveyed via texts, tweets, posts, or the role-playing avatars in VR games: digital spaces whose hidden rules are wholly humanmade and that, intentionally or not, skew patterns of behavior toward the values that they favor.

This is a topic worthy of a separate essay. I'll only note here that our separation from (and loss of intimate personal knowledge of) the natural world has become trebly dangerous. The peril is physical, as the storms and fires of climate change and the pandemics spurred by our invasion of the wilderness shatter modernity's illusion of utopian control. And the peril is also political and spiritual, as we continue to lose those isolated spaces where we can escape the social strictures of our everyday lives to better gauge who we now are and want to become. As Hester Prynne, suffering within an oppressive social order, says to her love-child Pearl in *The Scarlet Letter*: "We must not always talk in the market place of what happens to us in the forest."[2] But in Google's, Amazon's, and Facebook's America, where we carry the marketplace in the palms of our hands, the unregulated forest has disappeared, our every search corporately surveilled, our attention seduced, our behavior "nudged" toward mammonite ends.

In this age, as in others, we need our literature to probe the insidious aspects of our shared social setting, but that doesn't have to exclude reorienting glimpses of a natural world which, however much concealed, still surrounds and grounds us. Searching for models that show how that can be done, I've found myself rereading Anton Chekhov's "Gusev," Virginia Woolf's *To the Lighthouse*, and W. H. Auden's poem "The Fall of Rome."

2

The second realm of inquiry is the one, however, that interests me more now. This realm proves harder to define—which is, in part, why I'm driven to explore it—for it involves those qualities of literary art that precede representation. One way to approach it might be to ask, where does the *language* of a story take place? What is the linguistic equivalent of setting? Or this: what is the primary medium for language's meaning, the grounding that holds Woolf's tide-scrubbed Isle of Skye and Auden's decadent Rome, that feeds or sustains any literary work's symbol-laden themes?

A cautionary concession before I proceed: language can never be fully separated from its meanings, which are its first and final reasons for being. Words exist to represent something to someone. Though statically defined in our dictionaries, they are co-created over time by a community of fellow-users, and rich with connotations, they are fed by tradition but evolve over time. In our daily exchanges in person or on the page, the *medium* of a word, however we define it, is not the primary message—though to cite Marshall McLuhan's playful correction of his well-worn

---

2. Nathaniel Hawthorne, *The Scarlet Letter* (New York: New American Library, 1959), 225.

adage, it can *massage* that message, reshaping it in subtle ways that bear examination by authors eager to exploit for artistic effect every dimension of the words they use.

What would those other dimensions be? If we exclude the belief that words are imbued with a mystical power all their own, a force beyond the material logic of cause and effect that can summon or engender, curse or bless, we're left with our portals of perception: the pre-representational medium of our words as a sensory experience. The acquisition of language was, arguably, the most consequential event in differentiating our species' development from that of the other intelligent apes. The obvious advantages speech provided were only achieved, though, through reduction and abstraction, a strategic impoverishment of sensory experience; to be represented in language, the world had to be rendered and conveyed in a much narrower way.

However *rose-sweet* or *putrid* our descriptions may be, the words themselves, other than in scratch ads for tony colognes, have no aroma; no matter how often we've had to *eat our words* or how many slices of letter-bedecked birthday cake we've consumed, neither our talk nor our texts can be tasted; and unless we're blind and read by Braille, we don't experience language through the agency of touch. For most of us, the sensory dimensions of the language we use are limited to just two: we see words (when they're written, printed, or posted) and we hear them (when they're spoken, chanted, or sung). Even those two, though, aren't equally influential. Sound is by far the more primal, powerful, and potentially, therefore, the more useful medium for the literary artist. I reason as follows.

Evolution: For most of human existence, language was conveyed through sound alone. If we take the Greek completion of the phonetic alphabet as a handy time marker, widespread literacy is, on an evolutionary scale, a very new development. As we were becoming homo sapiens, the thinking species, the progression of our intelligence was rooted in and wedded to oral language alone for tens of thousands of years, and during that time our minds acquired an acute sensitivity to sonic nuances: changes in pitch, tone, rhythm, and inflection that can elaborate, amend, or, in the case of sarcasm, negate the literal meaning of our spoken words. The invention of writing radically increased our store of knowledge, but it didn't negate our foundational relationship with and dependence on the spoken word.

Ontology: The development of the individual recapitulates the development of the species linguistically as well as physically. Language is learned first through oral mimicry. As expressed in words, love, rage, compassion, and curiosity are first conveyed through speech alone, our core vocabulary deeply etched in our auditory memories before we learn to read and write. It's also revealing that when teaching language to young children we rely so often on musical devices—exaggerated inflection, refrain, rhyme, and various meters.

Daily Experience: Our most meaningful moments—including formal rites of passage such as baptisms, graduations, marriages, and funerals, as well as our most intimate interactions with family, friends, and lovers—are enacted through the spoken word. Writing allows us the luxury of reflection, but the events we tend to reflect on are oral ones. To overstate the case for clarity's sake: we live our lives through speech; we reflect on them through writing. (Though, as a student pointed out to me, the proliferation of texting—the hastiest and least reflective form of today's written communication—may be changing that ratio.)

Verbal Comprehension: The primacy of language as auditory pattern over language as visual shape can be demonstrated in another way. Even when silently reading we often internally voice the words on a page; this is especially true, I believe, with literary works and when any text, fictional or not, is difficult to understand. Note, though, the reverse is not true; there's no common equivalent translation from sound into sight. We don't normally visualize the words we hear to aid our comprehension or intensify our pleasure. If we are, metaphorically, a bilingual species, then speech remains our native tongue, writing a crucial but nevertheless still secondary language.

The Aesthetic Limitations of Visualized Language: Consider the process of reading. To experience it in the way a preliterate person does, try studying a page printed in a language whose letters you can't read—in my case, Arabic, say. How graceful the shapes of its words appear to be; though I haven't a clue as to what they might mean, I do find them orderly, even beautiful, and can appreciate that page as a kind of abstract graphic art. How difficult it is, though, to perceive a page of printed English in the same way. My proficiency is such that I instantly convert its visual shapes into mental concepts. The process is reflexive, and because the visual dimension disappears from consciousness so quickly, authors have difficulty employing it for artistic effect.

There are exceptions, of course, such as calligraphy and concrete poetry (sometimes call "shaped verse"), but as most any anthology will demonstrate, they're more supplementary than central to the literary arts. It's also true that authors make decisions concerning layout and lettering, but note how many of them—the use of italics and ellipses in prose, or line breaks and extra spacing in lyrical poems—are cues that score how the authors want us to voice their words. Any explanation for this limitation of sight-based language remains conjectural. I suspect our visual intelligence, newly yoked to the task of redirecting words through the portal of our eyes, is simply not adept yet at doing both things well at once. That may change as evolution works its way on us through another hundred thousand years, presuming we survive. But in our age the printed word can't do nearly as much to massage the messages we convey as the spoken word can.

3

The observations made so far hold true for all genres of written language, whether a novel, article, email, or poem. This seems a sensible approach, for to isolate the special aspirations of literature, we need to establish first the nature of the medium from which it's composed. Let it be noted, then, that the primary strengths and weaknesses of language as a mode of representation emerge from two of its most basic features.

1) *Our words are abstract*: that is, they bear a relation to the objects or actions they describe only through the mutual agreement of their users. In languages based on a phonetic alphabet like ours, the words we read don't visually resemble what they mean; nor with the exception of a small percentage of our vocabulary—*hush*, say—do the individual words we voice and hear sound like what they mean.

2) *Our words are sequential*: their abstract signs are delivered and received in a linear fashion, "one damn word after another."

Abstraction is what makes language so compact, so efficient; consider how much can be conveyed in so little space or time, the length or duration of a single word. *France* is a verbal concept that refers to some two hundred thousand square miles of diverse geography, along with a complex mix of natural, cultural, and historical facts, yet through the use of a single spoken syllable or six printed letters *something* of that country's nature can be evoked and shared. And though linear sequencing is a restraint necessary for comprehending language both spoken and written, that reductive artifice does resemble one crucial aspect of our natural lives. Word follows word as moment follows moment, day follows day. Whether aloud in speech or in print on the page, our words reenact an existential limit we can't escape: the mystery of time, the future's foggy text, how we can never know for certain what will happen to us next. Language, too, is trapped in time, and so can mimic the suspense inherent in our lives.

Each of these strengths is accompanied, however, by a critical weakness, a distortion through incompletion. As we've seen, the efficiency of abstraction can only be achieved through a radical reduction of reality's particulars, of its scope and density, its sensory texture. And by converting our perception of the world into the artifice of words, we are always in danger, too, of misconstruing them for the world itself: the abstract sign for the multidimensional thing it describes. Wordsworth was alert to that peril, if in a limited way, when in *The Prelude* he criticized the then emerging field of natural science, dismissing its reductive reasoning as

> . . . *that false secondary power by which*
> *In weakness we create distinctions, then*
> *Deem that our puny boundaries are things*
> *That we perceive, and not that we have made.*
> (Book II, 216–19)

The same critique could apply, however, to Wordsworth's own endeavor, for language itself is a "secondary power," and as a language-dependent species, we are constantly in danger of mistaking the "puny boundaries" of our favorite verbal concepts—political or economic, scientific or poetic—for the richer reality they were fashioned to represent. To amend Isaiah's indignant definition of idolatry's sacrilege: our land, too, is "full of idols," but rather than just "bow down to the work of [our] hands," entranced and enthralled, as we are today, by our digital machines, we are also tempted to revere and obey the virtual realities our verbal minds have made.

Abstraction's distortions are the more radical perhaps, but the linear nature of verbal communication also reduces, and so misrepresents, the world we experience in a crucial way. For though it is true that our lives are sequential in one profound sense and that our languages are adept at evoking the suspense of living in time, any single moment of consciousness has a multidimensional complexity that "one damned word after another" cannot easily suggest.

Returning to the subject of setting in the traditional sense, let's assume I'm standing in a living room at a wedding reception, conversing with a guest whom I've just met. Even as I'm absorbing his words and imagining my response, I'm also watching his gestures and interpreting his facial expressions, aware more vaguely too of the book-lined shelves behind him; of the cheesy scent of canapés warming on a table; of the aftertaste of the Thai-spiced shrimp I recently ate; of the faint aching in my thigh from a muscle pulled in a pickup game; of the recorded chamber music (Haydn, I believe) playing softly in the background, and whose harmonies interweave with the voice of that guest and with the rattling of ice as he gestures with his glass.

Ranging from self-conscious to subliminal, my awareness of that scene in the living room exists all at once for me, yet my words can only recover it one feature at a time, in a list that risks extending too long. For the more complete my description is, the more it violates the simultaneity of the experience. In movies and plays the entirety of the setting (its sounds and sights at least) can be present for their audience to perceive. Not so for the reader of a novel, memoir, or narrative poem; as every fiction writer knows, evoking and sustaining a sensory-based setting through an inherently abstract and linear medium is a technical challenge that never goes away.

These observations about the limits of language are helpful in two ways. First, I want to observe how easily we can use them to define by opposition the special mission of poetry and fiction, how and why they differ from other kinds of verbal expression. Literature, in this sense, is remedial, redemptive; among other ambitions, it strives to save our words from their native weaknesses. (This is surely in part what T. S. Eliot implied about the poet's mission when he wrote: "Since our concern was speech, and speech impelled us / To purify the dialect of the tribe."[3]) Self-corrective, literature aims to recover through the very agency of language itself those qualities of our complex, sense-drenched experience of life that everyday language, especially when written, tends to exclude. What, after all, are the unique features of literary language? Each answer I find—its sensuality, particularity, and depth; its reliance on imagery and musical effects; its attempts to create subtle ironies and symbols (to make

---

3. T. S. Eliot, "Little Gidding," *Collected Poems: 1909–1962* (New York: Harper, Brace, & World, 1962), 204.

its words, that is, have two meanings at once)—works to counteract the evisceration of abstraction or the reductive impact of linear sequencing.

The second assertion I would make, and the one I want evaluate in detail here, is how essential sound proves to be to that revivalist mission. Because we can't smell or taste or (unless we read Braille) touch our words but *can* hear them directly, in the same way we can hear a bell or a bird, the stirring of an oar or the rustling of wind through the needles of a fir, it is the *sound* of our words, whether spoken aloud or internally voiced, that saves them from the vacuum of arid abstraction. Sound gives our words a kind of flesh, a wet and breathy incarnation that echoes or evokes the tangible world they intend to represent. As the primary medium for language's meaning, sound comes first; it precedes the ideas our words convey, just as the natural world that surrounds and grounds us still precedes all the names we assign to its myriad features.

Not only does the sound of a word embody its meaning; unlike its visual shape, that word's auditory pattern can naturally coexist with its abstract definition. In the mind of an auditor (or, too, of a reader who internally voices a story), the action, object, or idea expressed doesn't instantly supplant a word's hiss or scratch in the way it replaces its cursive curl or printed slash. We can easily perceive both the lyrics and the song; can catch the nuances of a speaker's accent—her Scottish burr, say—even as we grasp to our delight or irritation the joke she tells or the curse she shouts as her car speeds past. Our natural ability to do just that, simultaneously attend to the sound and the abstract sense of the words we hear, is the basis for all of literature's musical effects; it's why we can discern and take pleasure in its rhythms and rhymes and tonal inflections—why, too, the adept manipulation of those effects is the most potent tool we have to massage the meanings, animate the feelings of the messages we craft.

As should be obvious by now, in asserting the primacy of sound I've been answering as well that elementary question I posed at the start. For insomuch as setting is an orientation of the self through our senses and sound is language's primary sensory dimension, it too constitutes a site where a story takes place. Any fictive landscape, whether urban or rural, is also a soundscape, and one whose combination of consonants and vowels, with their various pitches and patterns of stresses, can evoke emotions and stir sensations simultaneous to the characters' actions and to natural events. Phrased differently, the lyrics of a story can have a music all their own.

As every stylist knows, the orchestration of that music adds another dimension to the challenges and rewards of fictive representation. For even when wordless, music can penetrate deeply, evoking moods all its own, stirring our hearts and even urging our flesh to sway or dance. In weighing how to employ that power within an art form whose music, unlike a film's soundtrack, isn't a separate accompaniment to the ongoing story but incorporated within the words themselves, the traditional answer was expressed long ago by Alexander Pope in his didactic poem "An Essay on Criticism":

> *The sound must seem an echo to the sense.*
> *Soft is the strain when Zephyr gently blows,*
> *And the smooth stream in smoother numbers flows;*
> *But when loud surges lash the sounding shore,*
> *The hoarse rough verse should like the torrent roar.*[4]

In such an aesthetic, the music of a story, play, or poem has been composed not just to mimic but also to animate the immediate meaning of the people, places, and actions described. The abstract conception of a scene—King Lear, say, raging on the heath—is charged phrase by phrase, beat by beat, with a sensory enactment, a soundtrack composed by the words themselves.

To succeed at that, authors train their inner ear to discern the subtle but potentially evocative differences between short and long vowels, sibilants and fricatives; they strive to ascertain which rhythm best conveys the mood of the characters, the pace of their actions, or the features of their setting, whether manmade or natural. And so, although only a small percentage of individual words sound like what they mean, the careful selection and placement of words within phrases and sentences can greatly expand the range of that mimicry. By doing so, prosody in prose as well as in poetry becomes an artful exercise in onomatopoeia writ large.

Consider the following brief speech from the final scene of *King Lear*. Distraught, the play's reckless king and father is addressing the corpse of Cordelia, his only truly loyal daughter, whose murder has been caused in part by his own foolish pride.

> *. . . . . No, no, no life!*
> *Why should a dog, a horse, a rat have life,*

---

4. Alexander Pope, "An Essay on Criticism," Part II: https://www.poetryfoundation.org/articles/69379/an-essay-on-criticism.

> *And thou no breath at all? Thou'lt come no more,*
> *Never, never, never, never, never! (V, iii, 305–8)*

As T. S. Eliot argued in an essay on Yeats's work in the theater, the poetic beauty of any particular line in a verse play is dependent on its placement within the action, the sublimity of its sound inseparable from the meaning of its narrative site. Eliot then cited as his sole example that very string of five *nevers* quoted above, observing that while the line constituted "one of the most thrilling" in Lear's tragedy, we could scarcely know whether it was "poetry or even competent verse" if we read it in isolation, unaware of the context of persons, places, and actions that ground it.[5]

The immediate context is, of course, a father bending over his murdered daughter's corpse, and the line is thrilling—that is, it rises to the pitch of poetry—because its form so fully fits the matrix of meanings that animates the moment in all its emotional, thematic, and existential registers. Note, for example, the line's relentless repetition of a single word, a rare and risky tactic in any form of verse, and then consider its multiform propriety at this point in the action—how it succeeds in suggesting all at once: the intensity of a father's grief; the eternity of mortality itself (the never that goes on forever); and the very human need, in the midst of an unexpected grief, to repeat the awful message over and over in order to comprehend it.

The music of the line also coheres with the meaning of the scene, befitting both the nature of the existential fact (death) and the climate of the psychological instant (grief). After two full lines of monosyllabic words in strictly iambic feet (and THOU / no BREATH / at ALL?), Lear's horrified apprehension of the reality of Cordelia's death climaxes with a sudden reversal into a stuttered array of repetitive trochees (NEVer / NEVer / NEVer . . .). Rhythm and diction fuse. The sound of the line mimics its sense as each word—carved from hard consonants and short vowels and a stifling of stresses—becomes an isolated metrical foot in itself. Each poetic piece is arrested in time and sealed off from the whole, like the corpse from the fold of living relations. Each sound event, in its clipped, short-breathed diminishment, reenacts the cruel truncation of the real event. *Dead* the sounds sing as dead the words say: she's *dead, dead, dead, dead, dead!*

---

5. T. S. Eliot, "Yeats," in *Yeats: A Collection of Critical Essays*, ed. John Unterecker (Englewood Cliffs: Prentice Hall, 1963), 61. The subject of the essay is Yeats's work as a dramatist.

4

As in verse plays and narrative poems, the sound of our prose can also be employed to echo the sense of the stories we tell—but shouldn't we aspire to something more as well? If, in the words of Wallace Stevens, "we live in a place / That is not our own and, much more, not ourselves / And hard it is in spite of blazoned days,"[6] shouldn't the sites of the stories we write strive to suggest the alien features of that harder place too—a setting immune to our feuds and moods and self-conflicting needs, and whose nature eludes the puny boundaries of both our rational reasoning and our romantic imagery?

If that too becomes a goal for story-telling prose, then the mimicry of fiction would have to expand beyond the trials of its characters, whether coders or carpenters, evoking as well both the daunting scope and the omnipresent strangeness of the creation that sustains us but "is not our own . . . not ourselves." And if we agree with Emily Dickinson's associated claim that "art is a house that tries to be haunted,"[7] we're obliged to ask how the words we choose can possibly represent a ghostly otherness whose insinuating presence can frighten or astound us, but whose essence either way confounds each attempt of our limited intelligence to name and therefore tame it.

Such a challenge is somewhat analogous to the one we now face in the traditional realm of fictional settings: the urgent need to recover a hint of the wilderness, even as we wrap ourselves ever more tightly in our manmade habitats. While remaining true to our immediate condition, contemporary fiction still needs to resurrect a tactile sense of the Nature that gave birth to human nature and that can extinguish it too. We need to be reminded of the boar's skull that has been hidden behind the cashmere shawl in *To the Lighthouse*. Now more than ever, we need to catch a glimpse of the "altogether elsewhere" evoked in Auden's poem, where "herds of reindeer move across / miles and miles of golden moss," indifferent to the fall of Rome.[8]

The analogy between these two challenges to fictional representation finally fails, though, for summoning the ghost of a place that's "not

---

6. Wallace Stevens, "Notes Toward a Supreme Fiction," *The Palm at the End of the Mind: Selected Poems* (New York: Vintage, 1972), 210.

7. Emily Dickinson in a letter to her admirer Thomas Higginson, 1876. The full sentence is: *Nature is a Haunted House-but Art-a House that tries to be haunted*. See: http://archive.emilydickinson.org/correspondence/higginson/l459a.html.

8. W.H. Auden, "The Fall of Rome," *Nones* (New York: Random House, 1951).

our own" requires something further and more difficult. It asks that we evoke the *meta*-physical realm that surrounds and grounds the natural world too; it demands that we find ways to suggest the mostly supersensory reality that allows the boar, the reindeer, and ourselves to exist, even as it seems "unendowed with . . . pity"[9] for our individual fates. This is a challenge that has haunted me for years, the professional expression of a personal ambition to recapture on the page the flavor at least of my most transformative experiences: the urge to create what I called in my first published essay a "literature of awe."

From very early on I've wanted to read and write stories that, even as they probed the complexities of our social and psychological selves, supplied a sense of those deeper dimensions that fund all forms of earthly existence. I wasn't hoping for a body of work that focused solely on climactic moments of revelation in its characters' lives, for such experiences are rare, and it would misrepresent the human condition to suggest otherwise. But I did and do want stories whose houses are haunted with the *possibility* of revelation, hints of the metaphysical seeping through their sense-drenched depictions of our physical world and the crises that abide here.

Even if the characters, trapped in their travails, missed those hints, such a story's readers would still have a chance to be haunted by them. They'd have the opportunity to sense, however incompletely, an order of being that dwarfs our own, a realization then arising, not as doctrine but awe-struck sensation, that all our stories combined cannot come close to the whole story, that "under every deep a lower deep opens."[10] They'd sense that even "in the mud and scum of things / there something alway(s), alway(s) sings,"[11] and though its lyrics may be alien, its melody strange, this much at least is made palpably clear: man is *not* the measure of all things.

But since our stories are made from words, and words themselves are the most manmade of measures, reductive in ways already defined, a perceptive reader might protest that my lifelong goal, a literature of awe, is impossible to achieve. If so, I wouldn't disagree, not entirely anyway, but would qualify my admission by reminding such a critic that nothing we aspire to capture with our words is perfectly achievable, that even the

---

9. Ibid.
10. Emerson, "Circles," *Selected Essays* (Chicago: Peoples Book Club), 205.
11. Emerson, "Music." See: https://www.all-creatures.org/poetry/music.html.

best of sentences is incomplete and so in some way insufficient. Artifice is not genesis. A bird on the page is not the same as a bird in the hand.

Still, we only can work with what we have been given, including the limits of articulation, and in the analogue worlds that fiction builds, some depictions do come closer than others; *their* bird on the page can summon at least the shadow of a swift as it pulses across the thought-space in our heads on buoyant thermals of imagination. Such ghostly silhouettes, as weightless and fleeting as reawakened memories, are the best that we can do; in our prose as in our lives, "the imperfect is our paradise."[12] We're exiled east of Eden where the impossible, though not reachable, *is* approachable by degrees, in shades of verbal likeness through our rhythms, rhymes, and imagery.

Even so, that same critic might insist, surely awe is far *less* approachable than any of our other emotions or sensations. For isn't it triggered by glimpses of spaces whose scale and features have no obvious analogues in our everyday lives? And doesn't that absence then stymie our need to find a likeness that succeeds in binding the strange to the familiar, the ineffable sensation to a tangible thing: a simile that then supplies a tentative name? And isn't that why, along with widened eyes, our natural response to the experience of awe is the dropped jaws of silence? When ambushed by the unplumbable otherness that always surrounds us, we're naturally struck dumb.

Again, I wouldn't disagree, only insist that the difficulty of the mission doesn't negate the necessity of my committing to it. When setting out to write the most complete accounting of this multidimensional site we all share, I'm compelled to pursue the perimeter of our perceptions as well as their center. Because like love and loathing, lust and disgust, awe is one of a limited number of natural responses to the reality surrounding us—and because that response has profoundly transformed the person I've become—I've had to search for ways to evoke it on the page. The nagging question for me, then, has never been whether to pursue a literature of awe, but how I might do it. And the best, if still imperfect, answer that I've found is through its music.

Because the sounds of our words both precede their abstract meanings and also breathe through them, their patterning might weave into simulated being not just our private thoughts and social spaces, or even Nature's unadulterated landscapes, but also hints at least of those outer

---

12. Wallace Stevens, "The Poems of Our Climate," *The Palm at the End of the Mind: Selected Poems* (New York: Vintage, 1972), 158.

bounds and "lower deeps" that surround them all. Such an ambition expands Pope's claim that "sound must seem an echo to the sense" onto the metaphysical plane. It demands we assume a new impossible task, one simultaneous to staging the comedies and dramas of the human circumstance. It asks that we somehow rearrange our stories' sounds in ways that echo a voice portrayed in one of Stevens' final poems: that of a "gold-feathered bird" who, perching in a palm "on the edge of space" and "beyond the last thought," sings "without human meaning, without human feeling, a foreign song." *That* is the song, however distant, faint, or fading, I've sometimes overheard and want my stories' words to voice: its music "of mere being."[13]

Notes on Composing a Literature of Awe

- Nearly every story about embodied beings has a location, and its readers need to know where they are within that fictive space the author has imagined, whether that place is Mars or Manhattan. And because words are sequential, their descriptions disappearing line by line, page after page, a sense of that setting and the time frame within it must be periodically revived in the reader's mind.

- Narrative prose cannot assume all the freedoms allowed a lyrical poem, which isn't obliged to establish and sustain such a three-dimensional place, and whose brevity and spacing naturally allow for more grammatical and syntactical experimentation.

- Given the brevity of their work, poets can expect readers to revisit their lyrical lines to clarify their meanings and savor their feelings; James Joyce notwithstanding, fiction writers can't. Not only are there too many words, arrayed in dense paragraphs instead of spaced lines, to expect that effort; such a demand constantly undermines the integrity of the imagined world. Readers can't "suspend disbelief" when on first reading they cannot clearly grasp what they're meant to believe, when the fictive world remains confusing and opaque, just words on a page.

- Phrased differently, narrative prose needs to heed the distinction between *mystery* and *confusion*: between a) the suspense of not knowing what will happen next and the associated challenge of

13. "Of Mere Being," Ibid., 398.

sieving nuggets of meaning from the flow of events, both of which mimic the drama inherent in our everyday lives, and b) a failure to clarify in its readers' minds where they are in fictive space and time.

- In a literature of awe, that representation of "where they are" will aspire to include hints of the metaphysical too—of that realm "beyond the last thought" whose song is "without human meaning, without human feeling."

- As the hiss of the Big Bang persists within the ceaseless metamorphosis of the present-day universe, the music of mere being—which is to say the song of genesis—continues to coexist within and around our transient myths of longing, love, and loss. In the words of Jean Gebser, the mystery of our origin is "ever-present."[14] The music of the spheres is always here, if only we could learn to attune our ears.

- Such a ghostly song will not conform to the puny boundaries of our mortal musicology. It won't resound with predictable harmonies. To be true to our condition, any attempt to represent the "foreign song" of origin must sound in some sense foreign, even as—and here's the crux of the impossible task—it's still recognized as singing. Imagine a pattern implied that can't be circumscribed by any school of thought or narrative plot; a sequence whose notes can't be foretold on any of our charts.

- Wallace Stevens again: "there was a myth before the myth began."[15] Yes, that *is* the presumption, the faith that drives the impossible ambition to trespass the usual edges of cognition. Yet even as a literature of awe aspires to evoke hints of that earlier myth, it still must attend to those secondary ones we're more consciously immersed in. The social and psychological story, which *is* rich with human meaning and feeling, cannot be slighted, much less sacrificed for the foreign song that isn't.

- Two ways of observing a clear night sky: to search for a constellation, a hero snatched from a long-ago myth whose figure has been projected onto a few selective points of heavenly light; *or* to widen our vision and surrender instead to the milky luminescence of the night-dome's countless stars. A literature of awe, though, asks for

---

14. Jean Gebser, *The Ever-Present Origin* (Athens: Ohio University Press, 1984).
15. Wallace Stevens, "Notes Toward a Supreme Fiction," Ibid., 210.

TOWARD A LITERATURE OF AWE

something more—that its authors substitute *and* for *or*; it demands that we provide both the plotted myth and the plotless splendor.

- Simultaneity is key, then, and sound—the ever-present origin of every word we speak or read—one necessary means. Like color in painting, sound in fiction can supply a nonrational access to the emotional and spiritual dimensions of our existence, and it can do so even as its words dramatize our actions, vivify our settings.

- Heraclitus: "No man ever steps in the same river twice." Yes, the river has changed and so has the man, but never entirely, and capturing that muddled mix of continuity and flux, which is the drama of metamorphosis, is a challenge confronting every time-based art, whether it's a plotted story, wordless dance, or string quartet.

- Rhyming is a powerful means to do just that. Inside a story's river-rush of words, a sound returns downstream, but in that new location, its soul has been supplied a slightly different incarnation. Something has changed but also been reclaimed, a continuity affirmed by the sonic rebirth that the rhyming word sings. "The king is dead, long live the king."

- Some of the instruments available: full rhymes, off rhymes, alliterations soft or hard, assonantal chimes, bursts of unanticipated tempos that flirt, like evaporating dreams, with a shapeliness that never quite coheres into a rule-bound scheme.

- If we think of each of those rhyming repetitions as a sound event, then a literature of awe will strive to multiply their numbers and orchestrate them then into an entire musical environment, so many rhythmic connections, echoes within echoes, polyphonic threads with dissonant discrepancies.

- Some of those sound events will heed Pope's imperative by echoing the sense of the ongoing narrative: the moods of its characters, the temper of their actions, and the nature of their immediate setting. Others will hint at an order beyond the bounds of human thought and even Nature's untamed spaces; they'll sing a song of mere being, which, without human meaning, "is not the reason / that we are happy or unhappy."[16]

---

16. "Of Mere Being," Ibid., 398.

- Still, that multiplication of sound events mustn't disturb in any major way the syntax of the sentences containing them; nor should the meaning of any word be slurred to create an audible return. Reason can't be sacrificed for rhyme or meter. The foreign song has to abide within the familiar depiction without distorting it. In a literature of awe, each verbal house must be soundly built, even as it strives to be haunted.

- A model of the goal ironically recast in a visual mode: consider watching a juggler at work. One ball tossed then caught is monotonous; the tick-tock of two seems merely robotic. Keeping three in motion might seem at least admirable. With four or more, though, we begin to lose track of how many balls are arcing in the air; perfectly timed, the blur of their motion, like so many spokes on a spinning wheel, becomes too fast to keep count. Awe can surge in when the mind loses count.

- Now, to amend that model so it better represents the condition of our lives: replace those balls with knives.

9

Phoenix?
(An Inquiry into the Art of Uncertainty)

one inch ahead . . .

The one orbiting the Earth, the other the sun to escape the atmospheric haze that cushions but also blurs our short-lived stay here, the Hubble and James Webb telescopes have been recording celestial events as far as 13 billion light years away—a once unthinkable penetration into the depths of time as well as space. Some of that imagery is now available online. With the click of a mouse or a finger tap, we can summon at home a technicolor show of pinwheeling galaxies, of stellar births and cataclysmic deaths whose clarity and depth, when compared to the pictures Galileo first sketched, highlight the extent of our perceptual progress. This is how far and fast our vision has been stretched by our native inventiveness: from Jupiter's moons, first spied by human eyes in 1610, to a supernova's blaze on the universe's rim; from a Rembrandt that catches the subtle glow of being in some mundane merchant's face from Holland's bourgeois past to images that capture the spawning of stars ignited in the wake of the Big Boom's blast.

And yet, strangely, even as we've made stellar time and space collapse, it is also still the case, as the Japanese say, that "one inch ahead / the whole world / is dark."[1] The future's not the past, and when facing the many choices we must make—whom to love, where to live, how to best

---

1. W.S. Merwin, *Asian Figures* (New York: Atheneum, 1973), 44.

behave to spare ourselves the pain and shame of failure—we remain encompassed by a haze, an existential fog we can't dispel or jet beyond. We "want clear spectacles," a poet long ago complained, our "eyes are dim," and the problem he decried hasn't really changed. Now, no less than in 1610, when Galileo's Europe teetered on the verge of both scientific progress and sectarian slaughter, our "understanding's dark, and therefore will / Account of ill for good, and good for ill."[2]

Not in every instance: that's way too certain in itself. But frequently enough to sound a warning bell.

How so? . . . Oh, say, once upon a time, having received a prophecy that he will slay his own father, who just happens to be his city's king, a young man chooses to flee his home in Corinth to avoid that awful crime. And who among his peers—in a tribe that believes in oracles and patriarchy, in the sanctity of kings—could say his choice is not a righteous one? That same young man, now a stranger in a strange land, defends himself when challenged on the road, and who—in a tribe that, schooled to survive in a war-prone era, highly values martial valor—could blame him, really, for taking up the fight and slaying his opponent? Having fled and fought at the proper times, our hero now proves his mental mettle by answering a riddle that not only saves his own life but also rids the nearest city of a murderous monster—and what citizenry, saved at last and lacking a leader, wouldn't see in such behavior the makings of a king? What queen, having lost her only son years ago and her husband more recently, wouldn't find in such a man an ideal second chance, the best possible person to father her children and extend the royal line?

And yet, as that story plays out in *Oedipus Rex*, as clear spectacles are found but twenty years too late, each of those judgments proves "dim" in the extreme: each has "account[ed] ill for good" in a radical way. The consequences of so many apparently best possible decisions prove to be monstrous instead: patricide, regicide, ongoing incest. Oedipus, the city's old savior, is revealed to be the man who, while on the road all those years ago, killed its prior king, and that slain leader, it turns out, doubling the violation, had been his real father. The ideal second husband has been exposed instead as the queen's first son, a man absolutely banned from her marriage bed. And their children, a source of hope and joy just the

---

2. Edward Taylor, "The Accusation of the Inward Man," *The Mentor Book of Major American Poets,* ed. Oscar Williams and Edwin Honig (New York: New American Library, 1962), 32.

day before, will now be shunned as the dreadful embodiments of their parents' sacrilege, their sins made flesh.

Oedipus did try to "fly from the wrath to come"[3] that was predicted by an oracle, but though brave as well as smart, his understanding still proved dark. Intending to run away, he actually ran toward, following the path that mapped his fate's peculiar hell.

> ...... *no ship exists*
> *To take you from yourself.*[4]

Dissonance (if you're interested) . . .

If this were a class, and let's pretend it is, a student might interrupt now to complain that the plot of the play just described is not sufficiently "realistic" to remain "relevant" to our more advanced lives. As an experienced teacher, his professor shouldn't be surprised by such a claim, yet it irritates him still; he loathes especially its rote condescension to the thinking of the past, an attitude he finds both lazy and vain. Opening up a bit, let's admit that this teacher is a little too given to such moments of indignation, and that, recognizing this, he has worked to cultivate a set of classroom tactics to refine these over-reactions of his, aiming to turn the heat of their aversions into a kind of edifying light.

And so, calming down, he tries to assume now the perspective of this student—whose name, let's say, is Chad. He starts by acknowledging that, yes, *Oedipus Rex* is an ancient text, the oral myth it draws on far older still, and so, certain of its features, like the politics they practice and gods they worship, do seem alien to us, systems of thought we've long ago moved beyond. A belief in oracles, for instance, he readily admits, seems superstitious to us now—or, yes, "unrealistic" if that's the term that Chad prefers.

Having established some common ground, the teacher can move on to subtler issues now: to literary thinking as a formal way of knowing the world. For this is a class in fiction writing, and he's been charged with teaching these fifteen would-be authors how to think inside the form. He starts by discussing two wholly different species of accuracy, highlighting the distinction between the exact equivalences of math and the apt

---

3. John Bunyan, *The Pilgrim's Progress* (New York: Rinehart & Co., 1957), 11. He is citing Matthew 3: 7.

4. From Lawrence Durrell's translation of the C. P. Cavafy poem "The City," which he included his novel *Justine* (New York: Pocket Books, 1967), 256.

semblances of metaphor. Rising from his seat and pacing before the class, he contrasts the very different obligations which, in their common aim to convince, the logic of an argument and the likeness of a simile must each fulfill. For convenience, he calls the former "logos-minded thinking," the latter "mythos-minded thinking." (These are terms he's used before, but insomuch as their origin is Greek, as is the tragedy whose reality and relevance have been called into question, he hopes to convey the implicit message that if familiar words like *logic* and *myth* can still capture for us crucial aspects of experience, then so too might a story first conceived in that same language, however long ago.)

The professor quickly focuses on mythos-minded thinking, which, as an author himself, he practices as well as teaches. To his advantage, he has already talked about the nature of effective figurative language. Borrowing a phrase from a Josef Conrad story that they read together at the start of the quarter, he has defined metaphorical thinking as the art of uncovering "the secret sharing of apparently dissimilar things." And he has stressed while doing so the emotional power of apt surprise: how convincing it can be when two seemingly dissimilar objects or subjects are suddenly shown to be alike or aligned.

Citing one of his old teachers, he has warned his students, however, that "every likeness implies unlikenesses" as well. Strictly speaking and contrary to Macbeth's bitterly eloquent observation, life is not entirely like "a poor player / that struts and frets his hour upon the stage."[5] Nor are Hamlet's troubles wholly akin to "slings and arrows,"[6] for although that image does evoke the sense of danger the prince of Denmark feels, the overt aggression of those physical weapons fails to suggest the subtler dimensions of the ongoing threat—the courtly flattery and lies that conceal a horrid crime, his uncle's faux concern and mother's self-deceptions. Using models like these, as well as ones taken from the students' own stories, the class has discussed in detail the art of fashioning such imagery. Key among the points of craft endorsed has been the necessity of managing that inevitable tension between the likenesses and unlikenesses inherent in any metaphorical comparison.

"As the adept magician directs the attention of his audience away from the slick mechanics of his tricks"—the teacher has said, using a figure of his own—"authors must divert their readers' attention away

---

5. *Macbeth*, V, v, 24–25.
6. *Hamlet*, III, I, 58.

from those inevitable unlikenesses, allowing the resemblances to prevail in the end."

Now, however, using that same base of knowledge, the teacher decides to shift his tactics. Now, given the task of convincing the class of the reality and relevance of *Oedipus Rex* (and, he suspects, of ancient literature more generally), he chooses to emphasize the significance of the *un*likenesses instead. The impression of resemblance must triumph, yes, but only eventually, only in the end. The *sharing* must be apt, the teacher now insists, but it also must be, initially at least, *secret*. Because the obvious, by definition, lacks the persuasive power of surprise, the expected connection, reduced to a cliché, fails to provoke the shock of recognition—that knowing-charged-with-feeling which is the intended affect of the aesthetic experience and which can make of mere words a palpable simulation of the sensible world.

Perhaps the teacher will pause now to cite the following terse aphorism in verse:

> *Dissonance*
> *(if you're interested)*
> *leads to discovery*[7]

Or perhaps, borrowing from the psychology of the senses, he will simply assert: "no perception without difference." Our awareness of events *as* events, of news *as* news instead of noise, depends on our recognition of multiple sorts of difference, of dissonance. Figure against ground. Light against dark. A sudden sound emerging from a meditative silence. ("Oh, say, like a smartphone chirping in the middle of a class," the teacher adds, eliciting a laugh, for this is a well-established peeve of his and a comic motif now shared by the class.) "No perception," he repeats, "without difference." At a higher level of awareness, beyond these mere atoms of near-instant perception (a flash of color, burst of sound), we also recognize the likenesses supplied by larger, longer patterns. But a pattern is itself best defined as a memorable series of perceptible differences.

"Take music," the teacher says, well aware of its importance in his students' lives, the degree to which pop lyrics have replaced both sacred and literary texts as their most trusted emblems of truthful feeling. "Take your current favorite song. What is the pattern of its melody but a specific sequence of variations in pitch and duration? No variations (no

---

7. William Carlos Williams, *Paterson*: https://archive.org/stream/PatersonWCW/Paterson-William_Carlos_Williams_djvu.txt.

discernible differences in pitch and duration), and there is no perception of a pattern, no news within the noise—there is no song. And at yet a higher level of awareness, that initial pattern of differences is itself then varied. The song's earlier "news" has been refreshed, *re*newed through further thoughtful differences, a play on expectations that deliberately restages the powerfully persuasive experience of surprise.

"We're talking about *art* here, folks," the teacher says, deliberately appealing to an ambition which, despite their embarrassed avoidance of the word itself, the best of his students secretly share. "And in art, managing the relation of likeness to unlikeness lies at the heart of its serious game-playing. Too much likeness, too much repetition and, as with the ticking of a clock, the surprise of recognition quickly dissolves into a dull hum, the dozy buzz of inattention. Yet too much unlikeness, too many changes, and the surprise of variation blurs instead into the featureless fuzz of apparent randomness.

"News in each case degrades into uneventful noise. The knowing-charged-with-feeling that art aims to stage fades into a numb or dumb insentience. When pursued in excess, these apparently opposing aesthetic tactics become alike. In their dimming of consciousness, in their failure to affect us, they become, ironically, *an*aesthetic."

"But how far is too far?" a student blurts out—it's the one whose interior monologues can sometimes catch the true pitch and sway of the anxious mind at work. "What does 'pursued in excess' really mean for *us*?"

"Very good, Carl," the teacher says, as he nods in his direction, "— that *is* a crucial question. And, I confess, not an easy one to answer."

wrong is right

And because it won't be easy, the teacher pauses briefly to reconsider tactics. He knows that, raised in a how-to, self-help, twelve-step culture, his students will expect hard-and-fast answers. All their lives they've been trained to prefer those exact equivalences, modeled after math, that he can't provide because they do not fit the aesthetic sense of value he wants to profess—those ambivalent truths that treat feelings, too, as facts, and that cannot be reduced to immutable rules or bulleted advice of the how-to type.

PHOENIX?

"How far is too far? . . . Surely, there are outer limits of *some* sort," the teacher says, "ones set by the physiology of perception and our capacity for recollection. Though those, too, might be stretched by invention, our avid pursuit of clearer spectacles to know the world. But within those limits, the range of acceptable change or repetition can vary greatly. Our measures of artfulness are, as they say of some sculptures these days, site-specific. Unlike logos-minded thinking, which wants to imagine that, immaculate and chaste, its truths are freed of the limits of time and space, art is conveyed through our earthbound senses, and so is always, too, both culturally grounded and historically inflected. And so," the teacher notes, "even to approach answering Carl's excellent question, we'd have to know first which culture in which era, which art form, appealing to which sense or senses. And even then, the answer would remain to some degree subjective, and so susceptible to being contested.

"All of which is why," the teacher adds, reminding himself as well as the class, "Chad's questioning of the reality and relevance of an ancient Greek play is plausible and so permissible here. Permissible in a way that, say, a similar challenge to the truth of a geometric proof, also first produced by those same Greeks, would never be.

"How far is too far, then? At what point does repetition so hypnotize and variation so randomize that they achieve the opposite of art's intention, dimming awareness, inducing *in*sentience? No easy answers here," the teacher says again. "Depending on a person's taste, the preferred ratio of likeness to unlikeness can vary from the minimal to the radical. Think of the disagreements we've already had within this class when discussing your stories. Or consider today's music scene, where performances can range from the robotic melodies and chiming rhymes of some viral hit to the deliberate torque and scat of a jazz session's riffs."

(Suddenly uncertain, the teacher pauses. Because he is human, he must imagine options and choose among them, but without knowing enough to guarantee the outcome. Because he is human, he has intentions, ones strongly shaped by his profession. And so, to think at all, his thoughts must be, to a large degree, site-specific: physically placed, culturally grounded, historically inflected. His current locale is a university classroom in Seattle, Washington. His primary intention is to convince a group of student writers of the reality and relevance of *Oedipus Rex*. The strategy he's chosen so far has been to draw on this class's six-week history, especially their past discussions on metaphorical thinking as "the secret sharing of dissimilar things." Because within those past discussions he has tended to emphasize the sharing over the dissimilarity, and because he began today's defense of *Oedipus Rex* by acknowledging significant differences between our cultural site and that of the ancient Greeks, the teacher now suspects that he should continue to stress the importance of dissonance to mythos-minded thinking. And so he makes what he judges to be, given his intentions and the current context, the best possible decision about how to persuade Chad and the class. He might be wrong, he knows, and if he is, he will be accountable for this discussion's failure; he might be wrong, but he's made his decision. And he has had to do so, as is often the case with creatures fated to be free, in a real-time instant, much more quickly than this logos-minded description—carefully reducing the rich simultaneity of a moment's consciousness into a sharp-edged but slow-footed linear sequence—can ever suggest. Its account, too, is only a fraction of the truth. Even at its most accurate, logical analysis must also traffic in unlikenesses.)

"Yes," the teacher says, after a pause. "Let's consider, for a moment, a jazz session's riffs. Let's think about the importance of dissonance to *its* version of artfulness."

But before he's finished speaking, in the rich simultaneity of all this moment's thoughts and feelings, his memory starts replaying, oh so faintly, the signature phrase from "A Love Supreme." Just that quickly he is picturing again the black-and-white photo of John Coltrane on his old LP; he's lounging again in the messy living room where he first heard it played. And as another fact floats in with that wave of moody memories, he suddenly recalls, then chooses to recite, a quotation he first heard in that same place.

"Do you listen to jazz?" the teacher asks. "Anyone know the pianist Thelonious Monk?" No one does. "Well, Monk was the man who, catching the gist of jazz in just three words, once famously said: 'wrong is right.'[8]

"That's hyperbole, of course," the teacher quickly adds, all too aware of robotic rebellion's attraction to the young. "Wrong is *usually* wrong. But we're talking about art here, folks. And insomuch as art, unlike philosophy, pursues truth through the senses, and insomuch as there is no sensory perception without difference, art must supply the *dissimilarity* along with the *sharing*. Which is why, in simulating perception, in staging artful truth, the metaphors we write must provide both the figure and the

8. Widely attributed to the jazz pianist Thelonious Monk.

ground, both the wonder of the news and the welter of the noise from which it springs—or rather, a hint of that welter. In literature, wrong can be right because dissonance (if you're interested) can lead to discovery, because difference sparks the interest that awakens the mind to its surrounding place. Wrong can be right in the stories we write because . . . " And here he recalls another favorite line: "'the imperfect is our paradise.'"[9]

The teacher pauses, his stare slowly sweeping the class's circle of chairs, a single finger tapping the center of his chest. "*Our* paradise," he says.

This is the strategy for now: to draw on his students' tacit ambition. He will appeal to their desire (which he both encourages and admires) to become literary artists, their quest for those skills that constitute the guild of mythos-minded thinking. And so he points now to a professional connection, one that paradoxically transcends all the uniquenesses of the site-specific, even as it honors their sense-drenched appearance, even as it invites onto its stage "all things counter, original, spare, strange."[10]

From the anonymous authors of the original myth to Sophocles who revived and renewed it with his artful script, from Conrad to Ralph Ellison, from Herman Melville to Alice Munro, a continuity persists, the teacher now insists—a common approach to the enduring task of a mind mapping its place. Despite the very real differences between, say, Aeschylus's Greece and Conrad's U.K., and, too, the genuine idiosyncrasies of each separate author's temper and taste, they share the same graces and obligations of mythos-minded thinking. For each author the Eden of his or her artfulness depends on that special species of accuracy that, in successfully simulating the act of perception, admits differences as well as likenesses. *Their* version of paradise is that garden of delight— and delight, the teacher notes, is a literal translation of the Hebrew word *eden*—that bravely accepts the limits of the senses, those boundaries that come with being site-specific. Theirs is a delight that admits the pain of imperfection. And because the *wrong* of that pain is true to our experience in every age and place, it is, in a very real sense, also *right*.

---

9. Wallace Stevens, "The Poems of Our Climate," *The Palm at the End of the Mind: Selected Poems* (New York: Vintage, 1972), 158.

10. Gerard Manley Hopkins, "Pied Beauty": https://www.poetryfoundation.org/poems/44399/pied-beauty.

LIVING IN LANGUAGE

the news that STAYS news

"This is what they do ... what you and I try to do," the teacher slyly adds, then pauses to gauge his students' reaction. He's flattered them, he knows, by preadmitting them to the guild of artful thinkers. But if his students both accept that such a guild exists and admit that they wish to belong to it, then he is already much closer to persuading them that *Oedipus Rex* might still prove real and relevant to today's student-author. And this tactic has arisen naturally because the professor has long believed in what he just professed—both in the relevance of the myth and in the reality of the transmillennial guild. More grandly still, he actually believes, with a conviction that has ripened throughout these middle years, that the imperfect *is* our paradise.

And though he's stressed at first the confraternity of artists, the teacher also believes, more grandly still, in the common grounding of the existential. He believes that each sentient person (ancient or modern, local or foreign, mythos-minded author or logos-minded engineer) shares a plight: the anxious fate of being free. Which is what he now says. Aiming to link the mission of the author to the condition of being human, the teacher tells his students that as homo sapiens, the thinking creature, we must imagine options and choose among them—but without knowing enough to guarantee the outcome. If the preferred figure for knowledge is light, the teacher now insists, then we are at best translucent thinkers. Moment by moment, day after day, as we try to navigate our way past the next inch and through the next hour, we do so staring "through a glass, darkly,"[11] and each of our metaphors mimics in miniature that ongoing drama.

"This is what we do, what you and I try to do: we simulate the drama of consciousness itself. We restage not just the facts of that drama but its temper too. We reanimate that state of mind, both eager and anxious, where the rewards of recognition are always shadowed by the very real risk of misapprehension.

"And if a metaphor succeeds, if the reader finds its connection both surprising and apt, then the experience of discovery will be, well ... " the teacher pauses, oddly shy, as if he feels himself unworthy of the word now brimming on his lips, " ... *beautiful*. And it remains beautiful however ugly or outrageous the specific occasion that its slings and arrows are aiming to depict. At a deeper level of simulation beyond its evocation

---

11. 1 Corinthians, 13: 12.

of the narrative moment, each apt metaphor sparks in us a profoundly reassuring hopefulness. The recognition it initiates renews our faith that we can, after all, make a kind of sense of our amazing place—make sense despite the narrow scope and scale of our site-specific minds. More to the point here, its accuracy proves so powerfully persuasive *because* it admits those same limits. Mythos-minded truth seems especially real (and so relevant to us) because *its* variety of news includes a semblance of the noise that confuses our days.

"And as with the part," the teacher now adds, extending his arms in an expansive gesture, "so too with the whole." (This is the route back, the tactical pivot he's planned all along. As the artful magician, at just the right moment, redirects our attention back to the coin that, abracadabra, has reappeared in his hand, the teacher will now return to *Oedipus Rex*, hoping that his timing, too, will do the trick—that it will supply the surprise of recognition, the light out of heat that serves to convince.) "To animate awareness and convey their savvy news, our artful stories, too, are infused with differences."

As proof, the teacher cites the deliberate distortions of fairy tales and fables, their overt rejection of the merely documentary. He reminds them, too, of the value of stories from other cultures—how the fitful strangeness of, say, a Nigerian play or Columbian novel can reawaken an awareness of our own default presumptions about the real and the relevant. "No one knows England," he tells his class, rephrasing then an adage whose source he can't recall, "no one knows England who only England knows.

"And as with the plots of other cultures," he adds, completing the sequence of analogies to bring them all the way back, "so too with the myths of distant eras. There *is* no perception without notable differences, and the oldest stories from our own tradition can sometimes supply the most edifying kinds of dissonance. Still, let me be very clear about this. I'm *not* endorsing the sort of ancestor worship that rotely adores the artifacts of our tribal past merely because it is *our* past. Emerson got it right, I think: 'our admiration of the antique is not admiration of the old, but of the natural.'[12] That at least ought to be our goal. Refusing nostalgia's gauzy glow, we should admire our oldest myths only insomuch as they can clarify for us what's natural in our lives, what's real and so still relevant.

12. Ralph Waldo Emerson, "History," *Selected Essays* (Chicago: Peoples Book Club), 17.

"And with *that* crucial task, we need all the help we can get. For a species whose inventions can radically change the shape and pace of everyday experience, any notion of the natural is periodically tested. And because our site-specific minds can only see through a glass darkly, we find it hard to extract the germ of the natural from the chaff of passing fashion. What is essential to the human experience? What is truly lasting? These are questions that must be posed and reposed, repeatedly contested."

(In support of this last point, and as a further means of opening up about the person who professed it, let me add this: although he just quoted him, the teacher himself doesn't entirely agree with Emerson's understanding of the natural—they have their differences. And because the context seems right, he now chooses to cite another author with whom he often disagrees.)

"Ezra Pound wrote this," the teacher says, and turning then, he prints on the board a sentence first composed many years before, the ghost of a thought reassuming in chalk its original form. "He wrote: 'Literature is news that STAYS news.'[13] And since the news that STAYS news can serve as a reasonable definition of what we mean by the natural, we might also say this: that just as wrong can be right and the imperfect be our paradise, the *artifice* of the literary can best convey the heart of the *natural*.

"What has stayed true, and what has not? Which features have proven to be mere cultural costume, as opposed to those that still actively calibrate our ongoing lives? By the simple virtue of their age," the teacher insists, "our ancestral stories can help illuminate the difference between the two, and so serve as a vitally effective reality check. When we enter *their* fictive sites, ruled by long-dead gods and extinct local customs, the noise of the ephemeral can seem more obvious and so, too, amplify by contrast the news that's still natural—the news we need to know to navigate our way through the here-and-now.

"So you were right," the teacher says, addressing Chad again: that student whose dissonance, whose daring to doubt the reality and relevance of *Oedipus Rex*, has triggered this improvised lecture, which, interrupting the normal course of the class, might prove clarifying, but then might not. "Right to call to mind all those features of the Greek antique—kingship, patriarchy, life-altering oracles—that *didn't* stay news.

---

13. Ezra Pound, *ABC of Reading* (New York: New Directions, 1960), 29.

"But even noting those differences (and all the more persuasive, perhaps, because of them), doesn't there remain a continuous link between our *now* and his *then*? Isn't the fate Oedipus suffers—that, despite the best intentions and an impressive array of talents to enact them, his knowledge is insufficient to avoid a catastrophic ending—a familiar one? Though heightened in the way that myths often do and costumed to fit another time and place, although not *equal to*, isn't Oedipus's story still *like unto* ours?

"Think about it," the teacher says, his stare again sweeping the class. "Walk a mile in Oedipus's shoes . . . or should I say, his sandals?"

to know or not to know . . .

The teacher pauses, relieved to note his students' wry smiles, the contagious animation of a little muffled laughter: they've followed him this far, they "got" the joke. The truth be told, he isn't sure what sort of footwear Oedipus would've worn—it's just the sort of fact he tends to forget. But the medium of the joke was the real message intended, the comic interplay between the walk-a-mile cliché and his instant correction, that repetition with a difference (*sandals* for *shoes*) aiming to revive the truth embalmed in the moribund phrase.

All too quickly, though, his buoyant relief deflates into doubt. *Do they get it*, the teacher wonders as he stares through the fog obscuring the moment? Not the part but the whole? Not the small joke but the larger one that can get us all, that might soon get them? After walking a mile in Oedipus's shoes—in his sandals? slippers? sheepskin boots?—do they recognize themselves, their own potential lot, in the plotting of the myth?

Rereading their expressions, he suspects not. Abstractly perhaps, for his students are smart. But not in such a way, hearts aligning with their thoughts, that they will walk-a-mile differently in the days ahead. Surveying the class, the teacher doubts that his students believe in the actual and amazing fragility of "the facts"—in how tentative our grasp of reality can be. And who could blame them, raised as they've been on the logos of progress, the mythos of magic, the teeth of their souls rotted to the pulp on the cotton candy spun by ten thousand happy endings? And, too, by all those IPO-funded utopias to come? No, his students aren't convinced, and so he'll have to try again.

"Remember Chad's story?" he asks the class.

"*Phoenix?*" a young woman quickly says. She's the one, he recalls, whose images are potentially lovely but whose clumsy syntax can throttle their beauty in the midst of its expression, twisting the folds of a sensual rose into the knot of a logical maze.

The others nod—they remember it well, just as he expected. Once again, his tactics have shifted. He'll use a story of their own—better still by Chad—to plumb the secret sharing between the old Greek myth and their current lives in the Pacific Northwest.

"That's right—*Phoenix?* Can someone recap the basic facts for us?"

Together, they do. In this limited sense, the class behaves like a real community by drawing on a common core of experience, conversing and correcting to fashion together a consensus version of the past—in this case, the summary of a story they've read and discussed. Meanwhile, unsettled by the sudden shift in subject, the author of *Phoenix?* sits silently among them. Reading Chad's face, the teacher recognizes all too well its species of uneasiness: at once flattered (we all want to be remembered) and anxious (but remembrance is also a form of judgment, and life's next rejection might be in the offing.)

With a two character cast, Jared and Erin, and a circular structure, *Phoenix?* had dramatized a painfully unresolved romance. ("Is there any other kind?" one of the students had joked at the time, his smile a thinly masked scar, his slumping body a pillow pummeled one too many times.) Together they recall the story's quick start. Jared is sitting in a coffee shop while working on his laptop, highlighting jobs posted on a website, when his phone receives a two-word text out of the ether: "Follow me." The plot then retreats in time to its central concern, depicting Jared and Erin's torturous affair, its alternating poles of attraction and repulsion. The long flashback doesn't end until the next-to-last page when, after their final fight, Erin acts on a cousin's invitation and abruptly moves to Phoenix, Arizona, her true motivation captured in the final words of her farewell text: "*No mas.*"

Although the story had suffered from melodrama, the teacher had admired that use of the Spanish, a small touch that subtly suggested Erin's current commitment to abide *there*, in the place of her escape, to adopt its foreign ways. Better still, he liked Chad's willingness to leave, as the question mark in the title clearly conveyed, the problem unresolved. The story ends with Jared still staring at Erin's latest message, still pondering its sudden invitation (or was it a command?) to follow her to Phoenix, still weighing whether or not to take this last chance for a better future with his ex. (Or would it turn out to be the misery of the past merely restaged in a new locale?)

But now, charged with persuading the class of the reality and relevance of *Oedipus Rex*, the teacher is less concerned with the quality of the story's artifice than the character of the natural that it might represent. And so when he asks the class to reconsider the dilemma Jared faces, he quickly narrows the task at hand. He's not concerned for now, he says, with either the artfulness of the circular structure or the decision to leave the drama unresolved. Nor does he care to hear what they, as empathetic readers, think that Jared *ought* to do—though that, too, would make for an interesting discussion some other day. No, he wants them to focus instead on the predicament itself, on Jared's either-or choice as an event representative of the crucial decisions we all must face. He is asking them, he says, to think and think hard, about the fate of being free.

(*This is going nowhere,* a silent voice observes, that critic-in-residence who haunts his head, neutrally assessing all he says and does—*you're being too abstract.*)

"Take Hamlet," the teacher quickly says by way of self-correction. "Now *there's* a man who's facing a stark predicament, the harshest of either-or choices. How's he phrase it in the play?" The teacher pauses. "His most famous line?" he quickly cues, after panicking a bit: this is one of the very few literary quotations he expects them to know.

"You mean, *to be or not to be?*"

"Right, to be or not to be—that *is* the question. And not just for Hamlet. The capacity to kill ourselves is the most extreme expression of our native autonomy. And in the context of the play, that's not the only stark decision that Hamlet faces. How should he respond to the ghost of his father, its horrible story of regicide and fratricide, its plea for revenge? In the middle of the play, to believe or not believe what his father's ghost has told him, *that* becomes for a while the most pressing question.

"Now let me ask you this." (Pacing back and forth behind his desk, he has spotted his copy of *Oedipus Rex*, which he now waves in the air—a little too dramatically, the critic-in-residence silently complains.) "In Sophocles' revision of what was, already, an antique myth, how does the hero's dilemma get restaged? Using Hamlet's own words as a handy template, how can we phrase the painful dilemma that Oedipus faces as the play proceeds?" This time, he doesn't bother waiting to provide some cues: "To be or not to be, to believe or not believe . . ."

"To know or not to know," a student softly says.

(He's the one who rarely speaks but whose total engagement is never in doubt. Turning toward him, the teacher now notes that he is wearing a t-shirt whose own two-word text—*questioning authority* . . . —skews the cliché just enough to make it interesting again. Converted from a hectoring command into a gentle participial phrase, the old bumper-sticker sentiment now reads like a personalized caption: an accurate if slightly disconcerting description of what is going on right now, behind the usual veil of silence that this student presents . . . disconcerting, that is—the teacher wryly notes—when *you* happen to be the authority in the room.)

"Exactly," the teacher says. "To know or not to know: that's *his* fateful question now. As a man shaped by his time and place, Oedipus believes in oracles. He believes that it *is* natural that an unsolved murder can curse a city with plagues and famine, and so he promises, as that community's leader, to find the covert killer of the old king, Laius. But once the shape of the evidence begins to become clear, does he really want to pursue the answer he promised? The ironic bind of the plot makes him both the curse of Thebes and its potential savior, both the author of the crime and its assigned avenger.

"Using a much later play to clarify the challenge that he faces, we might say this. We might say that in Sophocles' renewal of the ancient myth, Oedipus has become Hamlet and Claudius rolled into one. And given the first glimmers of self-recognition, does the just avenger really want to know what he himself has done?"

Pleased with his comparison, the teacher pauses for a little self-congratulation, only to discover just a moment later that he's lost his flow of thought.

"Let's think about that," he says at last, stalling. And, silent then, he does.

the new heroic virtue

"Know thyself," the teacher starts again. Folding his arms against his chest, he hugs his open copy of *Oedipus Rex*. "Now *there's* a text message we might examine when thinking about Oedipus and comparing him to Jared. For those were the words inscribed on the temple of Apollo at the Oracle at Delphi. This most modern of sentiments, the ethical essence of enlightened individualism—an adamant endorsement of self-awareness—was stamped in stone at one of the Greeks' holiest sites.

PHOENIX?

"For Sophocles and his contemporaries that two-word command represented a meaningful shift in emphasis: a revaluation of the heroic character, as it had been dramatized in Homer's epics. Along with the fierceness of Achilles and the wiliness of Odysseus, the new Greek hero must also now possess a moral self-awareness. And so," the teacher says, "in trying to accommodate the new ethos with the old, Sophocles does what the artful usually do. He reenacts a familiar pattern but with a telling difference. Giving the antique myth a contemporary gloss, he focuses on that phase of its plot most relevant to the new ethical sense: that recalibration of virtue, centered in Athens, that places the highest value on an accountable individualism rooted in self-knowledge.

"And if that's the new heroic virtue," the teacher says, "then it has to be tested. No pussyfooting around for Sophocles. He doesn't bother with the merely difficult case but picks and probes the near impossible one. For surely if any of the old mythic characters has a plausible excuse for avoiding the truth about himself, that character is Oedipus. From the host of traditional stories he might revive, Sophocles selects the one that supplies the most difficult trial for the new Greek ethos. Through magnifying that one short phase of the old mythic plot when the middle-aged sovereign is charged with saving Thebes by solving the mystery of its old king's murder, this tragedy deliberately intensifies both the excruciating difficulty and the civic necessity of moral self-awareness. The spirit of the age is demanding of each citizen 'know thyself,' and although by turns as furious, paranoid, and terrified as Hamlet, this reimagined Oedipus finally heeds that high command. Alone among the cast, he stays committed to the new heroic task: he solves the crime committed by himself.

"Where an older hero, like Achilles, would sacrifice his life for the tribe, this new type willingly surrenders his ethical standing. Oedipus becomes heroic through freely choosing the agony of disgrace over the anesthesia of ignorance. The old myth has been replayed but with a crucial shift in emphasis. Through a set of artful variations, an old mythic figure has been reborn as the most relevant of contemporary Greek exemplars.

"Does that make any sense?" the teacher now asks. "This is slippery stuff, I admit—but not unrelated to points I made before. We might say this: that *Oedipus Rex* supplies just the sort of jazzy cover to a standard hit that Monk himself applauded. For here, too, *wrong*—or rather, the self-discovery of wrongs—finally proves *right*. Here, too, the admission of the very worst of imperfections paradoxically defines the best that one can be. In Sophocles' cover of the old oral myth, we're given a hero who proves his moral stature through the very act of relinquishing it."

"Confession," a student says half-aloud, as much to herself as to the class. She's the one whose prose gravitates toward intricate magnifications of mundane moments, the one who prefers the still-life of wonder to the theatrical motions of theme-driven plot. And turning toward her now, the teacher notices for the first time a small silver cross which, dangling from her neck, fitfully reflects the room's overhead lights, blinking out now a double message: *symbol . . . substance / symbol . . . substance.*

(Has she worn it all quarter, the teacher wonders? Is her cross one of those fragile facts which, saved from oblivion, are only made real and relevant by the demands of the moment? How many other facts are still awaiting the justice of his scrupulous attention? How many ghosts, like Hamlet's father, are lurking in the fog and begging to be heard?)

"That's an excellent point," the teacher says. "Something of the Athenian spirit still abides in our religious lives. The Christian tradition has long accepted that admitting our personal wrongs against man and God is spiritually right. And, say what you will about this play's reliance on superstition, it's hard to imagine a more radical endorsement of the political value of enlightened individualism, which is as well a hallmark of our democratic credo. In *Oedipus Rex*, the pursuit of self-awareness becomes the very source for securing social justice; knowing thyself is not only compatible with, it's inseparable from, the heroic act of saving the community."

everyone knows that no one should say . . .

"Speaking of communities . . . " a student interrupts and then pauses, his eyebrows raised, his palms turned up. The teacher stares at him dumbly: he knows he's being cued, but now *he's* the one who doesn't get it.

"*Phoenix?*"

"*Our* response to Jared's dilemma?" another fills in.

"Right—Jared. I haven't forgotten . . . well, not entirely anyway," the teacher adds, acknowledging his students' skeptical smiles with one of his own. "Let's put it this way: let's say that as a good American (no irony intended), as a worthy heir to the culture that revived Athenian individualism for its own place and time, Jared shares some of those values we've been discussing here. Let's just say that, as the ruler of his own life, Jared is being tested in the way that Oedipus is within the play."

The teacher hesitates: something is wrong here, something's not quite right. And in the rich simultaneity of his consciousness, he becomes aware now of both a dryness in his throat and a flaw in his comparison: *substance . . . symbol / substance . . . symbol . . .*

"Let me take that back," he says after clearing his throat by coughing twice. "The differences outweigh the likenesses there, don't they? Jared's not really like *that* Oedipus, the one restaged for Sophocles' play. He's not a middle-aged man who, in order to craft the best possible future, first must account for a long and weighty past."

(*No, that would be you*, the critic-in-residence coolly observes.)

"No, given his age, Jared's more the prince of prediction than the king of retrospection. Which means that, to get a better likeness, we need to magnify an earlier phase of the myth. If we line up the two plots, the Jared we find on both the first and last page more resembles the young Oedipus who, after traveling to Delphi, has just heard the dreadful prophecy. Each has received some shocking news, and the dilemma they now share, the question they both face is . . . "Again he supplies the old sequence of cues. "To be or not to be, to know or not to know, to . . ."

"Go or not to go."

It's the author himself, the teacher notes with surprise. Chad has spoken for the first time since questioning the relevance of *Oedipus Rex*, and there is something about his voice—a hitch of hesitancy, the premonition of a wince—that triggers a caution, begging a study of his face and posture.

"Right," the teacher finally says and tries to nod reassuringly. "To go or not to go—that's Jared's dilemma, too. He's received Erin's plea (or is it a command?), that two-word text out of the ether, and he has no choice now but to choose. Even to pretend that he hasn't received the message, to hit *delete* in his memory as well as on his phone, would be a freely made decision, one as consequential as any other. The message has been received, 'follow me,' and sooner or later he'll have to respond. And not only is fate, in the form of Erin, forcing Jared now to choose; the range of options has also been reduced, in practical effect, to just these two. Soon, very soon, on the next page or the next of Jared's life-story, he'll have to say 'I will' or say '*No mas*.'

"And let's assume, too, that *our* prince will be heroic in the Sophoclean sense. Let's assume that, hoping to make the best possible decision,

Jared *will* strive to know himself. And not the Romantic version—that glossy celebrity in splendid isolation—but the character fashioned from the ongoing marriage of mind with place. The self as a house inspirited by ghosts, some menacing, some mentoring; as composed by values, some logical, some mythical—some conscious, most not. Let's assume that our prince from Seattle will probe that house, and so know his self in all its resonant relations. Jared as son, Jared as friend, Jared as both would-be author and economic man, the person who chose this posting over that one when highlighting jobs. But, most importantly, Jared as lover. And not Jared, the star, adored in isolation, but Jared *with* Erin."

(Watch it, the critic-in-residence now whispers in his ear—*you be careful here*.)

It's just a bodiless voice, one ghost among many in the busy haunted house of a middle-aged self. But it's also the one he knows best, the ghost he trusts most. *Watch it*, the critic has advised, and the teacher now agrees. They've become, one might say, secret sharers. Like pilot and captain, their inner conversations steer the teacher's actions, measuring together, through the scrim of dim eyes, that murky discrepancy between two uncertainties, always trying to realign what actually *is* with what, in their view, *ought* to be—the true with the good. And the critic's warning him to be careful here has reminded him now that, just last week, Chad had given them both some cause for concern.

It was one of those anecdotes that teachers share with family and friends, a potential contribution to the latest concept in "reality television": *America's Funniest Classroom Incidents*. But unlike the Flagrant Plagiarist or the Drooling Addict, Chad had been, up till then, a model student, and this incident occurred well into the quarter when the rules about smartphones had long been set. Nevertheless, in the midst of a lively discussion on time transitions, Chad's phone rang out—or rather *sang*.

It was one of those irritatingly chipper tunes, reminiscent of ice cream trucks or merry-go-rounds, that seem to guarantee with animatronic sappiness that this incoming call WILL MAKE YOU HAPPY! Worse, contrary to the usual routine, when the offending student would effuse apologies, Chad made no effort to turn it off. Instead, he removed the phone from a backpack at his feet, lifting it very slowly, as if heeding an alarm whose danger, though real, he had yet to define and so couldn't disarm.

All discussion quickly ceased. The sappy tune still played. Now the obvious but oblivious center of attention, Chad appeared to read the caller's ID. Never looking up, he murmured in a voice both anxious and grave, as if he were, say, a surgeon on call or the president's national security adviser: "I have to take this." At which point, he rose, turned, and, after bumping into a desk, exited the room without another word.

The latch clicked shut. A moment passed before the remaining students, their amazement resettling like the shaken snow in a paperweight's globe, turned back to the class, expecting a response to Chad's rude behavior. It was, the teacher might joke when being interviewed by the host of *America's Funniest Classroom Incidents*, "one of those lead-or-leave moments." Determined not to extend the disruption, he merely shook his head in mute disapproval, and then, pushing ahead, restarted their discussion.

But though everyone made an effort, the focus had been lost, and the students were distracted even as they talked. For the university in question—I was remiss, perhaps, in not mentioning before—is state-supported and routinely underfunded, some of its buildings cheaply constructed. And so it came to pass that, despite the closed door, Chad's voice, now busily engaged in that call he *had* to take, was radiating from the adjacent hall and through the room's porous wall with distressing clarity. Fate, as formed by a complex interweaving of freely made decisions—by governors, legislators, architects, and schedulers—was decreeing that *this* class now receive *these* oral messages out of the ether. Someone's private self was leaking into the commons, and what were they, as stewards of that commons, to do about it?

The emphasis was on *they*, the deliberation plural. For this would turn out to be one of those tacitly made group decisions that are all the more grounded in the silent agreements that fashion any community's character. When in Rome, most choose to mind the ethos of its place. And so it came to pass that, given the civic demeanor of the Puget Sound region—with its site-specific blend of Scandinavian calm, Asian decorum, and West Coast live-and-let-live-ism—it seemed good to the class then, it simply seemed right to pretend together that they were not overhearing every word of Chad's side in what was turning out to be an intensely personal conversation. Among those facts that they tacitly agreed not to acknowledge, while feigning full attention to a formal discussion on time transitions, was the obvious consonance between the phone conversation taking place in the hall and the plot of a story they had just discussed a week or two before—a story called *Phoenix?* whose narrative dilemma, centering on an unhappy romance between Jared and Erin, had been left unresolved.

All of which should clarify why the teacher is quick to agree to *be careful here*, but doesn't yet explain why he chooses to proceed at all—why he is willing to risk wounding or offending the very student he most hopes to convince.

In fact, despite the frequent awkwardness of their prose—which, after all, he can help them correct—the teacher has come to admire his students' willingness to expose these sketchy shadows of their most vulnerable selves. And if he were inclined, he might show Chad now how this fictionalization of his own life story related to earlier points in their discussion. He might note, for example, that even though the most artful translation of your substantial self into the symbolic ghost of a fictional character necessarily results in distortions and revisions—even though Jared can only be at best *like unto* and never *equal to* the whole truth of Chad—it is precisely that tension between likenesses and differences that can spark a revelation.

The same aesthetic tactics that alert a mind to its given place can also awaken that mind to its own peculiar nature. Just as wrong can be right and the imperfect be our paradise, self-awareness can paradoxically arise from the deliberate self-estrangement of fictionalization. *Distance*, he might say, crafting an artful variation on his earlier citation:

> *distance*
> *(if you're interested)*
> *leads to SELF-discovery*

Or he might choose to cite another favorite line from Emerson, noting how such a literary strategy "remedies the defect of our too great nearness to ourselves."[14]

The teacher might say all of these things but chooses not to. For the irony of classes such as these—so apparently free, so conducive to self-expression, and where, given an apt context, students are licensed to use almost any fucking word, describe any ugly human action—the irony of discussions in moments like this is that their success still depends on a decorous reticence. The search for truth's elusive traces requires the suppression of truth's most flagrant fact. In this case, everyone knows that no one should say what everyone knows: that Jared has been fashioned as Chad's symbolic ghost.

---

14. Emerson, "History," 4.

PHOENIX?

In this silence that follows the critic's warning to be careful here—a silence whose brevity, I confess, is being violated by my ongoing attempts to capture the actual and amazing richness of the moment: the glint of a silver cross; the soft touch of an open book against the teacher's chest; the words of those mythic ghosts who, though thousands of years old, still haunt his current hopes, still customize his actions; all the weave and weight of fate, including the history of this class *and* the decorum of the region *and* the politics of acoustics *and* the archeology of emotion as it is currently being mined from the face and posture of a certain student-author—out of this same superabundant silence, the teacher notes a subtle but significant shift in mood: his students' peaking interest.

Because the members of this class did hear Chad's most intimate voice leak into their room just the week before, and because they too are of the age when most romances remain unresolved, they not only can, they *want* to read themselves into the story of Jared's dilemma. They're eager now to know what will happen next.

Through this shift in tactics, this turn toward *Phoenix?*, the teacher has won his students' engagement, just as he intended—but what will he do with it?

a beautiful likeness . . .

"Yes," the teacher says, glancing at the clock. (Does he have enough time to pull a rabbit from his hat, to complete somehow a surprising yet apt sequence of thought?) "Let's presume that, in deciding whether to go or not, Jared will be as committed to self-awareness as Oedipus once was. That fated to be free and facing this decision, he will thoroughly search the haunted house of self in all its resonant relations: Jared as son, Jared as friend and, especially, Jared and Erin as former lovers."

"The scene at the creek," a student interjects.

"Yes, the scene at the creek and the one that followed it."

"You mean their fight in Erin's jeep."

"Yes, the whole messy mix of desire and discord, of love turned to rage, of longing blurred with fear and then frayed to sheer exhaustion. We're presuming this—that whether or not he is aware of its history, Jared will be a true heir to our tradition of self-reflection. Because that *is* how it works."

Brows raised, still amazed himself by the nature of the news he is about to convey, the teacher allows his gaze to sweep very slowly the arc of his class.

"Ideals inscribed in languages long dead, policies shaped by forgotten debates in now-ruined forums, distant battlefield reversals whose annals have been lost . . . this is how it works for a species whose thinking is historically grounded: even *un*recalled, ancient events continue to haunt our present-tense lives. They still constellate our thoughts and customize our actions, consciously or not.

"And so even if he hasn't read *Oedipus Rex*, it is not unreasonable to expect that Jared would value introspection. And we're going to presume not only the urge to know himself but the competence to do so, for they're not the same thing. And not only the competence to know himself but also the will power to apply that self-knowledge on behalf of the good, whatever the good might mean on this occasion. And there's more. In our role as mythos-minded thinkers, we're going to grant him not only the will to strive on behalf of the good but also those skills that can transform good intentions into substantiated facts, the ideal made real and relevant within the matrix of his everyday life. Can we agree on that too? No? . . . Yes? . . .

"Good," he says. "But it *is* a lot, I admit, and so before we move on, let's be clear on this too: the status we're assigning him through the artifice of our fictionalizing is heroic, not divine. Our Jared will be intelligent and effective but not omniscient or omnipotent; he'll be virtuous but not immaculate. Given the circumstances, he will be the best that he can humanly be—which is to say, the best that *we* can be.

"Yes, let's be clear on that too. Because it *is* our topic here. It's the one that we've been approaching since Chad chose to question the authority of this play." (Unfolding his arms, the teacher now lifts the paperback book above his head: how thin, how light, how *immaterial*, it seems—so little mass yet so much lasting momentum within the human sphere.) "What's the best that *we* can be, this class of student-authors and their middle-aged professor in postmillennial America? And does that still relate in any credible way to Sophocles' play—which was, I want to stress again, his attempt to revive the reality and relevance of an already ancient myth?

"That's not to say," the teacher quickly adds, "that Jared's life is exactly equivalent to yours or mine, but his is the far more familiar story. There's much less dissonance, a higher ratio of likenesses to differences.

We not only recognize his place—the coffee shop, the smartphone, the jogging shoes or hiking boots; we also share many of his deepest views and values. We're not likely to accept, as he's not likely to accept, either the righteousness of kingship or the truthfulness of oracles. Imagining ourselves as Oedipus in Corinth might be a stretch, but it should be easy to project ourselves into Jared's predicament. We all agree, don't we, that *his* version of the dilemma 'to go or not to go' is one that remains especially real and relevant for us?

"Good," the teacher says, after scanning the class. "So let's do what we've been trained to do. Let's put *ourselves* there. In the coffee shop, sitting at a table, scrolling through the job postings on a laptop's screen: so many separate links to possible futures, so many other lives we might choose to lead—none of them, though, in Phoenix, Arizona. And now the phone pings. And now, assuming Jared's fate, we read that unexpected text, its sudden invitation to follow Erin: yet another possible life to live, another complication in our attempt to map what ought to happen next. We squint, we stare through the looking glass darkly. Should we say 'I will,' or should we say '*No mas*'?"

The teacher pauses, deliberately this time, using the delay to intensify suspense. And as he makes his students wait, he senses the mood in the room shifting again, less eager than anxious, as if this discussion, too, is a call they *have* to take, but one whose message they now doubt WILL MAKE THEM HAPPY!

"At some point, after all, Jared will have to decide. He can ignore or repress, he can ask for advice or wait for a sign. He can court and then cow to his own oracle at Delphi—oh, say, use that day's horoscope as his definitive guide. But because the message came to him, because *his* is the life that must be lived in the aftermath of its reception, Jared has no choice but to choose."

The teacher pauses. He's hearing, I might say, two conflicting voices in the ghostly ship of self, two would-be pilots for his captain, one insisting *pull back!*, the other *steer close!* A moment passes before he decides, and as he points then to Chad, the teacher can sense the anxiety of the class magnify: everyone knows that no one should say what . . .

"Am I right about that, Chad? That however hard he might try, Jared can't avoid the duty to decide?"

Chad blinks, then nods, exhaling a soft *yes* less spoken than mimed.

"Good," the teacher says. "Jared's fated to be free, he *has* to choose—as do you, as do I every day of our lives. But in this case, remember, that we're also allotting him, through the artifice of our fictionalizing, the best possible traits for making up his mind.

"Now, given those presumptions, this is *my* claim about the natural: that in making the best possible decision, our hero is still very much akin to Oedipus in Corinth. Yes, a lot has changed in the three thousand years from the myth's conception to our story's completion. If this likeness is to hold, I'll admit, it will have to survive some serious cultural dissonance. Jared and Oedipus speak different languages, practice different customs, trust different mental measures, worship very different gods. And, yes, as the beneficiary of progress in many fields, Jared is empowered in ways Oedipus is not.

"But our advances in technology haven't eliminated the underlying quandaries of being and knowing. The moral life—that is to say, the fate of being free—is not amenable to a technical fix, nor can it be reduced to some final solution cast in the image of a mathematical proof. Whether the message takes a month to arrive by sandal-wrapped feet or less than a second by wireless signals, the latest news still intrudes on our tranquility; it still demands a response from us. Now as then, moment after moment, day after day, we have to decide what's real, relevant, practical, valuable—what actually *is* as measured against what *ought* to be. The answers may vary widely from tribe to tribe, but those questions, at their base, have stayed the same.

"And though there can be considerable variation between persons or ages, the *final* limits on the accuracy of our decision-making haven't really changed. Some minds are naturally sharper than others, some cultural spectacles do prove clearer, but even at our sharpest and clearest we still remain translucent thinkers. Our minds, like our bodies, are inextricably wed to their limitations. Measured metaphorically, the fallibility of our thoughts shadows very closely the mortality of our flesh: they make for a true and, one might even say, a beautiful likeness.

"Does that make sense?" the teacher asks, surveying the class. "It ought to sound familiar at least. For all I'm really saying is this: I'm insisting again that 'the imperfect is our paradise.' As the swimming mammal must swim or die, the thinking mammal must think to survive—it must, that is, make up its mind. All the while, though, and *now* no less than *then*, the certainty of the task is inextricably wed to the uncertainty of its results.

"Or so *I'm* contending," the teacher now says, tapping his chest. "Although we've made Jared an heroic figure, the best that he can humanly be, he's no less vulnerable to error than Oedipus in Corinth, no less accountable for those errors than Oedipus in Thebes. Despite his good intentions and an impressive array of talents to enact them, it's simply true that our hero, too, might suffer a calamity, and one ironically fashioned from what seemed at the time the best possible decisions."

I'm sorry to report

"*Calamity?*" Carl says.

"Jared's going to *murder* his father, *marry* his mother?" another student adds, and there's no disguising her skepticism.

"Come on, guys—you know, if you've been listening, that isn't what I meant. Not the same fate literally. Not *equal to* but nevertheless, in significant ways, *like unto*."

"But what fate could possibly be like *that?*"

"We need an example," the girl with the cross suggests.

"Something site-specific," *questioning authority* . . . quickly adds, and so thoroughly has he been trapped by the terms of his own argument, the teacher has to laugh.

"Fair enough. You're right: calamity is far too abstract. I've been theorizing, not dramatizing, as a mythos-minded thinker should. So let's say it, do it—let's think this problem through together. How could a character who seems so right go so wrong, and what might that wrong specifically be? We need a possible scenario, a plausible plot. We need," the teacher says, revising a definition that he's used before, "a narrative sequence with calamitous consequences—with *unforeseeable* calamitous consequences.

"But first, to get that plot started, Jared has to make up his mind. Which means that we, as good readers-turned-authors, have to make up *our* minds about his likely behavior. For our purposes now, it doesn't really matter which of the two options he picks, but we do need a decision. So let's just say that, after hours or days of astute introspection, after knowing himself and minding his place, Jared chooses . . . "

"To go," a student insists. It's Amanda, the one who recalled the scene at the creek, and she clearly has formed an adamant opinion as to what ought to happen next.

"Sure—why not? We'll start with that. He emails Erin back . . . "

"Texts," another student corrects him.

"Okay, that makes sense. Cryptic message for cryptic message, he texts her back: to Erin's 'follow me' he responds with a yes. He types 'I will.' That, then, is the context we need to consider when assessing my claim that the fates of these men, though separated by two millennia of cultural change, can still be similar, if not the same. And to do that we have to examine closely the more familiar journey in relation to the stranger one. We need to compare the highway-drive-in-pursuit-of-true-love with the-dusty-flight-from-a prophecy-of-a-dreadful-crime-to-come. The differences are obvious, but there are also some likenesses, no? So let's make a list of those, starting with the most obvious ones."

"Well," Carl says, "if you want obvious, the two are about the same age."

"Right, and age does matter. Both heroes are still young; they're in that pivotal phase when the habits of a lifetime are still being fashioned. Neither, for example, is married yet, and that proves consequential to both their stories. What else?"

"Both were slammed with a message from out of the blue." (It's Rob, the student who had joked that all romances were unresolved.) "Their content's different, but both are the kind that would screw with your mind in a major league way."

"Right again—there's no doubt about that. Each has been forced to face an unexpected choice, a life-altering dilemma, and acting out of the best intentions when facing that dilemma, each has decided to . . ."

"Hit the road."

"Yes, but not in the lighter sense that phrase suggests. Ambushed by a message and faced with its stark either-or choices, each young hero chooses to go. Each makes the climactic decision to leave his home, and to leave it "for good," in both senses of that term. Although, to be honest here, we need to admit that, when hitting the road, Oedipus is running *away*—or rather, *thinks* he's running away—while Jared is running *toward*. And that one is motivated primarily by fear, the other primarily by love.

"Still," the teacher quickly adds, "we shouldn't exaggerate those differences either. Emotions, after all, are rarely pure. Oedipus's fear when fleeing Corinth is surely rooted in his love for the only father he knows, the one he mistakenly believes that he's fated to kill. And Jared's love is, just as surely, tinged with fear, a justifiable anxiety that things with Erin might fall apart again.

"Okay, that's good enough to start. We have some likenesses now to counter the differences, a baseline for comparison. The question, then, is this: how might Jared's story resemble the old myth? In what way or ways might his apparently best possible decision turn out to be disastrous instead?"

Because he doesn't have an immediate answer himself, the teacher reviews aloud, as a kind of prompt, the most relevant segment of the mythic plot: how, in his flight from Corinth, Oedipus has an apparently random encounter on the road, confronted there by a highly ranked stranger with four attendants; how the road is too narrow for both parties to pass, leading to a dispute, which then erupts into a physical fight; and how, after slaying that leader and three of his attendants, Oedipus continues on his way, completely unaware that he's just killed his real father—how, through choosing to run *away*, he's actually run *toward*, fulfilling the fate he was so desperate to avoid.

"Okay," the teacher says, for the prompt has worked: he's spied, he thinks, a plausible connection. "Let's try to imagine a similar encounter on the road from Seattle, not the same but akin—one converted to fit our time and place, our cultural beliefs.

"Jared, too, has left home with the aim of making a permanent move, but now a highway has replaced the cart-cut road, the walking stick upgraded to an automobile—to, let's say, given his fondness for camping, an old Subaru wagon. He's following his love, not fleeing a prophecy; nevertheless, he also gets involved in a dispute concerning right-of-way. He's in the left lane on a crowded interstate while traveling south at the reasonable speed of, say, five miles over the legal limit, when another car ... okay, let's think this through. To match this stage in the myth, it needs to be a pricey model, one that a wealthy man might use to project his power. So let's say ..."

"A new Beamer," a student suggests.

"Perfect. Jared's cruising along in the left lane, on his way to what he hopes will be a happily-ever-after ending, when a brand new, baby blue, eighty-K Beamer accelerates behind him, drawing too close, headlights flashing, demanding that this dull and dented wagon get out his way. A plausible scenario, no? And one that we've all probably experienced before.

"In any case, there he is, suddenly challenged. And having received *this* message out of the blue—the flashing lights, the spiffy grill in the rearview mirror—Jared has to make up his mind. He has no choice but to choose, and, sure that he's in the right, he refuses move. He won't change lanes, which, given the density of the traffic, would be difficult anyway (or so he judges), and he won't change speeds because going any faster would place him too close to the car in front of him.

"The confrontation continues for three or four miles, the tailgating driver only dropping back to accelerate again, headlights flashing. Finally, that driver takes a chance, passing on the right and then cutting quickly back in front of Jared. But there's not enough room, and just a moment later when that Beamer's forced to brake, their bumpers graze and the pricier vehicle flies off the road.

"Jared recovers just in time to see the German car spinning across the highway's divider and into a northbound lane, directly in the path of an oncoming jeep. There's a terrible crash and, I'm sorry to report, four of the five people inside the two vehicles, including both drivers, are instantly killed. One minute they were alive, and the next—after Jared was challenged and made up his mind—those four are dead."

The teacher pauses to survey the room. Directly introduced, the subject of death has skewed the mood of the group, whose eyes, it now seems, beg a release from their current assignment. They'd rather avoid thinking *this* scenario through.

"Responses so far?"

"Well," Carl says, "it's certainly melodramatic."

"Is it?" the teacher asks, stifling his irritation at the dismissive tone. "By that do you mean emotionally intense, which it certainly is, or implausible in the narrative sense, the sort of critique we apply to inept story lines? Because I have to say this: it doesn't seem all that implausible to me. A hundred or so people, real and so all too relevant to their families and friends, die every day on the nation's roads—that's a few hundred thousand in the last ten years. You and I might even know some of the victims."

(*Watch it*, the critic-in-residence warns again, and so the teacher softens his tone.)

"In any case, that's the new plot, the sequence with calamitous consequences I'm offering up. So let's review. We have two young men, living in very different cultures, in very different times, yet some likenesses still abide."

Placing the book down, the teacher uses two hands now to tally the results.

"Each receives a startling message out of the blue. Each chooses to go, to leave for good his longtime home. Each then has a violent encounter on the road, and after that encounter, each is about to proceed, whether to Phoenix or to Thebes, leaving behind a body count of four. The question's this: does our story—let me correct that—does *my* version of Jared's story supply a plausible parallel to the ancient myth?"

a-is-to-b as c-is-to-d

The teacher waits, sensing a resistance that he not only expects but actually prefers. To elicit its best voice, he knows where to turn.

"Go ahead, Jack," he now says to that student whose t-shirt's caption succinctly captures the role he plays within the class. "Show me no mercy: fire away."

"Those two chance encounters—they're not the same."

"True enough on the surface. But remember, I'm not saying they're the same, I'm saying that they're *akin*, that the likenesses surpass the differences here. And if that isn't the case—and issues of *likeness*, as contrasted to those of *equation*, can always be debated—then tell me why not?"

"Because it's not *his* fault," Amanda protests.

"You mean, because we're thinking comparatively here, that a car crash is not akin to a physical fight? That Oedipus *really* killed those travelers—club to skull, say, and not bumper to bumper—and so he is at fault in a way that Jared is not? You mean that while the latter's just an accident, the former's a crime?"

"Of course it's a crime—he *murdered* four people!"

"Okay. That's certainly an arguable point—though I'm not sure that upgrading the weaponry from the intimacy of a hand-held stick to the insulation of a two-ton car necessarily excuses *our* traveling hero from the same charge. And remember this too: we're thinking metaphorically here; we're measuring our truths *in relation to*. That is to say, we're not judging Oedipus as we would a contemporary American, nor Jared by all the virtues and values of ancient Greece. Instead, we're measuring the relation of two separate moral ratios: *a-is-to-b* as *c-is-to-d*, where a and c are individual characters and b and d are their separate cultural and historical grounds. Jared-on-the-highway-in-postmillennial-America with or against Oedipus-on-the-road-in-ancient-Greece.

"All of which is to say again that the context matters: the time, the place, the ruling beliefs and prevailing technologies. So let's remember this about the character who is, for us, the stranger figure: Oedipus belongs to a tribe that highly values martial ferocity and skill. Given the relatively primitive level of their weaponry, those cherished skills are, necessarily, of the hand-to-hand variety, and the Greeks have come to value them for the not inconsiderable reason that their culture couldn't have survived without a population adept at combat. By the standards of his own place and time, Oedipus's actions on the road are, eventually, judged to be a terrible crime, but not simply because he killed some strangers in passing—nor because he killed them with his own hands, rather than, say, forcing their chariot off the road and into a deep ditch. No, his actions are judged to be criminal because one of those strangers just happened to be both his own real father and the King of Thebes, and in beliefs hardly unique to the ancient Greeks, patricide and regicide are deemed utterly abhorrent.

"And let's recall, too, moving from his moral context back to Jared's, that our civilized aversion to violence of the hand-to-hand sort coexists with a peculiar tolerance for the bumper-to-bumper kind. Except for spectator sports, we don't value physical aggression any more. But we do value individual autonomy, especially mobility, especially the right to drive our own cars as far and fast, as unimpeded as possible. But that deeply valued preference of ours is sustained at an extraordinary cost. Far more Americans die on our highways each year than ever did in our so-called war on terror—the numbers aren't even close. Some thirty or forty thousand deaths, I believe. And those lost lives are just the start. They don't account for all the serious injuries, much less the so-called collateral damage, the ripple effect of so much grief and despair.

"We can imagine, can't we, another culture, with a different gauge on virtue and value, whose people would be appalled by these numbers, this slaughter? Who would find *our* tolerance of it on behalf of our autonomy—the trading off of so many lives, so much misery for the convenience of mobility—a communal crime in itself? Who would see in it, in *us*, a repulsive callousness, a barbaric crudity?"

PHOENIX?

a fatal difference

The teacher waits, noting as he does the clouds of uneasiness now shifting across his students' faces. They've been raised, he knows, to "celebrate diversity" but without being asked to mine the deeper implications of real cultural difference, its potential to challenge all virtues and values, including their own, including the notion that we should celebrate diversity. Hence their unpreparedness for the reactionary fury of 9/11 or the election results of 2016, the sheer rage of others to obliterate change, to exterminate the moral dissonance spurred by globalization or immigration.

Meanwhile, though, the class is still pondering his disturbing suggestion that Jared's actions on the highway to Phoenix might be akin, at least when viewed from one culturally diverse angle of vision, to those of Oedipus on the road to Thebes.

"So you're saying, then," a student finally asks—it's the one who wears the cross, her voice now thinned to a hesitant mix of skeptical resistance and disturbing self-doubt—"you're actually arguing that *Jared* is the one at fault?"

"I'm trying to go deeper than that. I'm not judging Jared alone and apart, as the absolute sovereign of his own moral life: that's just the narcissist's dream of unimpeded glory flipped into the rigid cartoon of unadulterated guilt. I'm insisting instead on the natural complicity of the human condition."

The teacher pauses, surveying the room: *you're losing them*, the critic-in-residence quietly notes, and he knows that it's true.

"Look, the distinction I'm trying to draw here is between the quality of a specific decision and the general condition that grounds *all* our decisions, ethical or not. I want to highlight the natural accountability that precedes any and all cultural definitions of right and wrong. But I have to confess that, on this issue at least, my version of Chad's story isn't helping us much, so let's see if I can find a better example."

Head down, the teacher paces now before his desk, seeing but not really noting two backpacks, a soda can, a scattering of jackets across the tiled floor—so many colors, textures, discernible borders, so many rich and vivid facts, which, in this site-specific moment of being and knowing, are all instantly dismissed as perceptual noise.

Finally, he recalls a recent item from the news. A middle school. In the Midwest somewhere, Iowa maybe—or was it Kansas? An eighth-grade class suddenly seized by an outraged parent. Some of the details are hazy but not the story's basic shape, or how he felt as a parent and a teacher when first reading it: an anger merged with fear, a surge of raw revulsion. Here was an event which, now as then, should never occur.

"Okay," the teacher says, nodding to himself, and then glances up, "—let's try this. If, say, a man armed with some sort of gun and a sense of injustice at who-knows-what? burst into this classroom and took us all hostage, it certainly wouldn't be your fault or mine, in either the criminal or the ethical sense. None of us chose, or would ever choose, to be placed in such danger. But despite our dearest wishes, the seizure of our class has become a real and terribly relevant fact. That's the new premise at least—the new sequence whose potentially calamitous consequences we need to think through. So let's do the work we're trained to do. Let's put ourselves there, which is to say *here*. Our room has been transformed from a place of learning into a makeshift prison, each of us recast from our usual role as student or professor into that of the innocent victim.

"And yet here's the point: even in the innocence of our imprisonment, each of us would be accountable for the decisions we made while being held hostage, decisions to be faced while under great stress and with potentially fatal consequences. Stress, I want to add, that is very much akin to the sort that Oedipus must have felt after receiving his prophecy, that Hamlet clearly suffered through after hearing from his father's ghost.

"To speak or not to speak—that would be *our* crucial question. And if so, what to say, which strategy to take: pleas for mercy? warnings about consequences? appealing to our hostage-taker's better side by attending to his story with a sympathetic ear? Or, moving from persuasive words to heroic deeds, should we act or not? And if so, how: go for the window? grab the guy's rifle? snatch the ten-pound *Intro to Bio* text that has been burdening your backpack all quarter long and try to knock the creep senseless? Or, more Odysseus than Achilles perhaps, sneak out that new phone, so miraculous in its many modes, to secretly transmit the crime in progress over the Web?

"All those possibilities and more would exist. And to pretend otherwise would be to fail to mind our current place. It's certainly not *our* fault that we've been taken hostage—we remain, on those terms, innocent victims. But that doesn't excuse us from being accountable for the decisions we make, that we *have* to make, while we're imprisoned here. Even when acting in good faith, each of us could make a terrible mistake. Given the natural limits of our minds, we could never know enough to know for sure what would work at any given time. Words we said (or failed to say), actions we did (or did not) take could make a fatal difference for every person in the room.

"One minute we're all alive. And then, in the aftermath of your or my decision," the teacher says; his extended arms, pretending to aim the hostage-taker's rifle, slowly sweep the class, "—and then we're not."

Behind him, as if a sound effect to punctuate their imaginary deaths, the room's clock now ticks. They're that much closer to the end of the class, sixty more seconds subtracted from their actual, not just fictional lives.

"That's the new scenario," the teacher finally says, "—and, out of it, the claim I'm trying to make about our natural state. What do you think?"

the ultimate no mas

"That's a pretty extreme situation," one student observes.

"I don't disagree. But the relevance of that observation would be? . . ."

"That eventually," another quickly fills in, "that at some point on any continuum, changes in degree become changes in category."

"That's very well said." The teacher nods, and then smiles when he recalls that this last speaker is the class's sole philosophy major. "And I do accept the general accuracy of your point. Nevertheless, I'm going to disagree with you in this instance. I'm going to insist that the extremity of the hostage situation, like the extremity of the Oedipus plot, serves to clarify our shared condition. Both highlight, I believe, the mix of vulnerability and accountability that is a lasting feature of our natural state.

"As Oedipus suffers to learn, no one gets to choose the conditions of his birth. We can't select the place, the era, or the families we're born into. I'm sorry to report—and we all know this, right?—I'm sorry to say that some people are born to parents who are little better than hostage-takers. And lucky or not, once we enter this life, we have no choice but to choose; we have to decide in every waking hour what to say, what to do. We're fated to be free, even though the menu of options is always beyond our total control—beyond yours, beyond mine, beyond Jared's too.

"After all," the teacher says, "Jared hasn't determined most of the features of the situation he now faces while driving south toward Phoenix. Fate—in the form of governors, state and federal legislators, highway engineers and, say, a landlord late for the key exchange, not to mention the many decisions on speed and lane changes made by a host of other drivers that day—fate has so arranged it that these two cars, an old Subaru wagon and a new BMW, are adjacent now in time and space. And sharing that same time and space, each driver has no choice now but to choose what he ought to do next. The resulting collision, I'll admit, is not Jared's fault in the legal sense. He did have the right to hold his lane, and judged as a formal jury would, the other driver was clearly the aggressor and so primarily to blame.

"Nevertheless, four people would *not* be dead now if Jared hadn't insisted, as Oedipus did, on his right of way. Nor would our hero have found himself in this awful situation if he hadn't decided, a few days or weeks before, to text *I will* to Erin's *follow me*. Four people are dead because, in part, of a series of decisions he freely made, just as two, or four, or all of us might die if you or I did (or didn't) go for the window or for the rifle, if we did (or didn't) say this word or that to our hostage-taker. And for Jared not to admit his complicity in these deaths and ponder its meaning would be to shirk the duty of self-reflection. Refusing to *know himself*, he'd cease to be heroic in the Sophoclean sense."

The teacher pauses, and the silence that follows is the sort he most loves, the kind he senses whenever he enters their library: a stillness charged with the resonant force of many minds thinking. Inspired by that feeling, he pushes the premise one step further.

"Of course, to make the challenge even worse, to further heighten the similarities between the ancient myth and our modern story, we could personalize those highway deaths. Let's say that, though his answer's still yes, Jared *doesn't* send a text. Let's assume that, as proof of the very spontaneity she has accused him of lacking, he is planning to surprise Erin instead. And let's suppose, too, that Erin, whose impatience we well know from earlier scenes, can't stand the suspense when she hears nothing back.

"And so it comes to pass that while Jared is packing his car, or waiting for his landlord to turn in his keys, his ex is talking to her roommates in Phoenix—two young women who once expressed, over retro martinis on the night they first met, a casual interest in visiting the Northwest. 'Let's just do it,' Erin now says, never admitting, perhaps even to herself, what her real motive is. 'Just call in sick and we'll jump in my jeep.' Those are her directions, but you see where *I'm* heading. That without violating our sense of the natural, without depending on superstitious oracles or the interventions of vengeful pagan gods, we still can restage an outrageous fortune that is very close indeed to Oedipus's fate on the road to

Thebes. For presented with the choice to go or not to go, both of Erin's roommates have chosen to hit the road, and, as a result, all three friends are now speeding unimpeded on a highway heading north.

"Let's put ourselves *there*, in that northbound lane, in their jeep's front seat. Let's see the action unreel from Erin's perspective. Now she's conversing with her friends, now singing along to a song she's streaming. Now she's silently rehearsing a speech she hopes to give when she crosses paths with a certain young man. And now, cued by some sign—the swerving of a nearby driver, the spewing of turf from the highway's divider—she glances toward her left, where a bright blue blur is heading straight for her.

"And so it comes to pass," the teacher says, and feels himself tense as he abruptly imagines what would happen next: the keening of shorn steel, the spray of shattered glass, the ricochet of fragments finding their random rest atop the shoulder's beveled pavement, scattered here and there within the tire-torn grass, "—it just so happens that Jared's choosing *I will* has ironically resulted in the ultimate *no mas*."

how mystery endures

Aware of the clock, the teacher now impatiently awaits his students' response.

"It's possible, no?"

"I suppose, but still . . ."

"Say it."

"The odds against it have to be phenomenal—a million, ten million to one."

"True," the teacher admits: he's annoyed, however, by this shift in ruling measures from metaphor to math, this invoking of the stats as the final authority.

"I mean, he'd be just as likely to be struck by lightning or win the lottery."

"The *megabucks* lottery," a second student adds, and the teacher watches as, a consensus coalescing, others in the class begin to nod.

"True enough," he says. "I don't dispute your math. But let's remember this: that however long the odds, someone does, eventually, win the lottery, megabucks or not."

The teacher pauses: although he's made his point, something still feels wrong. Pleased at first, and to the point of vanity, with the symmetry he forged between the two narratives, he fears he's gone too far, that killing Erin off has crossed that line where changes in degree become changes in category. The goal, after all, was heart-felt persuasion. The whole point of turning toward *Phoenix?* was to use the mythos-minded process of identification to make his students actively feel the ongoing relevance of Oedipus's tragedy—he wanted, he *still* wants them to believe in the actual and amazing fragility of things. But now, by pushing the likeness too far, he's supplied a story line that their heads can admit as an abstract chance but one that their hearts, comforted by the odds, can quietly dismiss: just a fact to learn and not a fate that they might live.

"Still," the teacher finally says, "I take your point. So let's delete *that* version of the story. Maybe Erin's jeep is in for repairs. Or maybe her roommates refuse the offer and, absent the excuse of playing their guide, she backs out herself. More likely if less exciting—truer to the characters as Chad has drawn them, I think, and befitting a romance that has already suffered too much surprise—Jared *has* sent Erin a text, and the whole temptation would never arise.

"And, too, if our main measure here is going to be the *odds*, then the most likely event of all would be the *un*eventful. Like millions of other dramaless passages on that same day, there would be no grazing of bumpers, no random encounter with a BMW resulting in four deaths, whoever those four might've turned out to be. In any case, we don't need a fortune *that* outrageous to dramatize the importance of Jared's decision to go Phoenix. He doesn't have to be complicit with anyone's death for us to recognize the scale of the difference his choice will make, that it *has* to make in the days to come.

"That's not to say that some crucial features won't remain the same. Jared might've shed most of his possessions, but he still carries with him the same predispositions, genetic or learned, the same history and habits. Mobility, after all, can only take us so far. No matter how fast we drive or hard we try, we can never fully flee from the symbols or the substance of the lives we have led. 'No ship exists,' a poet once wrote, 'to take you from yourself.' Still, by choosing to go our hero has changed nearly everything else."

"How so?"

It's Amanda, the one who insisted that Jared would go, and she now seems to suspect that the happy ending she imagined for him is about to be challenged.

"How so? Because our identities are never ours alone, because they're always being shaped *in relation to* the places we inhabit, the people we know. And by choosing to go, Jared has changed all the site-specific facts, natural and cultural, that will calibrate his days. In Phoenix he'll hold different jobs, make different friends; other ghostly voices will haunt his head, contending with the rest. There he'll encounter a different set of random events—a virus, say, that he unknowingly inhales while on his first or third job, or a life-changing book that he happens to spy on a yard-sale table. Or maybe he'll catch a flirtatious glance at, say, a concert in Tempe: that meeting-of-the-eyes while waiting in line which, choice following chance, might eventually affect his relationship with Erin.

"Though no one has died, Jared's reply to Erin's text has started a wholly new sequence of interactions whose consequences no one can predict. Yes, relatively speaking, we've made a lot of progress in the realm of prediction; thanks to science these days, we know a helluva lot more about the natural than the Greeks ever did. But that doesn't negate the larger point I'm trying to make about the fate of being free—how mystery endures in the midst of mental progress. How, the more things change, the more they stay the same in certain crucial ways."

let none presume

"I think that's *crap*."

The teacher rears back, then turns toward Jack, who, the sudden center of attention, is blushing now: he's as stunned, it seems, as the rest of the class by the rudeness of his outburst, questioning authority in a wholly different tone. Now where did *that* come from? the teacher wonders but knows he mustn't ask.

"Okaaay," he finally says as calmly as he can. "Crap in what way?"

"The old saying, I mean: the more things change, the more they stay the same. It's just a lame excuse that people use. An alibi for not taking charge of their screwed-up lives, for refusing to fight injustice in the world."

"Cowardly, you're saying."

"Yes, and *lazy*—an all-purpose cop out, a white flag to raise on any occasion."

"Which is why," another student says, turning back toward the teacher, "your point doesn't really apply here."

"Here?"

"To *Phoenix?*, to *your* extension of Chad's ongoing story. It doesn't apply to Jared."

"Or to Erin," Amanda adds.

"Or to Erin *with* Jared, as you keep insisting. In this version, neither one has quit. No white flags for them: our characters *are* taking charge of their lives."

The teacher surveys his class, feeling something like despair at this consensus they're now reaching, their collective misreading of the argument he's made. Not Chad, whose real life is too enmeshed in these events to escape ambivalence, who has yet to "take charge" like his fictive avatar. And perhaps not even Jack, whose unexpected outburst seemed to exorcize the ghost of a private dispute only loosely related to the discussion underway. But the others have now used his interruption to confirm their old presumptions about the range of our autonomy; they're reasserting their belief, American to the core, in each individual's innate authority to shape his or her own destiny.

"I *know* they're taking charge, or trying to take charge," the teacher says, his tone tainted then with a hint of annoyance. "That's how we defined Jared from the start, as both bravely self-reflective and practically effective, as the best that he, or we, can be. To keep the comparison fair, we've made him equal to the heroes in the old Greek plays. The tragedies, after all, are only interested in those who can and do take charge; they're obsessed with exploring how the best and brightest people can, nevertheless, both suffer themselves and cause unintended harm.

"No, surrender's never been an issue here. We've been assuming all along that Jared is as bold and smart as Oedipus, and we've admitted, too, that he has access now to knowledge and tools that no Greek possessed. Even so, my assertion hasn't changed. Oedipus's weapons and religion may be out of date but not the conditions that triggered his awful fate. Even with the best of our high-tech specs, our eyes remain dim in certain key ways. Moment by moment, day after day, we're accountable for decisions that, however well-informed and freely made, are vulnerable to error. A lot may have changed in our everyday lives, but that, I'm insisting," the teacher adds while turning back toward Jack, "*that's* remained the same."

The teacher waits, but having trespassed the bounds of civility once, Jack, he quickly grasps, is unlikely to speak, and the rest of the class, though clearly engaged, shows no readable reaction to the case he's tried to make.

"So," a student finally says, "—was it a mistake for Jared to choose to go?"

"We can't say yet."

"I know, but class is almost over. And you're always advising us that, when writing our stories, it's helpful to have an ending in mind."

The teacher smiles, less at the reminder that his snippets of advice sometimes take hold than at the need expressed. For the thinking creature, within whose supercharged mind imagination supplants instinct, the drive to picture likely endings is as essential to survival as food or sex. Whether in chanted poems, printed stories, or electronic texts, or in less formal conversations with family and friends, we're constantly probing what could, what will, what *ought* to happen next.

"By having an ending in mind, I meant a destination for the plot, a sequence finished or image revised, not a final judgment on the characters' lives."

"But still . . ."

"Yes?"

"What do *you* think?"

"I think . . ." The teacher pauses. With the session about to end, a few have begun to pack their books as quietly as they can, and their motion reminds him, as he studies his class, that the dilemma they're discussing is not entirely abstract—that, more than merely curious, someone in the room is truly desperate to discern what ought to happen next.

"I think this," the teacher says, keeping a watchful eye on Chad. "That if we had the time, we'd eventually find an artful ending to our story, but that's not the same as assigning a fixed and final meaning to the choice that Jared makes. I think this: that if Jared does aspire to know himself, the evaluation can't end. That the meaning of his choice, unfolding over time, will have to be examined again and again. I think . . ."

A bell rings and is so rudely insistent that he ceases to speak. As soon as it ends, his students begin stirring in their seats, and for once, if only in this very limited sense, the teacher does know what will happen next: a variety of phones are about to emerge, cupped in palms, their buttons pushed by opposable thumbs as the latest news from the ether is taken in. Anxious to supply an artful climax to this class in the few moments he has left, the teacher now grabs his well-worn copy of *Oedipus Rex*, flipping to the back—in a book, unlike our lives, the end of the story is always easy to find.

"Some final words," he now says, and the class looks up. Shuttling between realities, the collective imagination quickly adjusts, a Seattle classroom giving way to a Theban palace, as it once was crafted on an Athenian stage. They're on the final page, when the Delphic test of virtue has been met and passed. Oedipus at last knows himself, as does everyone else, and the same revelation that will save the city from its plague has already decimated the royal family. The queen who wed her son has hanged herself. The father-slaying son, who had once "towered up, the most powerful of men,"[15] has just been reduced to a self-blinded beggar, cast beyond the bounds of communal care. And now in the open air of Attica, where democracy has been founded, the chorus turns to face an audience of thousands.

"I think this," the teacher says, but theirs are the final words, so long preserved and carefully converted from tongue to tongue, that emerge now from his lips:

> . . . . *let none*
> *Presume on his good fortune until he find*
> *Life, at his death, a memory free of pain.*[16]

almost . . .

A silent moment passes. It's morning in early springtime; the Attic air is crisp, saturated with sunshine, and with the final scene enacted, the playwright and his actors await approval or rejection from the citizens of Athens whose benches rim the excavated hillside above them. Higher still, a glossy ibis—darkly feathered and long-billed, a seasonal migrant—glides on wide wings, the chevron of their shadow sliding over and through the amphitheater's crowd like the will of Apollo. Collective judgment will soon follow. More than six thousand miles and two millennia away, other

---

15. Sophocles, *Oedipus Rex*, trans. Dudley Fitts and Robert Fitzgerald (New York: Harcourt Brace Jovanovich, 1977), 78.

16. Ibid., 78.

classes are letting out, the voices of their students filling the hall with bird-like bursts of social display: so many pleas for attention, territorial claims, the lessons they've just learned now slipping away—for the moment or forever, happily or not, who can say for sure?

Searching for a marsh with the makings of a nest in its inter-tidal wash of birth and death, the glossy ibis passes on. Does the audience it leaves behind now choose to applaud? Do they sit in silent wonder, or indignantly baulk at the unexpected changes Sophocles has wrought in the ancient myth they know by heart? Do his differences *make* a difference? Do they startle and so rouse the habit-numbed senses of the festival crowd? Dissonance, it's been said, can lead to discovery—but only if you're interested, and the teacher worries now that he's failed to spur that interest, that he hasn't made a difference. Even so, he has nothing more to say. Channeling the play, making its final words his as well is the tactic he has chosen. And with its tragedy now over and the oracle of the clock having clearly spoken, he can only watch in silence, open book in hand, as his students slowly leave the sphere of his care.

The girl with the cross, the boy who lost in love, the master of metaphors, the aspiring philosopher, skeptical Jack (*I think that's crap*), Carl and then Amanda and then, trailing to one side, a still ambivalent Chad: some fifteen separate selves, their stories unresolved, each now exiting the class, moving out of this portion of their one-and-only lives and into the dimly glimpsed mystery of the next. All the entrails read, the gutted lambs and fatted calves; all the histories written and star charts cast, the data sets run; so many stories told and studies done to ease this same suspense now facing each of them—to moderate the mystery of what will happen next.

As if he too were expecting the imminent arrival of approval or rejection, Chad pauses by the door, phone in hand, scrolling for calls or snippets of text, and as the teacher watches over him, this last student in the class, his story's one-word title bursts back into mind. First *fee-nix?* the sound, as if a voice from the ether, an oracular prompt from whichever nameless goddess has replaced Athena. Then *phoenix?* the printed word, whose odd spelling recalls both its ancient Greek roots and its older meaning, the secret sharing of the sunbelt city with a mythical creature—that self-immolating bird who only dies to hatch again, who, happily or not, triumphs over death.

It seems strange enough, this cohabitation, within a single word from a long dead language, of the preliterate myth and the post-modern place. But now, recast by Chad's interrogatory title, the double meaning it encodes has been doubly questioned. To ask if Jared's passion should rise again from the spent fury of its ashes in the city of the sun is also to ask if our lives, too, might spiral on in endless cycles of rebirth. To go or not? To reemerge from the dust, or to suffer instead an irreversible *no mas?* Stories have been told and entrails read, but what do *you* think? Are we really one-and-done, or, feathers fledging out of ashes, do we burn to fly again? After this blaze of consciousness, after this paradise of pain and sun-steeped green, loosely netted by our words and imperfectly perceived, what will happen next?

We can't say yet.

At the Theater of Dionysus, where the final words of the chorus still resonate in the minds of its Athenian audience, few can cherish, on reflection, a past "free of pain." Few are likely to "presume" the imminence of "good fortune" when, at war again with Sparta and struck by plague themselves, most in the crowd have suffered the loss of someone they loved. No single mind, however fecund or firm, however willing to take charge, can shield itself from harm in times like these. In the seats as on the stage, even the man who "towers up" is susceptible to calamities, both natural and manmade. And of those about to judge this play, we might compare Pericles-the-leader, whose dignified oration over the bodies of the slain once roused the city with its patriotic fervor, to Pericles-the-father, who, a year or so later, was seen weeping in public after burying his own son. Here was a difference that made a difference, the news that stayed news: his son was gone forever—*his* boy had died, too.

More than six thousand miles and two millennia away—when all in or about the theater that day, the city's leaders and lackeys, its seers and slaves, when all their daughters and sons, and *their* daughters and sons have long been burned or buried, their physical remains dusting the plains and silting the marshes where migratory birds still gather to mate—the teacher now swims in the currents of consciousness.

As he watches over Chad, who lingers in the class while reading his messages, the reality of this one-and-only moment they both do and do not share seems rich beyond reckoning. He is awash now with memories and perceptions. The play of light on the glaze of each desk, another wave of student voices, the animated cipher of Chad's one-and-only face, the mix of moods that remains from teaching this class, reading this play: all here and now and haunting his head, all posing a challenge in the form of a choice. *Mark me,* this site-specific moment, this pause between bells, now pleads or demands, and long-committed to that task, the teacher says *I will*.[17] He chooses to know—to try to know; he wants to attend and somehow make sense of this superabundance now swelling within him, now swirling about him.

So many voices in the fog, so many claims on his attention, so many imminent messages simmering in the ether, surging across the epochs, so much historical momentum. He can hear, it seems now, within the carefree voices surging in the hall, the echo of crowds hailing the powers of long-forgotten gods. He can feel, it seems now, the whole history of meaning, the archeology of feeling layered within the words that articulate his thoughts. Borders are breaking down; categories blur and distances collapse, sunbelt cities into mythical birds. *There* inhabits *here*, *then* exists *now*, or almost, almost: out of the wall-less well of oblivion, the resurgent particularity of so many ghosts. Ghosts, he senses now, who've always been near, pleading for attention from the edges of extinction, waiting to be marked, to be thanked; who have helped him all along, a conspiracy of sorts, who have given him their language, given him their lore. Given as in *gift*, he realizes now in a surge of wonder and tender regard for all these generous ghosts emerging from the fog.

The legislators who once imagined a campus that didn't yet exist; the architects and craftsmen who, laboring hard to give that idea a material form, shaped this very classroom, laid this very floor; the former teachers of the teacher and the thinkers they assigned, including those writers whose works he's just cited—Sophocles with Hopkins, Conrad with Stevens—and all his other favorite authors, each conveying and sustaining even older voices, each conducting (even while amending) the history of the tribe; the archeologists and classicists who sifted through the shards, deciphering the maze of long-dead ways; the poet-translators who converted and resang the plotted verses of this play; from the preliterate bards who first sculpted in sound the Oedipus myth to the masons whose trowels once trued the walls that protect him now: they're all *here*, the teacher senses, they're swirling about him, swelling within him, charging these moments with meaning and feeling. Hidden by the fog of his inattention, they've *always* been with him. Each moment of each day has been and is, he recognizes now, a tacit collaboration, consciousness itself a secret sharing between the living and the dead, whose gifts are

---

17. *Mark me* is the two-word request voiced by the ghost of Hamlet's father, to which his son the prince replies with the equally brief promise: *I will*. The plot of Shakespeare's longest play is initiated by those four words: *Hamlet*, I, 5.

born again within the coursing of his thoughts, the sheltered movement of his limbs: they're born again and then again.

Gratitude alone seems too paltry a response to acknowledge such a gift, this inter-tidal flow that mixes and melds the living with the dead, nothing wasted or withheld. It buoys him now with joy, the cushioned comfort of belonging; it "remedies the defect of his too great nearness to himself." Loneliness becomes meaningless, it makes no sense at all, now that he knows his so-called private self is itself being woven from the voices of these ghosts, whose weightless presence he feels, whose essence he's on the verge of articulating now—almost, almost . . .

The teacher strains to label the soul of this sensation, its animating merger of mind with place, of age with age; to make it his own, he wants to mold within his mouth through some simile or phrase this moment's one, true immortalizing name. But soon, without a bell sounding or an apt image found, the intimation slips away. The ghostly company recedes like fading voices in a dream, and as they do, he feels again the pitiless extraction of *here* from *there*, of *now* from *then*. All too naturally, it seems, his inner vision crimps, a gate slams shut, and he's trapped again in that shadowy place of vigilant doubt, where only jeopardy is shared and "time and chance happen to us all."[18] There, because danger warrants fear and the body has evolved a rote mind of its own, a peripheral motion is now yanking his attention toward the classroom's only door.

The alarm proves false, though; no enemies are found—it's just the last of his students slipping into the hall. His duties are now done, his watch is finally over. The teacher hears himself sigh; his posture slumps, and just that quickly, exhilaration imploding into sheer exhaustion, he's too spent, it seems, to entertain another thought.

the work of wonder

And if I had the time, I might strive to recover the hidden field of meaning, of being and feeling, he's too tired to explore. How, far away and long ago but simultaneous in that theater of the imagination whose reality perpetually awaits our engagement, a glossy ibis spirals down to meet its own shadow, floating on the shallows of a reed-riddled marsh. From Africa to Attica, from sun-dried sky to sea-washed shore, this migrant's journey nears its end. Its wings, beating backward, brake its staged descent while

---

18. Ecclesiastes, 9:11.

its elongated legs, perfectly adapted for just this purpose, are dropping down now to slice through the water's diamond-bright surface, rooting themselves there in the saturated ground.

Meanwhile, in other realms where stone fences have been laid and livestock corralled, more fateful choices are being made. A crowd applauds a play. The latest war-time widow weeps aloud, her keening unrestrained, as if she alone has just discovered the injustice of the world. And while a pack of wolves begin to stalk a farmer's grazing goats, a sightless beggar taps his cane, searching for mercy on cart-cut roads.

Although all are in motion, carried on the currents of hunger, hate, or hope, the earth itself is turning at a pace no eye can quite discern. For each and every substance in its planetary garden, reformation is the one inescapable rule: evolution and extinction, accretion and erosion, the throttled body of a queen serenely decomposing while a partridge dances wildly to infatuate his mate, and, unobserved by human eyes, a molten mountain rises from the trenches of an ocean. Here, within this sphere of mandatory change, simply standing still requires an act of will, the posture of the ibis straining now against the sucking of the tide and the wind's pulsing motion.

Can any of our schemes possibly account for all the interlinking winches of individual intention that animate each moment? In prosperous Seattle, a hundred students, moving in a hall, miraculously coordinate a collisionless passage to their separate destinations. In an Athens under siege, dreams of revenge coexist with the surreptitious raids by plague-infested rats, one of whose fleas will soon end the life of Pericles—but not before he's forced to bury his sister and another of his sons.

Can something so wrong ever seem right? Should we simply curse these imperfections in the paradise we're given, or still strive to preserve—within the ashes of our anger, the urns of our despair—an ember of delight? For three straight days during their springtime Dionysia, the Athenians would stage a new series of tragedies. Should we follow their example and, even as we celebrate the season of renewal, "ask for mournful melodies"?[19] These questions may be old, but since no one's life in the end is "a memory free of pain," they still must be posed, asked over and over by those fated to be free.

In the meantime, there are so many riches to assay here, so much pain to parse and beauty to acclaim. Each instance is a feather shimmering

---

19. W. B. Yeats, "Lapis Lazuli," *Selected Poems and Two Plays of William Butler Yeats*, ed. M.L. Rosenthal (New York: Collier Books, 1962), 160.

with an iridescence that, if glimpsed from the right angle, just might supply every shade and hue to vivify the story of our visible world. Illumination, though, is not equivalent to control, nor can devotion purchase our exemption. No tribal god survives or theory contains the massive torque and surge of metamorphic history, its ceaseless merging of choice with chance. And each conceptual advance, to our eventual surprise, also reinscribes an irreducible mystery.

Everything changes, but this remains the same: the climate of our awareness. We know, *exactly* now, when the sun will set and tomorrow's tides will ebb. We've learned to tap our trees when their sap is at its sweetest, and in the aftermath of Eden, our capacity to plan a better future is bound to admitting the fact of our own deaths. But it still remains the case that, during the passage of each astounding day, no one knows for certain the intricate array, much less the ultimate purpose, of what will happen next.

Not the eloquent orator praising the dead. Not the anxious lover staring at an unexpected text. Not the water bird, which, after anchoring its feet, refolds its wings in finely modulated movements, like eyelids seeking sleep. And not the author of that man who, utterly expended by the work of wonder, now shuts the slender book he cradles in his hand.

www.ingramcontent.com/pod-product-compliance
Lightning Source LLC
Chambersburg PA
CBHW020839160426
43192CB00007B/709